The Quotable Moose

The

QUOTABLE

MOOSE

A Contemporary Maine Reader

✳

Edited by Wesley McNair

University Press of New England

Hanover and London

University Press of New England, Hanover, NH 03755
© 1994 by Wesley McNair
All rights reserved
Printed in the United States of America   5   4   3   2
CIP data appear at the end of the book

Published by special arrangement with Nightshade Press.

Contents

Contents

TRAVELERS' ADVISORIES

NEIGHBORS AND KIN

Contents

Contents

Introduction

The map explains a lot. In contrast to the rest of the New England states, Maine is big—almost big enough to contain the collective land mass of all the others. It takes as long to get from the coastal city of Portland to the northern town of Fort Kent, as to travel from Portland to New York City. If Maine's twisted and knotted coastline were unraveled, it would be 3,500 miles long.

On the map the states around Maine show a tangle of super-highways; neighboring New Hampshire alone is crossed by three of them. Maine has only one, route 95, which, dangling its small adjunct 495, traverses the entire state from Kittery to Houlton. Otherwise, there are three primary roads—routes 1 along the coast, 2 across the state's mid-section, and 201 going straight up into Canada—then, an assortment of spiderlegs, the more tenuous ones reaching toward the north.

All the rest is not-roads—enough white space to recall that even after Maine was granted statehood in 1820, a large section of the state was still considered part of the American frontier. Even today, four-fifths of Maine is covered with forests. Together with its lakes (approximately 2,200) and rivers and streams (more than 5,000), those forests possess wildlife of all kinds, more abundant by far than may be found in the other New England states. It was the sense of Maine as a wild territory beyond the reach of civilization that brought the first white settlers here, many of them renegades seeking escape from the confinements of life in the Massachusetts Bay Colony. Later, Maine's wildness inspired a literature and art of exploration, attracting writers like Thoreau and painters like Church and Lane to the state's less settled locations.

The tradition of journeying into the unknowns of Maine con-tinues in this reader. In poems, short stories, and essays, authors or their characters travel on foot, by car, on skis, in boats or canoes, making their discoveries about the territory and sometimes the self as they undertake or recall their hikes, drives, and voyages. The truth is that even though an entire section of the book has been devoted to Maine travels ("Travelers' Advisories"), journeys of one kind or another take place throughout *The Quotable Moose*. There is no more characteristic theme in the contemporary literature of Maine than the theme of the journey.

When they write about the settled life, writers in Maine tend to concentrate on villages and towns—a fact not so remarkable in a rural state whose biggest cities are by American standards more like big towns in their size. Large urban centers happen where there is modern industry; in this state, supported mostly by tourists, the primary industries of fishing, farming, lumbering, and paper manufacturing go back to the last century. Cut off from economic change and slow to adopt the urban styles more common elsewhere in New England, Maine's towns and their people offer writers sources that are increasingly unique: regional values and folkways, pockets of ethnic tradition, traces of dialect still untouched by the middle-American speech of radio and TV. Authors in *The Quotable Moose* have made use of such sources, citing also a certain sort of hybrid, a cross between the old and the new, which Maine's slow change has wrought. One writer, for instance, refers to "an old monster highway maintenance garage converted into an eating place"; another speaks of "pucker-brush suburbs." A third, determining that the illicit affair is urban in its origin, describes a Maine version that takes place at a Grange Hall dance "with your head up against a splintery upright . . . while wearing a thermal undershirt, while holding a can of beer stiffly, politely off to one side during the kiss."

However the characters we find in this volume may be carrying on, whether their stories are comic, sorrowful, or uplifting, what most typifies them is that they appear to us in the context of knowable communities or families, and place. Is this why they seem in general so sympathetic, eccentric, and vivid? In any case, they have an authority that distinguishes them from their counterparts in much postmodernist literature.

If the period style of today's literature calls for irony and skepticism rather than belief, the work that appears at the end of *The*

Quotable Moose represents still another departure from contemporary writing. There, Maine authors often turn to themes of affirmation. Little wonder that the natural surroundings of the state influence them as they do so. For Maine's geography includes, in all seasons, mountains, lakes, rivers, forests, meadows, and seacoast in combinations as various and beautiful as one could find anywhere. The spiritual and sometimes ecstatic writing that geography has inspired is among the most moving of the book, offering a last, lovely glimpse into the meaning of the map.

And how has the book's writing, on which Maine has had such an impact, been organized? As has been hinted, the units of *The Quotable Moose* underscore themes that the Maine map has helped to create. So sections of the reader relate to journeys, community life, and nature visions. But the sections have also been chosen and arranged to lead the reader step-by-step into the realities of Maine. The reader enters the volume, in part one, through the "arrivals" of assorted Maine people and creatures. Richard Gillman opens the section with his poem, "Together Among Monarchs." Coming upon a field of monarchs that have themselves just arrived, he and his father experience an uplifting of spirit that matches the flight of the butterflies they observe. Later on, a poem by William Carpenter traces the remarkable transformation of Bucksport, Maine, when it receives the unlikely visit of Equadorian sailors, and a Franklin Burroughs essay offers the compelling portrait of a hunter who introduces his small-town neighbors to a freshly killed moose he has hung in his garage. In his essay "Into Woods," Bill Roorbach arrives in the town of Farmington where, after a checkered history of work as a tradesman, he sets out to renovate an old house, assisted by the father who first got him "into woods." Just behind the feisty humor of the piece are the complexities of Roorbach's relationship with his father and the affection he feels for him.

Nor do the section's arrivals occur only in the towns of Maine. In Jacquie Giasson Fuller's spirited short story "Cecile's Dog Bo," we find ourselves in one of the state's few cities. There, Maureen, an ex-Floridian, is initiated into the life of Maine by her Francophone roommate Cecile, who also introduces Maureen to her unpredictable dog and her confused love-life. Edward Holmes' "Blitzkrieg and the Nautical Plow" takes us to an island on the Maine coast. In its dryly humorous, Down East style, Holmes' essay shows what happens when farmers hitch a savvy horse newly imported from the mainland to a plow made with seagoing equipment.

It is not difficult to find winter, Maine's longest season, in this reader. Winter appears in all four of the book's parts, never more menacingly than in "The Bird Feeder," a narrative poem by Robert M. Chute that appears in the second section. The readings of this unit, "Travelers' Advisories," present a wide assortment of journeys that extend our awareness of the state and its people, and sometimes reveal the underside of Maine life. Baron Wormser's disturbing verse "Somerset County," like the Chute poem, fits the latter category, associating the fatal accident of a truck driver with the hard realities of life in one of Maine's poorest counties. Fatal accidents are the theme in Amy Clampitt's poem "Handed Down" as well, in which fisherfolk on the coast of Maine repeat stories that feature "the names/of the dead, kept alive, they still hold onto."

Other readings in the section concern journeys that are less worrisome. To take the trip Robert Kimber writes about in "No Night Life"—from Allagash Village in northern Maine all the way south to Temple—one only need consider how much gas there is in the car, and how to appreciate "the real life of the night." In "Maine Eats," the journey is culinary; by following the intriguing directions of the essay's guide, John Thorne, the traveler will discover some of the state's best vernacular restaurants, and the true flavor of Maine besides. The issue of eating comes up once more in Richard Aldridge's verse recollection, "The Cornfield," where the poet's uncle accidentally drives off the road into a field carrying two passengers, Aldridge and his aunt. The poem's unpredicted and charming conclusion, which involves a sandwich, a sunset, and holding hands, is best left to the enjoyment of the reader.

Each of the first two sections of *The Quotable Moose* hints at what sort of people live, and have lived, in Maine. The third section, "Neighbors and Kin"—the reader's longest—gives the subject full play. Cathie Pelletier's short story "Civil Defense," about a family in northern Maine in the 1950s, shows a grandmother's struggle with the prospect of being placed in an old folks' home, and the impact of that struggle on her granddaughter, Mandy, Pelletier's central character. Ironically, the civil defense shelter Mandy's father plans throughout the piece offers no refuge from the dark insights that come to her at the story's end. In her essay "Cold Spring Nights in Maine, Smelts, and the Language of Love," Alice Bloom's topic is not family but neighbors, whose ways she, being "from away," attempts to understand. Beginning with questions about a smelting expedition ("What rush of blood or signal do they obey, and how do they know it?"), Bloom goes on to probe the frustrating sufficiency of her new friend Hilde, and finally, the submerged emotional life of country men in Maine, who, even when they seem most extroverted, conceal the "larger creek of their deeper feelings."

Urban neighbors are portrayed in poems by Betsy Sholl and Kenneth Rosen. Sholl's "Bird Lady" is a lively dramatic monologue that presents the eccentric character of a street person in Portland. Rosen's "Stormy Night" depicts a speaker who is compelled to assist a ragged group of ethnics trying to free their car from snow, though they trouble and repel him. By placing us close to their action, both poems force us to consider our own attitudes toward people outside of society's mainstream. "Wish," by Monica Wood, a short story set in a mill town, introduces still another distressing neighbor, who upsets the family of the narrator by the serious neglect of his dog. However, in the story's complex and moving climax, where the family's father, long ill, dies and the neighbor's attitude is altered, we are uplifted by a love that transforms grief and includes all creatures.

What do we learn about the Maine character from the people gathered in section three? If we are to be guided by Elaine Ford's story "Bent Reeds," in which a falling out between two old Down-Easters is retold by a third of the same kind, Mainers tend to be proud, guarded in their feelings, and independent to a fault. Yet Mainers also include the ethnics of Kenneth Rosen's poem— as different from Down-Easters as are the Francos whose ritual of the wake A. Poulin, Jr., touches on in his verse "The Front Parlor."

Such selections indicate that one must be careful not to stereotype the people of Maine, who are finally too diverse for simple characterizations.

The state of mind inspired by the state is similarly hard to define, varying, as it does, according to who is inspired, and when, and where. Readings in the anthology's last section, "A State of Mind," suggest the range of interpretations and visions Maine has elicited from her writers. In the fiction of the section, the visions belong to characters. There is Robley Wilson's aging believer, Lyle Kennett, under such stress as a defender of the sea's creatures that his view of the ocean includes colors "he [has] never seen"; and there is Patricia O'Donnell's dreamy and troubled protagonist Albert Moss, so obsessed with the teachings of Wilhelm Reich that he leaves his family to travel from Maine to the West, just as Reich did 36 years before.

When the essayists of the last section write of Maine's meaning, they speak with considerable passion. To Carolyn Chute, in "The Other Maine," the true state, now being corrupted by developers and the tourist bureau in Augusta, is a place where a person has the freedom to be herself, without putting on "fifty layers of makeup" and her "best leather skirt"—where people can have "useful stuff around our yards," such as "tractor parts, truck tires," and "rolled up chicken wire." Richard Peek, whose essay "Piles" advocates the "family tradition" of a pile in the yard containing assorted "widgets," would agree with at least part of Chute's description.

For the more lyrical and suggestive disclosures and visions about Maine, one must turn to poetry, the genre that dominates the final section. Behaving like New England's earliest writers of verse, the poets collected here turn to nature for their meanings— for instance, to the peculiar quality of light that "catches the stones" in Robert Creeley's tiny lyric, "Waldoboro Eve"; or to the clarity of a certain night that leads us, in Gary Lawless' "Some Clear Night," out to a cove to learn "the true names of the stars." Like Lawless, many of the section's poets make us aware that the real world, in all its mystery and wonder, exists outside of the names we have given it. The signs of that world in "Ghosts, Balloons, Some Martians," by Kate Barnes, are "sparks from fireflies" that frighten a visiting Irish girl—who, significantly, does not know how to name them. Another sign, revealed in George Garrett's "How It Is, How It Was, How It Will Be," is the brilliance of snow, so various in its shining that the poet cannot find the one word to describe it. For Philip Booth in "Presence," where the world is once again a mysterious place "we try to make sense of," the more compelling mystery is "that we are here, here at all, still bearing with, /and borne by" that world. If one has the feeling in "Presence" of a poet stammering toward truth, of a syntax stretching to take all the wonder in, so much more does one value the vision Booth presents.

I am grateful for such a poem, and grateful for all the writings gathered here, which take us—through arrivals, journeys, communal relations, and inspired states of mind—into the life and inner life of Maine, showing how universal the local ultimately is. To the authors of this splendid work I extend thanks not only for writing it in the first place, but for helping me obtain permission when necessary to reprint it. For her occasional help in checking my responses to submitted manuscripts, I thank my wife Diane, always my most trusted reader; and for their work in computer scanning, thanks go to Mal Carey and particularly to Mike Kelleher of the Computer Center at the University of Maine at Farmington. I am grateful to the Rockefeller Foundation for a residency at the Bellagio Center in Italy, and to the University of Maine at Farmington for a sabbatical leave—both of which contributed to the completion of this reader. Finally, I offer thanks to Roy Zarucchi and Carolyn Page of Nightshade Press for their assistance. They are the ones, after all, who first saw the need for a contemporary Maine reader. Without their idea, the literary feast contained in these pages could never have been served.

WESLEY MCNAIR
Mercer, Maine
August 1993

Arrivals

RICHARD GILLMAN

Together Among Monarchs

My father and I were motoring
across an ordinary morning
when a field of red clover on a corner
arose in one small place
on wings. It arose in another.
From out of nowhere wings
were lifting the whole field.

Dozens, I yelled.
My father yelled Hundreds
and stopped the car.

The field was undulating
three to five feet high.
Before it rose beyond us
we left the car and got aboard:
an ordinary ninety-year-old man
and sixty-two-year-old son,
together among Monarchs.

My father went straight ahead,
I veered left.
We glanced at each other
between fliers, through flight paths.
Our knowing better was suspended.
We shook our heads,
smiles making our faces
round as children's.

For a while, from an old decade,
we thought of our nets, the race,
the clean, swift sweep, when
it wasn't enough to keep butterflies
in mind: when we loved them
for their beauty
with a light squeeze of the thorax
and a killing jar.

We lifted our feet high and slow
in the grass and clover,
reaching out and sometimes
touching, being touched by, wings.
One of my knuckles was dusted orange.

We got higher and higher,
feeling what anyone would feel when
the best of the impossible
suddenly shows up.
I don't know
what we looked like
to someone planted firmly on the ground.

When the Monarchs were filled
with clover juice,
set to head on to Mexico,
we began coming down to earth.
We stood and watched them,
spoke of the broad, strong wings,
the female's darker orange, thicker
veins, the male's hind-wing scent pockets
for sex, but most of all
their command of air:
how they slipped through it
as if they had been around it
since it had been around,
had taught it

how to be slipped through,
how to hold up a field,
a morning of time and
two men who wanted nothing dead,
nothing in the world.

Apparition

Driving home from Turner the back way in twilight, we went by the fairgrounds and I slowed down, stopping at an opening between two buildings. Out in the center of the racetrack the whole infield was completely white, filled with dandelions gone to seed, as if we had discovered where summer was hiding. On the far side of the track a horse and sulky floated into view, passing by like an apparition. Yet in a minute we heard a clop, clop, clop, and the horse and sulky sped by our opening going the other way, carving out the circumference of where summer lay undisturbed.

Mallards

Ella Mae Brown was driving home from Ellsworth yesterday through the light rain that had been falling since before noontime. Ahead of her, on the wet asphalt, two mallards sat as if they were floating on a river, a drake in full plumage and his hen.

Ella Mae slowed her white 1986 Mazda to a stop for the mallards, but the rig behind her kept coming from fifty yards down the road before the driver noticed and swerved the cab to the right. It lost its grip on the tar. It flipped to its side and snapped the flatbed forward against her. Then the cab went skidding in slow motion into the ditch and the two mallards flew off, following the winding direction of the road.

The driver of the rig broke his left hand. Ella Mae lay in her car, her eyes wide.

"What is it?" she said to Ronnie Kane who looked in at her and, without answering, bolted up the hill to the Chipman place to call the police and the ambulance.

Ella Mae could not see the outside of the Mazda. She lay in its untidy interior, not bleeding on it, but every rib snapped, and most of them lancing soft tissue. They were like a lot of fingers with long fingernails poking into a slowly leaking dike.

I know about this because Ella Mae lived in the town I live in, in a red house across the road from the post office. In summer, 2,000 people live here. But this time of year the number is half that. We spend a considerable time finding out about each other, and although not all of what we report is true, what I've just said about Ella Mae is certain. She was sixty-one years old and had lived in Hancock County all her life.

She used to clean for the people who come to spend the high season in their second homes, the big places that are banked in sheets of glass, and look out at the water of one of the two bays in town. On the summer water there are always ducks to look at, the black ducks, the rafts of molting eiders, and, more recently, the mallards.

Ella Mae cleaned the pine floors and the big window panes and the Formica kitchen tops of those houses. She was rumpled and neutral-colored, and I believe that she must have moved almost invisibly between those gleaming surfaces with her dust cloth and her bottles of cleaning aids. She told our postmistress, Cindy Chipman, that she didn't mind the summer people she worked for, although she couldn't say she understood them exactly. It was Cindy Chipman, a few years ago, who told me that Rufus Gray, the man Ella Mae lived with, liked to slap her around. But I was never sure of that.

When she was alive, we noticed the uncomplicated way she went about her life. Hers was a mild, everyday kind of face. But perhaps, when we think of Ella Mae now, we will remember first the way she died, how sudden it was, how it began with a notion to spare two ducks.

My husband, Fred, and I were driving in to Ellsworth to speak to Harry Lynch at the bank again about why we couldn't make our second mortgage payment. I had lost my job. Fred's job was still steady, but it didn't bring in what we needed, what with Carrie, our daughter, starting college in the fall. The money problems had forced other things to the surface. I was sitting on the passenger side, not saying anything, but thinking it was a time since I could remember feeling pretty, or even just finding a man—any man—attractive. I hardly wanted to cook dinner any more; I didn't care much if the house was clean. When Fred flopped down in a chair and flipped through a magazine, or turned on the TV, or even spoke to me, I felt a big rock—one of those rocks out on the barrens—had been pushed right through the front door and rolled across the floor. A big, heavy, grey rock.

"What did you say?" I would answer. He would say it again in a voice that sounded hollow.

I was turning over in my mind what I felt about Fred and myself, along with the fact that I had just celebrated my forty-eighth birthday, when we saw the two ambulances, the fire truck, the three police cars in the road. As we drove closer, we saw the people squeezed into the doors of Ella Mae's car, talking to her, not touching her. We saw what she must have seen, what their faces looked like. They were people Ella Mae had known for years, but now they looked like strangers. I put my hand on Fred's thigh. He clamped his hand over mine. We drove by the cab and the flatbed and the dozen or so other cars.

"It was Ella Mae," Fred said.

"Why? . . . What were they doing to her in there like that? . . ." I was shaking. The dreary weather meant something more, all of a sudden, than a rainy spring day. It meant the way life was and death could be for anyone: cold, strangely impersonal, people you knew looking right at you and half-scared to death.

"She must be hurt too bad to move," said Fred.

Jimmy Cousins, who is the medic for the Peninsula Ambulance Service, and Jay Carter, who is the driver, and Tom Carter, our policeman, finally decided to move her onto a stretcher and lift the stretcher into the ambulance. They had no other choice, although they must have sat there for a spell thinking it would be a whole lot safer to tow the car to the hospital with Ella Mae inside it.

She said "Hi, Jimmy" just before he leaned down with his smooth, careful hands to strap the oxygen mask to her mouth. Then the blood came up, spurting into the mask. Jimmy said that she shot him a look of pure panic and died.

I couldn't sleep that night. Somehow, Ella Mae's death and the troubles that Fred and I were having grew together in the dark. Then I thought about Carrie spending the night at Lisa Young's house; I decided the Youngs didn't even own a smoke alarm. I was lying on my stomach feeling a bone pinching into my left lung. I was sure that it wasn't my feelings that hurt like that, but something physical, dangerous in my chest. When I turned on my side, the pain moved down to the liver. When I lay on my back, it slipped against my heart. So I got up. The window was open. The air was cold with the smell of melted ice in it. The moon was old, only a blade left.

I went downstairs and Ella Mae was sitting at the oak table by the window. The thin edge of moonlight falling on her made a silvery outline along her skin.

"Ella Mae," I said at once, "I can't have you cleaning my house. It's too messy to clean, and anyhow I can't afford it."

That made her chuckle.

"I'm not here for that," she said. She looked around. I could tell that she was agreeing with me about the mess.

"This week got a little bit out of hand," I said, thinking that it wasn't fair, her coming at night, not calling ahead. What could she expect by not giving any notice? Then I remembered the most important thing about Ella Mae.

"You're dead," I said. I stared right at her.

It was her turn to feel uncomfortable. She looked down at her hands which were folded on the table top. I saw that she was wearing a short-sleeved shirt, in spite of the cold.

"May I get you a sweater?" I asked her, sorry for having been so quick.

"I don't think so," she said, rubbing her upper arms with both hands. "I'm fine," she said. So I sat down across from her.

"Wasn't that something," she leaned forward as she talked, speaking in a half-whisper, as if she thought someone else might overhear, "about Jimmy Cousins. You could have asked me a thousand times and I'd never have guessed it would be Jimmy Cousins I'd be staring at in the end." She chuckled again.

"Did it hurt?" I asked.

"It did," she said.

"I have always been afraid of that part," I blurted, "not so much the being dead, but the dying part."

"Me, too," she said. We sat soaking up the quiet of the room, with the little bit of light falling in on us through the naked branches of the swamp maple outside.

"Did you know that Jimmy Cousins is gay?" she asked me.

"No!" I said.

"I suspected it for some time," she went on, comfortable and confidential, "ever since his mother told me that when he goes to Bangor nights, no one—not even the ambulance drivers—can locate him. He doesn't leave a number or a street address. He was always such a quiet, caring boy, as I remember."

"I didn't know," I repeated.

"When he put that mask over my mouth, it was sort of tender, as if he felt how I was feeling. Not rough, like some men. I wanted to tell him then and there it didn't matter, his being gay. Not to me, anyhow."

"Maybe he knows that, Ella Mae," I said. I set my hand over hers which seemed chilly.

"You never can tell with men," she went on, "take Rufus, for instance. He was always completely positive the whole world was down on him, that everyone in town had him figured for a fool. It made him angry. Not because he didn't agree with them. Because he did."

"I never liked him," I said.

"Well, that makes two of you," she laughed softly. "You and him. I've come to think that people don't really learn anything new after a while," she went on, more to herself than to me. "This'll probably make him hate himself all the worse."

"Cindy told me he hit you," I said. Right away I could tell she thought I had gone too far. She looked out the window.

"What does Cindy know," she said. We sat for a while, not saying anything. I listened to the water in the frog pond by the house pouring off steadily into the ditch that drained into the cedar swamp.

"I'm sorry if he did that to you," I said. I couldn't help but think of her body, how it was the wrong shape and size for hitting and for accidents.

We heard Fred turn over in the bed upstairs. I started to think about his body, too, naked under the sheets. Even though he always cut and split the fire wood, it wasn't that much stronger than Ella Mae's, if you thought about it.

"Can you see the future?" I asked her.

"Try me," she said.

"What about Fred," I told her. "Will his dying be hard?"

She got quiet. She let her eyes focus somewhere outside the window beyond the maple. Her face looked tired, as if she had just finished cleaning one of those big houses.

"Yes," she said. My heart made a rubbery noise. But I felt as if it were news I'd been told already, told years ago and forgotten at the beginning, before I first noticed who Fred was, had singled him out specially. All those years were nothing but days, really.

The days no more than a few minutes. There were never enough of them to get things right, were there? And not many ways to protect ourselves. Ella Mae must have found out all about it, if she hadn't known the whole of it before.

"And me?" I said. "What about me?"

Again, her eyes looked away. Despite how tight I felt inside, I couldn't help but think that she must have been a pretty child, blond, with ruddy, round cheeks.

"Yes," she said.

"Carrie?" I asked. My throat sounded scraped.

Ella Mae looked straight across the table. "That's too far," she said. "I can't see that far."

I let go my breath. "Thank you," I said.

She pushed back the chair, sat up straight, and her eyes went around the big open room, taking in the sink where the dinner dishes sat in a pan of grey water, and the couch under the east window with the afghan on it that my grandmother had made for Fred and me when we were married. She looked at the scented geranium I have kept on the windowsill for five years. It was blooming now with little pink flowers all over it that smell, like the leaves, of cinnamon. Her gaze went down to the floor, to my winter boots with the thick treads, to Fred's old shapeless boots that he wears when he cuts wood, to Carrie's hot pink running shoes. Her eyes stopped at the woodstove that had quit giving off heat a few hours ago.

"It's nice here," she said. "I hadn't noticed before how nice it is." I was bone tired. She was alert, interested in everything, but I could hardly keep my eyes open.

"I'm exhausted," I told her. She turned to look at me, an immaculate spareness to her.

"I'm going to bed," I said. "Do you need anything?"

"I think I'll just sit here for a bit," she said. She smiled. "If I were you, I'd put a broom to it once a day," she made a half-circle with her arm. "It'll take you no more than ten minutes. You'll feel a whole lot better."

"Hold me, Fred," I whispered, shaking him. I didn't want Ella Mae to hear me, to hear the needy sound I was hearing in my voice.

He rolled over.

"Put your arms around me, Fred." He leaned forward, half-awake, to kiss me.

"No!" I whispered. "Not that! Hold me." And he did. His breathing was slow. I put my face into the springy hair of his chest. I knew he had fallen back to sleep because he didn't even feel my crying. There was no sound in it, just tears. Even then I was noticing how warm his skin was. It had a nice smell. It made me remember the time we had first undressed together.

I turned away, lying on my back, listening for any noise that Ella Mae might make downstairs. But there was no noise.

Except for Fred's breathing, and the water moving into the ditch, the night was wide and quiet. I began to relax. My mind was holding on to the picture of Ella Mae sitting at the table. Then I heard a low, sharp sound like somebody rubbing a cloth against glass.

"Damn," I said to myself. "She's washing the windows." But the sound grew louder. It wasn't Ella Mae busy at the windows but a flock of Canada geese flying north in the dark above the house. The sounds came from overhead. They were voices calling sharply back and forth to each other. I heard the wingstrokes. I listened to them fade.

The silence gathered itself up again to settle back on the house and the ground. Then I did hear Ella Mae push back the kitchen chair. I expected that she would sleep on the couch, which I have done myself before, and that she would wrap herself in the afghan because, with the fire out, she was bound to feel the cold.

The Ecuadorian Sailors

The Ecuadorian sailors arrive in Bucksport.
They stare at the American girls who stand
on the oil wharf in shorts and halters, eating
pistachio ice cream in the long Maine afternoons
as the sun drops behind the refinery. Evenings,
the Ecuadorians gather on deck. From the town hall
you can hear their slow, passionate music
as one of the officers, immaculately dressed,
sings something about love, about a man murdered,
a woman stolen in the night. The Bucksport girls
throw daisies to the Ecuadorians, who place them
behind their ears, and the officer sings about
a flower blooming in a forgotten place. The next
morning, the girls wear yellow flowers between
their breasts, but the sailors do not see them.
They want to shop in the American stores. They move
through Bucksport talking rapidly. Soon they find
Laverdiere's Discount Drug Store, where you can buy
anything. A line of Ecuadorian sailors streams
from the ship down Main Street to Laverdiere's.
Another line returns, carrying brown paper bags.
Where the two meet, they talk and touch fingers
like ants describing the source of food and pleasure.
Some have small bags with radios and calculators,
others have large mysterious bags. Two of them
carry a color television while a third holds the
rabbit-ear antenna and tells them where not to step.
One solitary man carries a red snow shovel, as if,
when he brings the shovel home to Ecuador, it

will snow in his village for the first time since
the Pleistocene. When Laverdiere's closes, girls
come to the ship with long dresses and daisies
plaited in their hair. The air fills with music
from guitars, with emotions like red and blue rain-
forest parrots that no one in Bucksport has ever seen.
Each Ecuadorian sailor invites a girl to dance
and speaks to her in Spanish, which she understands
fluently, like a lost native language, like words
uttered by eloquent red parrots in a country where
it is always afternoon. At night, among the oil tanks,
the girls all become women. They go to their houses
before dawn, but they are not the same, they have
new languages, new bodies, they have grown darker
and will wear flowers forever between their breasts,
even when the sailors have returned to Ecuador, even
when they marry and take their clothes off for the
first time in a lighted room, the flowers will be there
like indelible tatoos. Their husbands will grow silent
as winter, but it will not matter, they will teach
their children three or four words of Spanish, a song
about red parrots crying in a place of sunlight where
it never snows, and where the heart is everything.

Brief Afternoons

In the brief afternoons of February,
when the whole God question comes up
like a knock on the door from Jehovah's Witnesses—
no, not *like* them, but *really* them
and their stack of newspapers and questions, swirling
in the snow—I'm cautious, impatient, defenseless.
I guard the door like St. Peter or Cerberus,
The Word before it's written. We discuss the proof
of the snowflake, God's design and the sin of the self.
We require uplifting because of the chill
and the solitude, because we project onto the pines
endings and beginnings, the whiteness of snow
in the darkening quill of afternoon,
where January can no longer be corrected; December's
a parent's perpetual death and July a child's fairy tale.
But now they're at my door with their gloomy accusations,
and because of the lateness of the hour,
because I have no defense, no justification
outside myself, I invite them in for hot chocolate—
together, white man and black man, the lapsed
and the saved, we watch the wind push the snow,
we listen to the woodstove chatter and whisper and hiss.

FRANKLIN BURROUGHS

Of Moose and a Moose Hunter

When I first moved to Maine, I think I must have assumed that
moose were pretty well extinct here, like the wolf or the caribou
or the Abenaki Indian. But we had scarcely been in our house a
week when a neighbor called us over to see one. She had a milk
cow, and a yearling moose had developed a sort of fixation on it.
The moose would come to the feedlot every afternoon at dusk and
lean against the fence, moving along it when the cow did, staying
as close to her as possible. Spectators made it skittish, and it would
roll its eyes at us nervously and edge away from the lot, but never
very far. It was gangly and ungainly; it held its head high, and had
a loose, disjointed, herky-jerky trot that made it look like a puppet
on a string.

The young moose hung around for a couple of weeks, and it
became a small ritual to walk over in the summer evenings and
watch it. My neighbor, Virginia Foster, had reported it to the war-
den, and the warden told her not to worry: the yearling had prob-
ably been driven off by its mother when the time had come for her
to calve again, and it was just looking for a surrogate. It would
soon give up and wander away, he said, and he was right. But until
that happened, I felt that Susan and I, at the beginning of our own
quasi-rural existence, were seeing something from the absolute
beginnings of all rural existence—a wild creature, baffled and in-
trigued by the dazzling peculiarities of humankind, was tentatively
coming forward as a candidate for domestication. Mrs. Foster said
that if the moose planned to hang around and mooch hay all win-
ter, he'd damn well better expect to find himself in the traces and
pulling a plough come spring.

First encounters mean a lot, and in the years that followed,
moose never became for me what they are for many people in

17

Maine: the incarnation and outward projection of that sense of wilderness and wildness that is inside you, like an emotion. As soon as I began going up into the northern part of the state whenever I could, for canoeing and trout fishing, the sight of them came to be familiar and ordinary, hardly worth mentioning. You would see one browsing along the shoulder of a busy highway or standing unconcerned in a roadside bog, while cars stopped and people got out and pointed and shutters clicked. Driving out on a rough logging road at dusk, after a day of trout fishing, you would get behind one, and it would lunge down the road ahead of you. Not wanting to panic it or cause it to hurt itself—a running moose looks out of kilter and all akimbo, like a small boy trying to ride a large bicycle—you'd stop, to allow the moose to get around the next curve, compose itself, and step out of the road. Then you'd go forward, around the curve, and there would be the moose, standing and waiting for the car to catch up to it and scare it out of its wits again. Sometimes you could follow one for half a mile like that, the moose never losing its capacity for undiluted primal horror and amazement each time the car came into sight. Finally it would turn out of the road, stand at the fringe of the woods, and, looking stricken and crestfallen as a lost dog, watch you go past.

Of course you also see them in postcard situations: belly deep in a placid pond, against a backdrop of mountains and sunset, or wading across the upper Kennebec, effortlessly keeping their feet in tumbling water that would knock a man down. Once two of them, a bull and a cow, materialized in a duck marsh as dawn came, and I watched them change from dim, looming silhouettes that looked prehistoric, like something drawn by the flickering illuminations of firelight on the walls of a cave, into things of bulk and substance, the bull wonderfully dark coated and, with his wide sweep of antlers and powerfully humped shoulders, momentarily regal.

But even when enhanced by the vast and powerful landscape they inhabit, moose remained for me animals whose ultimate context was somehow pastoral. An eighteenth- or nineteenth-century English or American landscape painting, showing cattle drinking at dusk from a gleaming river, or standing patiently in the shade

of an oak, conveys a serenity that is profound and profoundly frag-
ile. The cattle look sacred, and we know that they are not. To the
extent that they epitomize mildness, peace, and contentment, they,
and the paintings in which they occur, tacitly remind us that our
allegiance to such virtues is qualified and unenduring, existing in
the context of our historical violence, our love of excitement, mo-
tion, risk, and change. When I would be hunting or fishing, and
a moose would present itself, it would not seem to come out of
the world of predator and prey, where grim Darwinian rules de-
termine every action. That world and those rules allow the op-
posite ends of our experience to meet, connecting our conception
of the city to our conception of the wilderness. The moose would
seem to come from some place altogether different, and that place
most resembled the elegiac world of the pastoral painting, an Ar-
cadian daydream of man and nature harmoniously oblivious to the
facts of man and nature.

I suppose it would be more accurate to say that the moose came
from wherever it came from, but that it seemed to enter the Ar-
cadian region of the imagination. I found it a difficult animal to
respond to. It was obviously wild, but it utterly lacked the poised
alertness and magical evanescence that wild animals have. If by
good fortune you manage to see a deer or fox or coyote before it
sees you, and can watch it as it goes about its business unawares,
you hold your breath and count the seconds. There is the sensation
of penetrating a deep privacy, and there is something of Actaeon
and Artemis in it—an illicit and dangerous joy in this spying. The
animal's momentary vulnerability, despite all its watchfulness and
wariness, brings your own life very close to the surface. But when
you see a moose, it is always unawares. It merely looks peculiar,
like something from very far away, a mild, displaced creature that
you might more reasonably expect to encounter in a zoo.

In 1980, for the first time in forty-five years, Maine declared an
open season on moose. Given the nature of the animal, this was
bound to be a controversial decision. People organized, circulated
petitions, collected signatures, and forced a special referendum.
There were televised debates, bumper stickers, advertising cam-

paigns, and letters to editors. The major newspapers took sides, judicious politicians commissioned polls. One side proclaimed the moose to be the state's sacred and official animal. The other side proclaimed moose hunting to be an ancient and endangered heritage, threatened by officious interlopers who had no understanding of the state's traditional way of life. Each side accused the other of being lavishly subsidized by alien organizations with sinister agendas: the Sierra Club, the National Rifle Association. The argument assumed ideological overtones: doves versus hawks; newcomers versus natives; urban Maine versus rural Maine; liberals versus conservatives.

At first this seemed to be just the usual rhetoric and rigmarole of public controversy. But as the debate continued, the moose seemed to become a test case for something never wholly articulated. It was as though we had to choose between simplified definitions of ourselves as a species. Moose hunters spoke in terms of our biology and our deep past. They maintained that we are predators, carnivores, of the earth earthly; that the killing and the eating of the moose expressed us as we always had been. The other side saw us as creatures compelled by civilization to evolve: to choose enlightenment over atavism, progress over regression, the hope of a gentler world to come over the legacy of instinctual violence. Both sides claimed the sanction of Nature—the moose hunters by embodying it, their opponents by protecting it. Each side dismissed the other's claim as sentimental nonsense.

I knew all along that when it came to moose hunting I was a prohibitionist, an abolitionist, a protectionist, but not a terribly zealous one. When the votes were counted and the attempt to repeal the moose season had been defeated, I doubted that much had been lost, in any practical way. The hunt was to last only a week, and only a thousand hunters, their names selected by lottery, would receive permits each year. It had been alleged that once moose were hunted, they would become as wild and wary as deer, but they have proved to be entirely ineducable. Hunter success ran close to 90 percent in that first year, and has been just as high in the years that followed, and the moose I continue to see each summer are no smarter or shyer than the one that had mooned around Mrs. Foster's feedlot, yearning to be adopted by her cow.

Late one afternoon, toward the end of September, the telephone
rang, and there was a small voice, recognizably Terri Delisle's:
"Liz there?" So I went and got Liz. She's old enough to have over-
come all but the very last, genetically encoded traces of tele-
phobia—just a momentary look of worry when she hears that it's
for her, and a tentativeness in her "Hullo?" as though she were
speaking not into the receiver but into a dark and possibly empty
room.

Terri is her friend, her crony. The two of them get together—
both polite, reticent, and normally quiet little girls—and sponta-
neously constitute between themselves a manic, exuberant sub-
culture. It possesses them. They are no longer Terri and Liz but
something collective: a swarm, a gang, a pack, or a carnival, hav-
ing its own unruly gusts of volition. They glitter with mischief,
laugh at everything, giggle, romp, and frolic, and I believe that,
with each other's help, they actually lose for a moment all con-
sciousness of the adult world that watches from within, waiting
for children to draw toward it. They aren't destructive or insub-
ordinate—that, after all, would be a backhanded acknowledgment
of civilization, maturity, and responsibility. They are simply be-
yond the reach of reproof, like colts or puppies.

But on the telephone, with distance between them, self-
conscious circumspection took over. I heard Liz's guarded and
rigorously monosyllabic responses: "Yep." "He did?" "Sure—I'll
have to ask Dad." "OK. Bye." And so she told me that Terri's
father Henry had killed a moose. Would we like to go over and see
it? "Sure," I say, all adult irony, "I'll have to ask Mom."

I knew Henry Delisle in a small and pleasant way. There were a
lot of Delisles in town, and Henry, like his brother and most of his
male cousins, worked over in Bath, at the shipyard—a welder, I
think. But like many other natives of Bowdoinham, he had farm-
ing in the blood. The old Delisle farm, up on the Carding Machine
Road, had long since been subdivided and sold, and Henry's neat,
suburban-looking house sat on a wooded lot of only two or three
acres. Even so, he had built himself a barn and a stock pen, and
he kept a few pigs, a milk cow, and an old draft horse named Ho-

mer. There couldn't have been much economic sense to it, just a feeling that a house wasn't a home without livestock squealing or lowing or whickering out back. He plainly liked the whole life that livestock impose upon their owners—harnessing Homer up for a day of cutting and hauling firewood; making arrangements with local restaurants and grocery stores to get their spoiled and leftover food for pig fodder; getting the cow serviced every so often, and fattening the calf for the freezer. He had an antiquated Allis-Chalmers tractor, with a sickle bar and a tedder and a bailer. There are a lot of untended fields in Bowdoinham, and plenty of people were glad to let Henry have the hay if he would keep them mown.

That was how I had met him for the first time. He had come rattling up to the house in his big dilapidated flatbed truck to ask me if anybody planned to cut my fields that summer. In fact somebody did, and I told him so, but Henry had too much small-town civility, which coexists comfortably with small-town curiosity, simply to turn around and drive off. I appreciated that, and so we chatted for a while—Henry sitting up in his truck, talking with an abrupt and fidgety energy, and I standing down beside it.

He remembered my house from his boyhood: "Used to be a reg'lar old wreck of a place. They didn't have no electricity down here or nothing. Winters, they'd cut ice from the pond. Had a icehouse dug into the back there; kept ice all through summer. Hard living." He told me a story I'd heard even before we bought the house, how one winter the eldest son had gone out to the barn to milk, as he did every morning, and had found his younger brother there, hanging from a ceiling joist. "Never a word or a note. That was a terrible thing to happen. Unfriendly people, but they didn't deserve that."

He laughed. "But they was *some* unfriendly, I want to tell you. I slipped down to the pond and set muskrat traps one fall. But they musta seen me. They pulled 'em every one out and kept 'em. I was afraid to ask—just a kid, you know. Probably still lying around in your barn somewhere." He looked at me and sized me up: "But I ain't afraid to ask now, and don't you be afraid to turn me down— would you mind me setting a few traps in that pond this fall? It used to be about lousy with muskrats." I hesitated at this—the pond was still full of muskrats, and I enjoyed seeing them sculling across it, pushing little bundles of cut grass ahead of them, or sitting out on a log, grooming themselves with a quick, professional adroitness. But I liked him for the way he had asked it, and there was something else. His country-bred practicality and local knowledge gave him an obscure claim—he was less indigenous than the muskrats, but far more so than I was. "Sure," I told him, "go ahead."

All this had taken place on a bright, airy morning in late July or early August, with the kind of high sky that would make anybody think of haying. Henry said he was glad he'd stopped by, and that I'd see him again once the trapping season opened. I reached up, we shook hands, and he backed the truck down the driveway. His windshield caught the sun for a moment and blinded me and then, as the truck swung up into the yard to turn around, I could see through the glass what I had not been able to see before. He had a passenger—a little girl sitting in the middle of the seat, right at his elbow. She did not look in my direction at all, but stared at the dashboard with that look of vacancy and suspended animation that you see on the faces of children watching Saturday morning cartoons. Henry grinned at me, waved goodbye, and the big truck went lumbering off.

That first meeting with Henry had been the summer before Elizabeth and Terri started school. Later, when they had become classmates and best friends, I learned that the girl I had seen in the truck was Stephanie, whom everybody called Tadpole. She was three years older than Terri, but that was a technicality.

Bowdoinham is a small, spread-out town. It tries to hold onto the idealized ethos of the New England village, but is in fact well on its way to becoming a bedroom community, a pucker-brush suburb. Like the state as a whole, it is full of outsiders moving in, old-timers dying out, and the uneasy sense of a lost distinctiveness.

The elementary school is the nearest thing to an agora that such a town has. Parents are separated by their backgrounds and expectations, and by the devious anxieties of people who feel that, in appearing to belong to the little unglamorous place they inhabit, they may misrepresent or compromise themselves. But children go to school, and it stands for the world. They make friends and enemies, and suddenly populate your household with unfamiliar names. It is as though you had sent them off as members and worshipers of a stable, self-sufficient Trinity consisting of Mama, Daddy, and themselves, and then had them return as rampant polytheists, blissfully rejoicing or wailing despairingly about the favors and sulks of capricious gods and goddesses named Tommy Blanchard, Vera Sedgely, Joanie Dinsmore, Nikki Toothacre, and Willie Billings. At school functions you would meet the parents of these entities, or, prodded by your child, would nervously call up Joan's or Nikki's mom, and arrange for that child to come over and play. And slowly, with no direct intention of doing so, you would find out about other families in the town—who they were and how they lived, how they regarded themselves and how they were regarded.

So we learned that Tadpole suffered from Down's syndrome. She was the first child of Henry and Debbie Delisle, born to them within a year of their marriage, when they themselves were just out of high school. Perhaps if they had had more education and experience they would have accepted the irremediable fact of their daughter's condition. As it was, they were mistrustful of the state and the school system and all the experts who came to help them and warn them and in some way to deprive them of the right to raise their daughter as they saw fit. Against every recommendation, they were determined to try to give Tadpole all the circumstances of an ordinary childhood.

When time came for Tadpole to go to school, Henry wrangled with the school board and the superintendent and the Department of Mental Health and Retardation. And finally everybody agreed that, for as long as it didn't create any disturbance, Tadpole could go to school with Terri. Word of that sort of thing gets around, and some parents didn't like it, fearing that what Henry had gained for his daughter would diminish the education and attention that their own children would receive. But I believe that most of us admired Henry and wished him well. He was his own man; in his battered old truck, with a tottering load of hay on it, or with Homer tethered to the headboard, he implied an old-fashioned resourcefulness and independence, which we could praise even if we

24

couldn't emulate. It was heartening to see a man like that acting out of the best and simplest human impulse, and sticking to his guns, even if, in the long run, the case were hopeless.

And of course the case was hopeless, although at first it didn't appear to be. Tadpole was docile and affectionate, and in her first year and a half of school, she enjoyed an almost privileged status among her classmates. It was as though she were their mascot, like the wheezy old bulldog or jessed eagle you might find on the side-lines at a college football game. You would see a crowd of children fussing over her in the schoolyard, alternately courting her as though she were a potentate to be appeased, or babying her with bossy solicitude. Liz would report on all that Tadpole had done or said, as though she were a celebrity, in whom we should take a communal pride. And we did take a kind of pride in her. Her being at the school with the other children seemed proof that humane flexibility, sympathy, and tolerance were still operative in this overgrown country. There was something quaint about it, some-thing from the putative innocence of the past.

But by the end of the second grade, Liz was bringing home bad news. Tadpole had begun to balk at going to school, and would misbehave when she was there. She was bigger than her class-mates, and her truculence threatened them. They retaliated as chil-dren would, by teasing and persecution. She regressed, growing more withdrawn and morose, and would go through days of not speaking, or of only muttering to herself. Public opinion hard-ened. I don't think there were any petitions or formal proceedings to have Tadpole removed; it was just one of those sad things that had become plain and obvious. Henry and Debbie had no choice; they had to give in to the fact that confronted them every day. The next year, Tadpole and Terri were separated, and Tadpole was sent to school in Topsham, where there was a class for what the state calls Special Children.

When Terri would come over to play, she seemed untroubled by the change. She was as quick and inventive as ever. I did not know Henry well enough or see him often enough to speak to him about the matter, and hardly knew what I would or could have said. He got himself transferred to the night shift at the shipyard that fall, and he must have kept Tadpole out of the special class a good deal. I would regularly see the two of them together in the truck—usually first thing in the morning, when he'd just gotten off work. But he told me one morning, when he'd come to check the muskrat traps, that he had changed shifts purely to give himself more time for the woodcutting, haying, trapping, ice-fishing, and hunting that seemed to be his natural vocations.

So on the September afternoon in question, Liz and I got into the car—none of the rest of the household had any interest in a dead moose—and drove over. It was nearly dark when we turned up into Henry's driveway. His garage lights were on. He had set up a worktable of planks and sawhorses along the rear wall; the moose was hanging by the neck squarely in the center of the garage. From the driveway, it looked like a shrine or a crèche—the brightly lit space, clean and spare as an Edward Hopper interior; Henry and four other men standing chatting, and, just behind them, the lynched moose. Terri came running out, excited as on Christmas morning, and took us in to see.

From the outside, the moose's head appeared to go right up through the low ceiling of the garage, but once inside I could see that, when he had built the garage, Henry had left out one four-by-eight ceiling panel, to give him access to the attic. He had put an eye bolt in a collar tie, centered above the opening, so that he could rig a hoist from it. It was a smart arrangement, enabling him to convert an ordinary two-car garage into an abattoir whenever he had a cow or pig or deer to slaughter. The moose he had shot was a cow, and she was a big animal, hanging with her head in the attic, her rump scarcely a foot above the concrete floor. A big animal but not, Henry said, a big moose. "She'll dress out about five-fifty. Just a heifer. She'd have calved next spring."

Henry introduced me to the other men—neighbors who had wandered over out of curiosity, and his cousin Paul, who had been his partner in the hunt.

We were somehow an uncomfortably self-conscious group; it was as though we were all trying to ignore something. Perhaps it was that Paul and Henry were still in their stained and ragged hunting gear, and were grubby and unshaven. The rest of us were in our ordinary street clothes, and only a few minutes ago were watching television or pottering around the house or having a drink and getting ready for supper. We had been in our familiar cocoons of routine and obligation, where the only world that matters is the human one. And now we were talking to men who were in another role, and we were abruptly confronting a large, dead animal, a thing from far beyond our lives.

I think it was more this awkwardness than aggression that made the man next to me, a bank manager new to town, speak the way he did. "Well, Henry. That's a weird damned animal. You sure it's not a camel?" Everybody laughed, but uneasily.

"Tell us about it," the man said. "How'd you bag the wily moose?"

Henry said there wasn't a whole lot to tell. The man asked him if he'd hired a guide. Henry said he hadn't.

"Well maybe you should have," the bank manager said. "If you had, you might have gotten yourself a bull. Then you'd have something to hang in your den."

Henry didn't answer. He got busy with a knife, whetting it against a butcher's steel. The man walked around the moose, looking at her appraisingly, as though she were an item in a yard sale. Then he said he had to get on back home, and left, and there was a general relaxing. Henry looked up.

Now he was going to tell us how you kill a moose, or how he had killed this one. None of us knew anything about moose hunting. The tradition of it had died out, and hunters—even very experienced ones like Henry and Paul—don't know moose in the way that they know deer. The hunt was limited to the upper third of the state, and a lot of people up there had set themselves up as moose guides, offering what was supposedly their deep-woods wisdom to anybody lucky enough to have a permit.

Henry snorted: "Hire a guide. You know what a moose guide is? He's a guy with a skidder, that's all. You go to his house and he'll take you out and leave you somewheres where he thinks there might be a moose, and charge you so much for that. Then you kill a moose and he'll charge you a arm and a leg to hook it up to the skidder and drag it out to your truck. So I go to this guy that's listed as a guide, and he explains it to me. And I say to him, 'Look.

Don't tell me a word about where to find a moose. Now if I get one, what'll you charge to drag him out?' 'Hundred dollars for the first hour; fifty dollars per hour after that,' he says. See, they got you. Law don't let you kill a moose less than fifty yards from the road. So I says to him, 'You prorate that first hour?' 'Fifty dollar minimum,' he says to me. 'Take it or leave it.' Musta thought I was from Massachusets. 'See you later,' I says. And that fifty dollar, hundred dollar shit ain't from the time he drives his skidder off his trailer into the woods. It's from the time he gets in his truck right there in his front yard."

Paul quietly removed himself from Henry's audience and went into the kitchen. It wasn't his story, and there was a lot of work still to do.

"We had topo maps, and I seen some good bogs. Day before the season opened we drove and scouted all day. I don't know much about moose, but I know a moose'll walk on a log road or a skidder track if he can, instead of bustin' through the bushes. About suppertime we see a cow cross the road ahead of us, and go down a skidder trail. We followed her down on foot. There was a bog in there at the end of the trail, about a quarter mile in off the road, and there she was, feeding. Her and another cow too. That skidder trail was rough, but I figured we might be able to get the truck down it.

"Opening day it was raining. We parked a ways off and walked up to the skidder track and down to the bog. Got there before day. When it come day, one cow was there. I looked at her. She looked good, but not extra good. Animal like a moose got a lot of waste on 'em. Big bones, big body cavity—not as much meat as you'd think. That's what they tell me. And they told me when you see a cow, wait. It's rut, and a big bull might come along any time."

Paul came out from the house with his arms full—wrapping paper, freezer tape, a roll of builder's plastic. He spread the plastic over the table, and he didn't make any effort to be unobtrusive about it. But Henry was occupied by his story. It was like something he wanted to get off his chest or conscience. Maybe he just couldn't get over the strangeness of the moose.

"It ain't like a deer. A cow moose calls a bull. That's what they say and it's the truth. We watched her all day, and ever so often she'd set right down on her butt and beller, like a cow that ain't been milked. So we set there too, and waited, but no bull showed. By dark she'd worked over to the other side of the bog. Shoot her there and you'd have to cut her up and pack her out."

Henry was standing in front of the moose. Her chin was elevated and her long-lashed eyes were closed. All of the things that had so splendidly adapted her to her world of boreal forest, bog, and swamp made her look grotesque here: the great hollow snout, the splayed feet and overlong, knob-kneed legs. In whatever consciousness she had had, it was still the Ice Age—she was incapable of grasping human purposes or adjusting to human proximity. Her death was almost the first ritual of civilization, yet she was in our present, suspended in the naked light of a suburban garage, and we could only stand, hands in pockets, as though it were something we did every day.

"So we come back the next day, a little earlier even, and I sent Paul around to the far side of the bog. This time I hear her walking in on that skidder track just before day, and she got out in the bog and bellered some more. We were going to give her 'til noon. I figured if a bull showed, he'd come up the track too, and I could get him before he hit the bog.

"By noon she was all the way out in the middle of the bog again, but Paul stepped out of the bushes, easy, so's not to scare her too much. Took her the longest time even to notice him. Then she started trotting toward me, but she'd keep stopping to beller some more. It was almost like she was mad."

One of the men chuckled: "More like she was desperate, if you ask me. If she didn't call herself up a boyfriend pretty quick, she was a dead duck."

"Well. Anyway, Paul had to slog out after her, keep shooing her along. I wanted her to get all the way out on the trail, but she musta smelt me. Stopped about ten foot from the woods and started throwing her head around and acting jumpy, like she might bolt. So I shot her there.

"We had a little work with the chain saw to clear the skidder trail out wide enough for the truck. Then we backed in and put a rope around her and dragged her out to dry ground. Used a come-along to hoist her up on a tree limb and dressed her out right there.

Then cranked her up some more, backed the truck under, and low-ered her in. On the way out, we stopped by that guy's house. I went in and told him we wouldn't be needing his damn skidder this year."

The whole time Henry talked, Paul kept coming and going, bringing out knives, a cleaver, a meat saw, and a plastic tarp. Eliz-abeth and Terri had examined the moose and then gone inside. I had been worried about Elizabeth. She was at least as sentimental as the average ten-year-old about animals; at country fairs she would lean against the stalls and gaze with pure yearning at Suffolk sheep or Highland cattle and especially at horses of any descrip-tion. But she and Terri had looked the moose over as though she were a display in a museum of natural history, something inter-esting but remote. They had walked around her, rubbed the coarse, stiff hair, and inspected the big cloven feet, and then gone about their business.

Now, as Henry finished his story, they returned, giggling. Terri was carrying a child's chair, and Liz looked from her to me, trying not to laugh. Terri ran up to the moose and slipped the chair under her rump, and then the two of them stood back and waited on our reaction.

It was comic relief or comic desecration. Because the moose's hindquarters were so near the floor, her hind legs were spread stiffly out in front of her. With the addition of the chair, you sud-denly saw her in a human posture, or really in two human pos-tures. From the waist down, she looked like a big man sprawled back on a low seat. Above the waist, she had the posture of a well-bred lady of the old school, her back very straight, her head aloof, and her whole figure suggesting a strenuous and anxious rectitude.

In the ready, makeshift way of country people, Henry had taken one of Debbie's old worn-out lace curtains with him, and when he had killed and cleaned the moose, he had pinned the curtain across the body cavity, to keep out debris and insects and to allow the air to circulate and cool the animal while he and Paul drove back home. The curtain was longer than it needed to be, and now Terri picked up one end of it, brought it like a diaper up between the moose's legs, wrapped it around the hips, and tucked it in, so that it would stay up. The effect was funny in a way I don't like to admit I saw—the garment looked like something between a pinafore and a tutu. It was as though the moose had decided, in some moment of splendid delusion, to take up tap dancing or ballet, and was now waiting uncomfortably to go on stage for her first recital.

Terri and Liz admired the moose. "She needs a hat," Terri pronounced, and they ducked into the house. What they came out with was better than a hat—a coronet of plastic flowers, left over from some beauty pageant or costume.

"Daddy, could you put this on her? She's too high for us."

She was too high for Henry too, but he pulled the little chair from beneath the moose, then picked Terri up and set her on his shoulders. He stood on the chair and Terri, leaning out daringly, like a painter on a stepladder, managed to loop the coronet over one of the long ears, so that it hung lopsided. She slid down Henry to the ground, stepped back and dusted her hands together.

"There. That'll just have to do. I think Momma needs to see this. Maybe she'll lend us some mittens and a scarf. Let's go get her and Tadpole to come see."

"Terri, Paul and me got to get to work on that moose right now," Henry called after her, but she was already gone. The other two men who had come over to see the moose said they had to go, and left, one on foot and one in his car. Terri and Liz came back out with Debbie and Tadpole. Debbie looked at the moose and laughed. Terri was pleased.

"Don't you think she looks like a beauty queen, Mom? We could enter her in the Miss Bowdoinham contest."

"Well I guess so." Debbie turned to Tadpole. "Look at Daddy's moose that he brought us, honey." Tadpole looked at it and walked over as though she wanted to touch it, but didn't. Her face had that puffy, numbed look of someone just wakened from a deep sleep, and her movements were slow and labored.

Debbie called over to Terri. "Now your Daddy and Paul have to start, and I've got to run buy some more freezer paper. You and Stephanie come with me, and we can let Liz get home for her supper."

Terri gave the moose a comradely whack on the rump: "Good-bye, moose. You're going in the freezer." Liz patted the moose too, but more tentatively. Then they all trooped out.

I stood talking to Henry for a few minutes longer. He looked at the moose with her cockeyed halo and tried to make a joke of it. "If she'd been dressed that way this morning, maybe I'd have got a bull." But his laughter was awkward, apologetic. His remark about how little useable meat there really was on a moose, for all its great size, had not been lost on me, and yet I felt that it would be right to ask him for something, as a way of restoring to him a vestige of the old role of hunter as public benefactor, bringer home of the bacon. So I asked him if I could have some of the long hair from the nape of her neck, for trout flies.

"Sure thing," he said, all business. "Tell you what: I won't cut it off now—don't want no more loose hair than I can help when we go to skin her. But when she's done, I'll clip some off and drop it by, next time I'm down your way. You can count on it."

I thanked him and left. Liz was subdued as we drove back toward home. You might have asked an older child what she was thinking, but not Liz, not for a few years yet. Besides, I wasn't so certain what *I* was thinking just then: two scenes alternated in my mind. One was a recollection, back from the previous November, a morning when heavy frost had sparkled white as mica on the dead grass, and I had been driving to work. I saw Henry walking across a stubble field, a big fox slung over his shoulder. He held the fox by its hind legs; its tail, curved over and lying along its back, was luxuriant and soft as an ostrich plume, and it stirred lightly in the breeze. I felt some sadness for the dead beauty of the fox, but it was Henry I remembered. He ought to have looked like a mighty hunter before the Lord, holding the bounty of his skill and cunning and knowledge of the ways of wild animals in his hand. But he was walking with a shambling hesitation, to keep pace with the daughter clinging to his other hand and trudging glumly at his side, beyond any idea of triumph or happiness.

The other image was of something that had not happened yet. June would come again, and I would be up north fishing again—this time with a fly that would have, wrapped in tight spirals around the shank of the hook to imitate the segmented body of a nymph or mayfly, one or two strands of mane from Henry's moose. And I would look up from the water, almost dizzy with staring for so long at nothing but the tiny fly drifting in the current, and there they would be—maybe a cow and a calf—standing on the other bank, watching me watch them, trying to fathom it.

Cecile's Dog Bo

Before I leave Florida, Daddy says, "But you ain't ever experienced a Maine winter."

"Sure I did," I say back.

"When I was stationed in Brunswick," he says, his chest getting a puffed-out look, "why, you was just a tot then. One year ol', about. We had us a Maine winter that year, all right. You're pickin' a heck of a place to go live, young lady."

"Daddy, I was *born* in Maine," I say. "All our life we traveled, one navy base to another. I never had nowhere to call home."

"*This* is home," Daddy says.

"*Your* home. We moved here when I was nineteen. But Maine is my *homeland*. I feel a need to see where I am from."

"Damned foolishness," Daddy says.

I come in late September, when it's pretty enough here to make you wanna cry. I drive around and look at trees for a couple weeks, stay in hotels. There's a bright-orange feel to things—people's faces shine, the sun follows everybody around. But after the leaves fall, everything changes; people's skin gets grey-colored, and they got worried expressions on their faces. Sky looks like it's having a good sulk.

So I get a job. I get a roommate.

❀

Later today it's gonna snow. I have the radio on at work, turn it up every time they give the news. The weather girl talks in them excited tones: "This'll be a *big* one," she says, "so batten down those hatches." They got a list of cancelings, including the shoeshop where my roommate Cecile works second shift—looks like she'll be home tonight, which I wonder how it will go. Cecile's on hard times.

I've had some bad trials in love, but I never lost a man to another woman. Cecile and I agree: that is the worst. You have no choice there; you just have to put your hands in the air and let go of your man.

And, to boot all, this guy leaves her Bo.

❉

"Won't be long now," someone says. Every time I look out the window my heart jumps up in my throat. Everything's grey-brown: the sidewalks, buildings, sky. The clouds'r so low it looks like if you take a good running leap you can slap 'em. I think: *I am about to see the pure, natural power of my homeland,* and my heart takes a surge.

Not that I ain't ever seen snow, 'though Daddy got sent to warm places, mostly. But Cecile shows 'me snapshots of the '79 blizzard, *seventeen* inches, she says—I flip through 'em, disbelieving: one of them shows just her head sticking out behind a sidewalk snow-bank. Her car's buried up completely. Bo's just a puppy, a *blur* on a hill of white snow.

Around eleven-thirty someone says, "Here it is!" and I run to the window, my heart filling up my throat so I can't talk. Everyone's watching me. "What'cha think, Maureen?" they say. It's *beautiful*. The flakes fall all gentle-like, like God's letting 'em slide out of His hands.

I call up Cecile. "Look outside!" I yell, and she laughs. I hear Bo's toenails slipping on the linoleum below her.

"Bo wants to say hi," she says.

"Put 'im on," I tell her. "Hi, Bo!" *Bonjour,* Bo!" I say. That's one of Bo's tricks. You ever heard of a French-speakin' dog? Cecile grew up talking French—*lots* of people 'round here do, so she taught him French, too. Everyone in our block says *bonjour* to Bo. "It's snowing out, Bo!" I yell. I can hear him breathing like crazy in the phone.

"He knows it's you," Cecile says, sounding far away. "Where's

Maureen, Bo? *Va voir Maureen!*" I can hear Bo's head banging on the receiver. "So." Cecile's voice is loud again. "This is Maine, Maureen. You like it?"

I make a noise of love.

At noontime the boss says, "Put down your weapons, gang, and make a run for it." Those folks who take an hour drive from Portland rush out the door. I walk slow to my apartment, feeling the flakes on my face, taking a few on my tongue—they taste sour. They're falling on everything—window railings, garbage-can tops, people's hats. The buildings are getting a lacy design to 'em. The wind whips around when I turn onto Pine Street, and the air is full-up of whirling snow, like elf-dust in a fairy tale.

I get to my building and go up the stairs; I come in the first-floor apartment. Cecile's vacuum is going, which is prob'ly why Bo ain't come running; he can't hear me. I take off my wet coat and high heels and walk over, and peek into Cecile's room. She's vacuuming out Bo's spot under the bed, where he sleeps. Her and Bo's rumps stick out while she runs the hose around back and forth; Bo's white tail whacks Cecile's rear end again and again.

Bo ain't really Cecile's dog. He belongs to her husband Robert. It's Robert's old trophy room I'm renting now—Robert's a bowler, a good one judging by the big trophies Cecile had to pack up. Cecile is not a dog-person, she claims, so when Robert calls asking on Bo, I hear her tell him: *"Come get your dog."* Robert says he can't; he's livin' with a woman who don't like dogs.

But when I suggest taking Bo to the pound, Cecile says, "No way. I couldn't do that, even if he wasn't Robert's dog. Imagine being put in a cold cage, preparing yourself to die. You ever been there, Maureen? The dogs *know*. They look at you that way—they know you're their last hope. I'm not takin' Bo there, no-sir. I wouldn't bring my worst enemy to the pound."

Bo starts squirming, barking at the vacuum cleaner. "Damn it, Bo, get out, get out, get out!" Cecile shouts. *"Va t'en!"* Bo backs out rump first, turns around, sees me and bounds over—I duck out of the way—Bo has a *powerful* leap. He sniffs me like crazy. Bo is nose-first at any event, any arrival; nose don't stop. He is smelling the pure odor of snow, I know. He's pretty, mostly white, with some black. Some kind of hunter, Cecile don't know which.

"Hi, Cecile!" I yell, so she won't be spooked when she turns the machine off and finds someone in the house. She looks around and waves the hose at me. Bo runs and splashes her face, whining, sniffing the vacuum hose. Cecile wipes the nose-goo off her cheek.

She says: "Yup, this is your space, Bo. Right under where Papa used to sleep." When Bo hears the word "Papa" his ears prick up. "No, Bo," Cecile says, shaking her head. "Papa's gone away. *Papa s'en aller.*"

Bo's ears go flat.

Cecile puts the vacuum away and we decide to go strolling. We bundle up warm; she put's Bo's sweater, which she crocheted for him, over his long legs. We laugh at him for a while—he looks like a little old man. He stares up at us, self-conscious, leans over and gives the sweater a careful sniff, like it's gonna blow up in his face. Cecile made him two—a red and a blue; today he is wearing his blue.

Bo is unpredictable, so he stays on a leash; we take turns holding him 'til our arms get sore. We walk around the block, go buy cigarettes. Bo jumps up and bites at the snow. A blue pickup truck whishes by and Bo stops dead. *Points.*

"See that?" Cecile says. She stops walking and the snow piles up on her shoulders. "A blue Ford Ranger. That dog knows blue from any other color. He sits in the window all day, watching for Robert's blue pickup. Robert is Bo's true master," she sighs, and we start walking again.

Bo crouches low and shakes off the snow. He looks displeased, grumpy. He sniffs a curbside and pees—makes me sad to see the clean snow dirtied up. It reaches to our ankles now, about three inches. Hardly any cars go by, just enough to keep the street shiny, so you can see the reflection of the stoplights in 'em. Everything's white and clean, pretty. I say out loud: "Pretty."

"So you like the snow," Cecile says. "You *must* be a Maine girl. Well, then again, there's plenty of Maine girls who hate the snow, go live in Florida soon as they can swing it."

"Florida's nice," I say. "But Maine's my *homeland.*"

We walk along; Cecile pulls off her mittens, lights a Winston inside her hands, and then starts crying, which she does every day for a little while. I let her go on, know she'll be better soon. I look around and breathe in the smell of snow, feel the cold, keep track of Bo, who sniffs at everything.

Then the UPS truck goes by. Cecile drops her cigarette in a hurry. "Oh, Jesus, hang on to 'im," she says, and she grabs Bo's leash so we're both holding on. "It's the UPS man," she explains to me. Bo sees the truck and starts bouncing in the air like a circus dog. He gives some loud accusing barks and strains against the collar 'til he gags.

"Sit!" Cecile yells. *"Assiz-toué!"* Bo pays no heed. His body bounds up and he snaps at the air again and again, like he's trying to eat up her words. The truck stops in front of us at a red light and the UPS man stares out—and don't those UPS men look alike? All across America. Brown suit, brown hair, brown eyes. Bo bares his teeth and growls back in his throat; white spit falls out the sides of his mouth.

"Shame!" Cecile yells. *"Non-non!"* But the wind comes tornadoing down and carries her voice away. It sounds small and high-pitched. The light goes green and the truck roars off. Bo watches it go, blinking his eyes in the falling snow; then he does a real nice heel by Cecile's side for the rest of the walk. "Don't know why it is," Cecile says, "Bo hates the UPS so much."

Well, at least she stopped crying, I think. I go back to looking at the winter wonderland. I sing Christmas carols in my mind. I feel the spirit of this realm inside me. I am a Maine girl.

❄

We've had eight inches by the time I'm lying in bed, ready for sleep. I listen to the wind hurry in and out the alleys between the blocks, like it's searching for something important it lost there, hear the big jingling sounds of the plows going by. Cecile's rocking in her chair, crocheting. I hear her say to Bo, "As if a Maine winter ain't bad enough. We're goin' this one alone, boy." I imagine him looking up at her, squinting his eyes, tryin' to understand.

And then I'm asleep.

＊

At four A.M. I hear a snow plow rumble by and then there's that awful sound Bo makes just before he throws up, which he does every morning since Robert left. He grunts some more, and finally the release comes. I hear Cecile's bedsprings.

"Thank you, Bo," she says. "*Merci beaucoup* for the nice gift." She goes in the kitchen; Bo follows along, his paws pitpatting on the linoleum.

I sit up, anxious to look outdoors. My window is white, opaque—covered with snow in a paisley-swirl pattern. I get up and go into Cecile's room. She's heaping paper towels on the floor; Bo sits quietly beside her, his tongue hanging out sideways.

"What would I do without Bo to get me started in the morning?" Cecile says. "Why, I just might sleep all the damn day."

Bo watches, shame-faced, while she cleans up the mess. I get his leash, throw my coat over my pajamas, put on my sneakers—don't own boots yet. I put Bo's red sweater on him and take him outside. I hold my breath when I open the outside door.

I'm not disappointed. The whole world smells like outdoor-dried laundry: *fresh*. The streetlights are like tall angels, their halos dim under layers of moving white wings. Bo and I step carefully into the trackless snow. We find a corner of the yard with a low drift—Bo crouches and pees, then we walk around the yard some more. The snow stings our faces—Bo looks up at me and then heads back for the door, pulling me along. He shakes the snow off his red sweater, and we go into the apartment.

Cecile has gone back to sleep. Bo stops to sniff the wet spot where he was sick, then crawls underneath the bed. I go to my room and lie down, and think how I haven't missed Florida at all. Next time Daddy calls I will say so.

❉

Cecile and I have no work because we're sitting on fourteen inches of snow, which is still blustering around. Cecile says that it is mostly wind now; the storm's about over. I stare out the window at the sky, don't see any change. But I trust her on this. She's lived twenty-eight Maine winters, after all. I was just born here.

We cook pancakes with warmed-up maple syrup that Cecile's father makes from his trees, and have what Cecile calls Canadian bacon, which I know as breakfast ham. Bo begs like mad. Cecile says *"non-non"* but later I see her pass him a little hunk. Then we sit in the living room. Cecile crochets a lap blanket while I watch *Price is Right*. Bo's at our feet, being good. Suddenly he cocks up his head and starts panting hard. I don't hear anything, keep watching, try to guess the price of the Creamettes. Bo gets up, goes in the kitchen. Hurls himself against the door.

"I'll take him," I say. "You went last time."

Bo is standing up, his paws on the frame of the kitchen window, looking out. I peek past his head, make out a blue truck behind the swirling snow. Some guy gets out. Bo goes to the door and pitches himself against it.

"Hey, Cecile!" I yell. "Come here a minute!" She comes in trailing a long green yarn. "That Robert's pickup?" I ask, pointing at the window. She looks out.

"I don't believe it," she says. Bo paces from the door to the window, bouncing himself off them, whimpering.

"So that's him?" I say to Cecile.

"That's him," Cecile says to Bo. *"Papa y'est chez nous."* She pats Bo's head while he stretches himself up, paws scratching against the windowpane, mouth and eyes wide open, to watch Robert walk toward the apartment building. Then Bo gets very still, except for his tail, which swings rapidly right and left like a speedometer-needle gone haywire. The doorbell rings. Bo begins to bark and flings himself around in circles.

Cecile opens the door and Bo gallops down the long hallway. The outside door is locked; Cecile walks toward it slowly. I stand back and watch. The upper half of the outside door has a glass window; Robert stands on the other side. He's brown-haired, with

a reddish beard. Big. Handsome. He smiles down at Bo and taps
on the window. Bo leaps and leaps.

"What do you want?" Cecile asks.

Robert has a mound of snow—looks like a white beret—on his
head. "I come for Bo," he says. His voice is soft behind the heavy
door. He doesn't look at Cecile when he talks, but keeps staring
down at Bo. Suddenly his face breaks up into a big laugh. "What
the hell you got on?" he says. Bo's still wearing his red sweater;
he yelps at the sound of Robert's voice, jumps up and hits the
doorknob with his nose.

"Listen, I don't know," Cecile says. "I don't know about this."

"Hey, he's my dog," Robert says. "And you been bitchin' about
my taking him for weeks."

"Let me think," Cecile says. "Bo, *assiz-toué!*" Bo sits, his
whole body vibrating. His tongue creeps out the side of his mouth;
he pants and looks up at Cecile like a child waitin' on permission
to go buy candy. She kneels beside him, holds his head in her
hands, smells and nuzzles him, stares into his eyes. Bo pulls his
face away from her and looks up at Robert.

"Okay, Bo," Cecile says, dropping his head. "Okay. *Va voir
Papa.*" She unbolts the door and opens it a notch—a cold wind
flings in a fistful of snowflakes. Bo pushes his nose into the door
crevice, forces his way out. He bounds up into Robert's arms, licks
him wildly; Cecile runs back in past me, a blur, her face in her
hands.

For the first time ever, I hear the kitchen clock ticking. I look
out the window. Bo's white fur blends into the swirling snow; the
red sweater looks like a bright box tumbling in the wind—it flies
up into the back of the blue Ranger, and Robert takes off. Cecile
lies down on the couch, bawling. I pick up Bo's stuff: his empty
food dish, yellow ball, Nylabone, blue sweater. I take them into
my room, pack them into my closet, far from Cecile's eyes.

❄

After the six o'clock news, Cecile's ready to talk. She says: "Did
you see who was in the truck this morning?"

"Yes," I say.

"*Monique,*" she spits out. "That blonde bombshell. She's had more men than I've got socks."

"That's what I hear," I say.

"Men are idiots," Cecile says, and she chokes up.

"Not *all* men," I say in a hurry. "You have to keep hoping."

"No, all men are idiots," Cecile argues, on the verge of crying.

"Well, but ain't some women too?" I say. "Like Monique?" Cecile stares at me. "And what about our fathers? Ain't they good men? My daddy thinks I'm crazy for moving to Maine, but he never tried to stop me. And your daddy seems nice, making maple sugar."

"Yes," Cecile says. "My father is a good man. He's kind; he loves my mother. He's easy to buy presents for."

"See? You have to have hope," I say.

But the night is long for Cecile. I hear her sobbing, hear the wind toss snow like shovelfuls of sand against the windows. Sometimes I can't tell if it's the wind or Cecile that's howling.

❄

At seven A.M. the doorbell rings. I have left my shade up all night, to watch the flakes rotating around the streetlamps; now the sky is clear, blinding-bright. I think something must be wrong—Cecile doesn't have any friends 'cept me, to come calling first thing in the morning. Cecile goes to answer the door; I shuffle into the kitchen, peek out the window, see Robert's blue pickup.

Bo busts open the apartment door and careens into the kitchen from the hallway, beelines to the spot where his food dish was, sniffs around for it. Cecile comes in a minute later. *Guess what!*" she says, smiling. "Bo threw up at Monique's. Here, Bo!" she calls, *"viens icitte!"* Bo runs over and sniffs her hands. "And *guess what.* Monique tol' Robert she's allergic to dogs." Bo tears around the apartment, looking for his food dish. "Do you have Bo's blue sweater?" Cecile asks me. "He came home naked and it's *frigid* outside. By the way, *dress warm* today. You are about to experience true Maine weather," Cecile says seriously. "You could freeze to death, walkin' to work, in this cold."

Bo comes and watches, his tail workin' like crazy, while I gather his stuff from my closet. "Hey-yo, Bo!" I say cheerfully to him. "Hey, you ol' dogger!" He knocks me aside, grabs his food dish in his mouth, runs back to Cecile.

"Down!" she says. I can hear him pitching himself against the kitchen counters. *"Couche-toué!"* The dog-food bag rustles and Bo starts barking. *"Tais-toué!"* Cecile yells.

I pick up Bo's things and go sit on the edge of my bed. Take a moment to look out the window. The snowbanks and drifts shoot up a blue glare that burns my eyes.

"Non-non! Assiz-toué!" Cecile shouts.

The street is noisy—people are clearing paths, shoveling out cars. Everything's clear and sparkly, like in TV commercials.

"Arrêt ça!" Cecile shouts.

I look at the long white snakes of snow weighing down the porch clotheslines, the breath-clouds hovering over the heads of the people passing by. I think: *I am in my homeland.* My heart jimmies up my throat again.

"Arrêt, arrêt, arrêt!" Cecile commands.

Bo comes running in, puts a big wet lick on my face, forces his snout into my hands. I give his withers the hard pounding he likes, then get up and go into the kitchen. I hand Cecile the blue sweater. "You know," I say, "I'm glad Bo's home. 'Cause didn't we miss Bo's true spirit here in the house? Wasn't the house lonely for it?"

"Yes," Cecile says, choking up again. "Part of what makes a home a home is the chaos, I guess. The nutsy stuff." Bo goes back and finishes his food and then hockey-pucks the bowl around the kitchen with his nose.

"You and I are prodigal souls," I say, crouchin' down to Bo's level. "We are *chez nous* again." I open my arms and Bo bounds over and licks me on the lips. "We have returned to our true homelands," I say to him.

The wind comes up and rattles the windowpane, and a little breeze seeps through the sash and blows on me. I shiver and go look outside, see people hunching their shoulders up under their ears, walkin' fast in the wind. I think how I ain't ever been one for the frigid cold, but I know it'll pass before long. Cecile says a

Maine spring is muddy, a Maine summer is hot, but the way I see it, that's what makes it a true homeland—the NUTSY stuff. Besides, when it's autumn again, there'll be them leaves for me and Cecile and Bo to drive around and look at. All them pretty, bright-orange leaves!

Into Woods

In a dive near Stockbridge in the Berkshire Hills of Massachusetts, I nearly got clobbered by a big drunk who thought he'd detected an office fairy in the midst of the wild workingman's bar. He'd heard me talking to Mary Ann, the bartender, and I didn't talk right, so by way of a joke he said loudly to himself and to a pal and to the bar in general, "Who's this little fox? From Tanglewood or something?"

I, too, was drunk and said, "I am a plumber, more or less." I was thirty years old, was neither little nor a fox, had just come to work on the restoration of an inn, and was the foreman of the crew. But that seemed like the wrong answer, and too long in any case.

He snorted and said to everyone, "A more or less plumber," then appraised me further: "I say a hairdresser."

"I say a bank teller," his pal said.

I didn't mind being called a hairdresser, but a bank teller! Oh, I was drunk and so continued the conversation, smiling just enough to take the edge off: "Ah, fuck off."

"Cursing!" my tormentor cried, making fun of me. "Do they let you say swears at the girls' school?"

"Headmaster," someone said, nodding.

"French teacher," someone else.

"*Guys . . . ,*" Mary Ann said, smelling a rumble.

"Plumber," I said.

"More or less," someone added.

"How'd you get your hands so clean?" my tormentor said.

"Lily water," someone said, coining a phrase.

My hands? They hadn't looked at my hands! I was very drunk, come to think of it, and so took it all good-naturedly, just riding the wave of conversation, knowing I wouldn't get punched out if

I played it right, friendly and sardonic and nasty all at once. "My hands?"

My chief interlocutor showed me his palms, right in my face. "Work," he said, meaning that's where all the calluses and blackened creases and bent fingers and scars and scabs and cracks and general blackness and grime had come from.

I flipped my palms up too. He took my hands like a palm reader might, like your date in seventh grade might, almost tenderly, and looked closely: calluses and scabs and scars and darkened creases and an uncleanable blackness and grime. Nothing to rival his, but real.

"Hey," he said. "Buy you a beer?"

My dad worked for Mobil Oil, took the train into New York every day early-early, before we five kids were up, got home at six-thirty every evening. We had dinner with him, then maybe some rough-housing before he went to bed at eight-thirty. Most Saturdays, and most Sundays after church, he worked around the house, and I mean he worked.

And the way to be with him if you wanted to be with him at all was to work beside him. He would put on a flannel shirt and old pants, and we'd paint the house or clean the gutters and mow the lawn or build a new walk or cut trees or turn the garden under or rake the leaves or construct a cold frame or make shelves or shovel snow or wash the driveway (*we washed the fucking driveway!*) or make a new bedroom or build a stone wall or install dimmers for the den lights or move the oil tank for no good reason or wire a 220 plug for the new dryer or put a sink in the basement for Mom or make picture frames or . . . Jesus, you name it.

And my playtime was an imitation of that work. I loved tree forts, had about six around our two acres in Connecticut, one of them a major one, a two-story eyesore on the hill behind the house, built in three trees, triangular in all aspects. (When all her kids were long gone, spread all over the country, my mother had a chainsaw guy cut the whole mess down, trees and all.) I built cities in the sandbox, beautiful cities with sewers and churches and schools and houses and citizens and soldiers and *war!* and *floods!*

And attacks by *giants!* I had a toolbox, too, a little red thing with kid-sized tools.

And in one of the eight or nine toolboxes I now affect there is a stubby green screwdriver that I remember clearly as being from that first red toolbox. And a miniature hacksaw (extremely handy) with "Billy" scratched on the handle, something I'd forgotten until one of my helpers on the Berkshires restoration pointed it out one day, having borrowed the little thing to reach into an impossible space in one of the eaves. Billy. Lily.

My father called me Willy when we worked, and at no other time. His hands were big and rough and wide, blue with bulgy veins. He could have been a workman easy if he wanted, and I knew it and told my friends so.

In my rich suburban high school in Connecticut we were nearly all of us college track, which meant you could take only two shop classes in your career there. First half of freshman year you could elect Industrial Arts, which was an overview: a month of Woods, a month of Metals, a month of Technical Drawing. Second semester, if you still wanted more, you went into Woods I, Metals I, etc.

I loved Woods. I loved hanging out with some of the rougher Italian kids, Tony DiCrescenzo and Bobby LaMotta and Tony Famigliani, all of them proud and pleased to be tracked away from college. I wanted to hang out with Tommy Lincoln and Vernon Porter and Roland Fish, the three black kids in my class, all of them quietly (maybe even secretly) tracked away from college. Wood shop was first period, and it was a wild class. Mr. Schtenck, our little alcoholic teacher, made no effort to control us and often left the shop for the entire period to sit in his car.

The rough kids used the finishing room to smoke pot, the storage room to snort coke. We all made bookshelves and workbenches and record racks and knickknack shelves and lamps and tables and guitar stands and frames for photos of our girls. The year was 1968, so we also made elaborate bongs and stash boxes and chillums and hollowed-out canes and chests with secret drawers. Wood shop (and along with it the very act of working with my hands) took on a countercultural glow, the warm aura of sedition, rebellion, independence, grace.

Sophomore year I signed up for Woods II, which was the advanced course. My guidance counselor, Miss Sanderson (a nice enough lady, very well-meaning, very empathic—you could make her cry over your troubles every time if you played your cards right), thought I'd made an error on the electives form. "Only one elective a semester, William. Surely you'd like a writing course! Journalism! Or how about Occult Literature?"

"Woods II," I said, flipping my hair. I had to get parental permission to take Woods again and thought a little note with my mother's neat signature would be easy to snag, but it was not. "Why do you have to reinvent the wheel?" Mom said, one of her phrases, something of a non sequitur in this case, her meaning being *someone else will build the furniture.* Her next question was, "What kind of kids are in that class?"

Dumb kids, Mom. Mostly Italian kids and blacks and, of course, Alvin Dubronski (the class moron) and Jack Johnsen (the plumber's kid!) and me.

My dad thought it was fine, especially with the alternative being literature courses where who knew what kind of left-wing occult hippie double-talk Mrs. Morrisey would tell you!

So into the wood shop again, every day first period (if I wasn't late for school; by that time I was hitchhiking to avoid the uncool school bus). I was the only college-track kid taking Woods II, maybe the only college-track kid who had *ever* taken Woods II, though the other kids got to take it semester after semester. And I got peer-pressured into smoking pot in the finishing room and occasionally even into blowing coke in the storage room, always a sweet, nerve-jangling prelude to another round of boring college-track classes.

One day when I was in the storage room with my high-pressure peers (and the two smartest kids in Woods II, maybe in school, both destined by their blackness for bad times in Vietnam) Roland and Tommy, fat Tony Famigliani stuck his head in the door: "The Stench is coming!" But Schtenck was already there, standing in the door. I saw my college-track life pass before my eyes.

"What are you little fuckers doing?"

"We're tasting coke, sir," Tommy said, the idiot, total honesty, as we'd all learned in Boy Scouts.

Florid Schtenck raised his eyebrows clear off his face and said, "Jesus Christ, boys, put it away—you want to get me canned?"

He never looked in the storage room again.

And later that year he stumbled and cut his finger off on the band saw. For two weeks then we had a substitute who made us file all our plans and actually checked them, stood beside us as we drilled holes in our wood or turned bowls on the lathes. It seemed an eternity before Schtenck came back and we could finally fill all the bong and hash-pipe and stash-box orders we'd been sitting on. *Sedition*.

The next year I took Woods II again, having secured special permission from the principal to go along with my parents' special permission and the special permission from Miss Sanderson. Senior year I signed up for the class once more—what the hell—but I don't think I ever got to school in time to attend.

Somewhere in there I stopped being a willing volunteer for my father's list of chores. Now he had to *command* me to help with his corny weekend projects. I had better things to do, things in the woods with Lauren Bee or cruising-in-the-car things with some of the guys in my various garage bands—minor-league dope runs into the Village or actual gigs in actual bars in Port Chester, where the drinking age was eighteen and we could get away with it.

At home things were quiet. Except for my long hair, you wouldn't have noticed that a teen was testing his folks. I was good at talking to my elders, and good at hooking grades without working too hard—college track—and very, very good at staying out of trouble. I was on the student council. I helped with the student newspaper. I went to the homecoming rallies and proms and parades. I memorized the headlight patterns of the town police cars (I still get nervous around those big old Plymouth Furys), could smell a cop from miles away, leagues away, light-years. I had a plan for every eventuality and an escape route from every party.

Weeknights I'd turn in early, out to my room over the garage, wait for the main house to quiet down, then slip out into the night. I was caught only once, coming home about five in the morning with a friend named Melanie. Someone had called me after I'd left, and Dad couldn't find me. He was asleep in my bed when Melanie and I walked in. I was grounded, and here was the punishment: I had to spend the next four Saturdays and Sundays helping him build a playroom in the basement—drilling holes in the concrete for hours to anchor the sills for a Sheetrock wall, running cable for a hanging light over the bumper-pool table, slamming up paneling, churlishly working side by side with my dad and his distinctive smell, Aqua Velva mixed with cigarettes and Head & Shoulders and sweat.

The college track barely got me to college. As part of my desultory rebellion I put off applying until well past all the deadlines, never lying to my folks, never lying to my guidance counselor, but showing all of them the forms ready to go, then just plain old not mailing them. My plan was to play rock and roll and maybe—if necessary—make money working as a carpenter, or maybe drilling holes in concrete, or maybe making furniture or bongs. Then Miss Sanderson got a list of our school's applicants from one of my supposed top choices, and I wasn't on it. Crisis! April already, when most kids were hearing from Colby and Yale and Michigan and the U. of Hawaii.

My trusty guidance counselor got on the phone and found some schools that would look at a late application. She was crushed for me, so crushed she spared my parents the full brunt of my dereliction. At hastily arranged late interviews, admissions counselors never failed to ask why I'd taken Woods II *six semesters straight.* Finally I was accepted by one famously lame school, to which I resigned myself; then, at the last possible minute and by great good fortune, I was put on the waiting list at Ithaca College, where, on August 21, one week before school started, I was admitted into the freshman class.

I never saw my father at work, and he never talked about his work, which I vaguely knew was Executive and had to do with Mobil Oil and was desky and involved meetings and much world travel and made us pretty rich. And because I'd never seen him at work, my natural adolescent impulse toward emulation had little to go on. What to imitate? How to surpass, destroy? What I saw of my valiant dad was his work around the house, and so, emulation gone awry, I set out to be a better home handyman than he'd ever be, the real thing, even, a tradesman.

Two dollars and fifty cents an hour was well known as great money, nearly double what I'd made stocking frozen foods at the A&P during high school. Two-fifty an hour was what truck drivers got, longshoremen, a full hundred rasbuckniks (my father's word) a week. I dropped out of Ithaca College in my junior year (just when most of my buddies were heading off for a year abroad), went back to Connecticut (not my hometown, God forbid, but one nearby), and went to work for an electrician.

Lawrence Berner was a former electrical engineer who'd thrown it all over at age sixty, a theory ace but a fairly clumsy worker, a guy who had actually tossed away everything and left the college track for good. Larry was British and Jewish and unconventional and very charming, all qualities that impressed me. Best of all, he was divorced, the first divorced person I'd ever seen up close. He was filthy of habit—decadent, disgusting (maybe not as bad as my friends at school, but Larry was *old*). He lived in his marital house, wife long gone, and had trashed the place—filled the garage with electrician junk, filled the kitchen with dirty pots and jars and cans and dishes, filled the refrigerator with his important papers (fireproof, he said), filled the bedroom with the most slathery skin magazines imaginable, filled the whole house with take-out cartons, TV-dinner tins, and his own filthy underwear. His living room seemed buried in death.

He paid me $2.50 an hour.

Working beside him (tradesmen often touch—four hands to pull the cable, four arms reaching into a small space, heads together to look into a service panel . . . *hey, hold my legs while I lean out over this here abyss*), I'd feel sometimes like I was with my dad. It was Larry's thin hair, maybe, or the Aqua Velva and cigarettes, or just regular old transference. I spent every day beside this parallel-universe effigy of my father, and I was mad at Larry almost always and desperate to impress him.

One day he said I had good hands, and that little compliment was everything—I glowed, I crowed, I told my friends, my folks. I stared at my hands late at night in bars, stared at them for hours, entranced. And my hands got callused, grotesquely callused, were always covered in cuts and scratches and dings and scabs that I hardly felt. Your knuckles never healed. And Larry mostly worked *hot,* meaning with the power on, because it saved time. I got shocks and blew holes in screwdrivers. I hit my head on rafters and slammed my thumb with hammers and fell off ladders and sliced my fingers (daily) and once even poked a screwdriver hard into my eye (the blade didn't penetrate the eyeball but rolled past it and into the socket so that old Larry had to pull it out . . . and we kept on working). I drove the truck sometimes, sweet-talked the customers, ate in diners, worked squinting with a Lucky Strike in my mouth. I put in panel boxes and wired 200-amp services and installed a thousand outlets and a million switches. I drilled holes for cable, sawed rafters, snaked wire through walls. I wriggled into crawl spaces, sweated in attics, dug trenches.

I got tired of it. All that *body* work. Like every college-track kid in America, I'd been taught that someone else would do the rough stuff if I'd just use my mind. I went back to Ithaca, pleasing my parents enormously. Suddenly I was a good student—all A's, excellent attendance, papers handed in on time—fully engaged in a tough fight against the possibility of being a tradesman, the possibility of taking Woods II for *life.*

But after the college track had run its course, I needed to make money. I failed tests for newspaper jobs (*twenty minutes: neatly type a 500-word story around the following facts . . .*), gagged at the thought of ad agencies, moved around the country for a long time, worked with cattle, bartended (which left your hands clean, at least), then landed in New York, where I got the bright idea to put up posters around the Village and SoHo and be a handyman. Independence! I did every sort of odd job for every sort of odd person, moving over the months and years to larger home repairs, leaving town to restore that Berkshires inn, coming back to sub myself out to contractors. I graduated finally to a specialization in kitchen remodels and new bathrooms, getting more and more deeply into it, hiring helpers, wearing suits to estimates, taking ads in fancy magazines, cracking the codes for admittance to the wholesale supply houses, getting good at all of it, twelve years in all, Woods II, until one day I woke up and realized I was about to take out a bank loan to buy a truck and some very expensive tools, about to start looking for a storefront, about to start paying my employees *on the books*.

I headed straight to graduate school.

My wife and I spent lots of our free time last summer looking for a house to buy up here in rural Maine (where I teach college), our first, an old farmhouse, we hoped. I kept telling myself that I had an advantage, which was my haphazard twenty-year fund of construction knowledge and restoration experience. I looked up at the beams and poked at the foundations and lifted the vinyl siding and pulled away carpets. I wiggled toilets and pulled on feeds and pushed on all the walls and ceilings. I got in crawl spaces and pried open hatch doors, inspected wiring, eyeballed plumbing, made the real-estate folks nervous.

And sometimes, in light of this commitment, this buying a house on a wee piece of our little planet, I thought about what would happen if the legislature shut down my branch of the University of Maine, or what would happen if I didn't get tenure, or what would happen if I just couldn't take the bureaucracy anymore and quit. Education presidents come and go, but people always need a plumber or someone to fix the roof, replace rotten sills, plaster the stairway wall. I could build furniture. Or renovate inns. I could take my clean college hands and plunge them into work, open all the old scars, stop being mincy and fastidious, once more revel in goo and slime, get into it: wrestle cable, kick at shovels, stand in the mud all day, hook my leg around ladders in the wind, lay tile, lift toilets and plunge my hand down that reeking fuzzy hole to pull the clog (poor Raggedy Andy one time, usually worse).

My wife and I found a house, bought it, moved in. And immediately my dad, now retired, came up to visit, tools in hand. The two of us got up early the first morning he was here and headed

out to the garage, a forlorn little outbuilding about to fall down
and stuffed to the rafters with the owner-before-last's junk (mostly
pieces of Volkswagens and cans of old bolts and misshapen gaskets
and used spark plugs and odd shims and clips). My plan was to
leave room to park a car, sure, but to build a wood shop, a work
space from which to operate while my wife and I renovate the
house (a neglected nineteenth-century quarter-cape with many ad-
ditions, the newest of which is a porch built in 1953, my own year).

So for hours my dad and I worked. We cleared out and sorted
all the junk, ripped down the cardboard that made the walls,
stopped to stare, to think, came up with opposite plans, argued,
convinced each other; then, having switched sides, we argued
again. Finally we jacked up the north side of the garage, replaced
the sill, dropped a corner post in cement, took the jack away, re-
built the wall. Next we shored up the south side, then added wir-
ing, finally installed a metal roof over the leaky old asphalt
shingles. We hit our heads and cut our fingers and ripped our jack-
ets. We peed in the woodpile. We argued, mostly about technique
and a little about the Education President (who was about to go),
but really, I guess, about who was in charge of the work in my
garage. And even though Pop was helping me for free, even buy-
ing some of the materials, I fumed and fulminated, almost sulked:
instant adolescence.

We rebuilt the barn-style sliding door and cut in a window. We
ate companionably in the Farmington Diner with sawdust and
plain dirt in our hair and new hammer holsters on our belts (the
acerbic Down East waitress looked me over, said, "Hi, Professor,"
and I introduced her to my dad); we went to the dump; we gabbed
at the lumber yard; we swung hammers, climbed ladders, cut
wood; we gazed at our work a long time in the dark when we
were done.

Pop said, "You saved that building," as if I'd done it on my
own, and we went on in the house to wash up.

Blitzkrieg and the Nautical Plow

"I was obliged to hire a team and a man for the plowing, though I held the plow myself," wrote Thoreau in *Walden*. He had moved from town to the edge of a body of water entirely surrounded by land. About a century later my wife and I moved from town to the edge of a body of land entirely surrounded by water. We too plowed. But at this point, the connection between the Holmeses' island experience and the Walden Pond experiment abruptly ends. Our plowing was far from harmonious; it was probably not even good economics.

We had what was literally an old gray mare, and getting her three miles out to the island in the first place was no easy feat. We also had the assistance of a lobster fisherman friend of ours, whose help was the more impressive when one considered that there were few things he hated more heartily than grubbing in the earth. From the outset it was obvious that the mare knew more about plowing than any of us did, and moreover, that she didn't really believe in it. She had led, no doubt, a hard life; she was tired, and wise in the ways of passive resistance. She could not hear "Giddap" at all until the third time, and then only after a whack over the rump. Watching her, we could almost see unoiled wheels revolving in her heavy head, corroded ratchets falling into place, and at last the appropriate message being telegraphed from her engine room to the reluctant legs: "Slow ahead." However, "Whoa," or even some unintentional and remote facsimile thereof, such as a slight cough, she heard and obeyed at once.

But even on those occasions when she moved willingly, "Blitz-krieg," as we named her—this was in 1940—Blitzkrieg offered no satisfactory solution to our problem. She was simply unable to turn over land like ours, which no plow or harrow had touched for perhaps twenty years. Faced with this apparent impasse, our lobster fisherman automatically thought of seagoing equipment. Up from the shore he transported a forty-pound anchor, two double pulleyblocks, and three hundred feet of half-inch anchor rod ("rope" to you, perhaps). With the plow at one edge of the field, the anchor dug into the turf at the other edge, the block and tackle between them, and the mare hitched up to the business end of the line, he surmised that we could plow the earth. And so we could. But the job was not that simple.

For one thing, Blitzkrieg now took an even dimmer view of our plowing practices. When my wife finally persuaded her to take a strain on the line and start across the garden, the mare saw approaching her what she knew quite well she should never have seen at all: a plow and plowman with no horse attached. She came to a quick halt, eyeing our nautical gear with one-third disapproval and two-thirds disbelief. It took more than patience to accustom her to passing this uncanny device and then continuing beyond the garden twice its width, forging through wild rose bushes and fir sapling, and finally into a spruce thicket. Still, under human power, we hauled the plow back each time, and the blocks apart, then shifted the anchor over for the next furrow.

All this made for an exhausting enterprise, and we nearly gave up the day the lobster fisherman, taking his turn at the plow, inadvertently rubbed the handle against his dungaree pocket and ignited about fifty kitchen matches that were loose in it. The resulting explosion, both chemical and verbal, was a traumatic experience for everyone. Blitzkrieg was adamant about not moving again until she had a bucket of water and a pan of oats.

A year later we plowed in the conventional manner, and after Blitzkrieg's death we turned to gasoline power, but the old heroic spirit had gone out of the thing; it was simply work.

In his second year at Walden, Thoreau hired no team; he just spaded up a smaller portion of earth and planted less. Like no small number of his moves, this one was wise enough. We took only a little longer to come round to it ourselves. Recently, I have refined the technique even further, though like many refinements, mine has an air of decadence about it. I don't plow at all now. I just write about it.

Moth at My Window

Against my pane
He beats a rapid
Pitapat
In trying to reach
The desk lamp lit
In front of me.
Wing flurries spent,
He crawls and toils
This way and that,
His whole self bound
To pierce the veil
He cannot see.

The glance I turn
On him, light
Spreading still across
My page, is one
Of interest in
The company.
Whatever time
I take to watch
Will be no loss
From my own toils
To pierce the veil
I cannot see.

Travelers' Advisories

❄

Somerset County

The log-crammed trucks smash the yielding air,
Whine like leviathan gnats.
Last week a trucker died at the wheel
On the way home from the mill.
He fell asleep. Or did he wake before?
The wreck looked like a freighter run aground.

One January day, a pulpwood driver tells me,
He skidded the better part of a quarter mile
Towards a stopped school bus.
He played the brake and gears
Like the valves of a trumpet, soft and hard.
And he said he saw himself as a boy:
"About eight years-old—
You forget that stuff."

If summer here is the sovereign remedy,
The pure swat of northern heat,
Its pleasure lies in ineffability
The true green that governs growing things
But is bound to retreat,
Bound to turn sullen and spare,
Bound to wait wordlessly in the spell of winter.
Patience was never a human virtue
And never will be.

At the end of August the air is so clear and light
A body could levitate,
Fly off without benefit of preacher or motor,

Shedding the responsible wrenches, the keys.
That's a *fantasy*—not a word I hear often
If ever.

Hard knowledge wants a sharp edge.
A pile of metal filings from lathe or saw is swept
To the floor or ground and forgotten,
The power of work needing that precision
And that waste.

Northern Lights

You never know what you'll run into once you head up into the hills, Gracie thought, as she left the shoe shop where she worked the late shift and began the long ride home. So many people got their cars banged up—or worse—when some moose got in their way, and a thousand pounds of moose can do a job on a car, not to mention a body inside. Jackson Wilmot, her nearest neighbor, he lost an arm when a moose came through his windshield and pinned it to the dashboard, held him there until someone came by and it was some wait since he was out on the South River Road where no one goes unless they're wanting to look at woods. Jackson went on disability after that, and though Gracie knew some people might like being home all the time, she was certain it wouldn't work for her. All those empty rooms and herself just rattling around in them, waiting to hear what Morris would say next.

Soon after he died, Morris spoke to her in the kitchen. Then it got to be a habit. He told her things, things she'd forgotten, like not to plant the Big Boys until after Memorial Day or when to pay the homeowner's, little things she needed reminding about, helpful things, but still, when the person who was doing the reminding was dead, it was unsettling.

If she hadn't sold Morris' truck after he died, Gracie thought, driving home after work late at night wouldn't be such a problem. At the time it seemed maybe she could get by with no vehicle, could rely on her sister Maxi to get her to work since they had the same shift, but that hadn't worked out, and now she had the Fiesta, bought used down to Farmington. But it was a tinny little yellow thing and she knew a moose flying at a Fiesta would do serious damage to both her and her car.

Gracie hunched over the wheel of her car as she passed Fenno's Grocery, then the Willow Bed and Breakfast which was still lit up. "That's what you do when you cater to people from away," Morris' voice echoed. Gracie shook her head, passed a hand through her hair as if to shake Morris from her thoughts. Usually Morris waited till she was home alone to speak to her. She passed the corn field that belonged to Rodney Strout; spikes of dried corn stalks rose out of the ground like spooks alongside the road. Then past the park that Lottie Pratt tended every summer for the children from the town, past the old cemetery where several of Morris' relatives were buried in the Snow plot, and then she was out of town.

And once out of town she realized that the night sky held a peculiar brightness, a film of grey sheen that illuminated treetops and fences and granite slabs where they lay at the doorsteps of the occasional house. The moonlight left silver slashes on the river's rushing water, and where the rocks stood up from the water, it covered them with white gauze. Morris' voice came at her then like a beam of light. "When the moon's full, unpredictable things'll happen," he said.

Gracie grimaced. "Don't be foolish," she told him.

Then, as she headed up onto the Ledge Road, the one that follows the ridge north of town, her Fiesta started doing something strange, something it had done a couple months earlier in the middle of summer when it was 'specially hot. But she'd had no trouble with it since September when the air stayed cool day and night.

It chugged, spit and sputtered, then evened out as she shifted into low gear. The tires spun on the gravel as she accelerated, and then the engine started that sputtering again. Morris had always said a car sputters when it's not getting enough gas. "Either downshift or gun it," came his words at her ear. Gracie's shoulders hiked up in defense, but it turned out the advice was good, as she discovered when she shifted down into second gear. Once up on the ridge, though, the car continued chugging; it lurched once, twice, evened out for half a mile, then chugged again until the engine died. "Switch off those lights," Morris suggested, "so you don't wear down the battery."

This was enough for Gracie. "Morris, I'm tellin' you, wait till

I get home to talk to me. I can't take this out here in the woods."
But she followed his advice and turned off the headlights. Around
her was just the silver bath of moonlight on the car's hood, on the
road before her, on the fields surrounding her, and ahead, on the
gas pump at Herbie Davison's car repair shop, a huge barn of a
business that set down the road from his trailer where he lived.

Gracie let the Fiesta coast to the side of the road near Davison's.
"You don't want your vehicle sitting plumb in the middle of the
road for everyone to see," Morris piped up. "God's sake, Morris,"
Gracie retorted, feeling her insides clutch up. She felt the Fiesta
slump into the soft soil of a ditch. Now even if it started up again,
she wasn't sure she'd be able to drive it off. "See what I mean?"
she snapped at the air around her. "You got to leave me alone."

That was the thing of it, this talking to Morris. She'd go along
as if he was really there and then suddenly she'd hear herself talking
to air and she'd wonder: Have I gone clear off the edge?

Gracie turned the key; the engine cranked, but it didn't catch.
She tried again, and before giving it a third try, she said, "I know
enough not to flood the thing, so you don't need to butt in and
tell me so." The car cranked but still it didn't catch. Gracie leaned
forward, stared at the night sky.

Up high like that, open fields all leading to the north, she could
see far off. A greenish glimmer shone against the black night.
"Northern lights," she exclaimed, quickly, so Morris wouldn't get
his word in first. Morris had loved the Northern Lights; sometimes
they drove over to route 17, all the way up to Height of Land, so
he could gaze at the sky. Sometimes she asked him to explain those
mysterious colors to her, the pinks and greens seeming unnatural
to her. Morris understood the science of it; he read books when he
wasn't hauling pulp, books about the stars and the planets and the
universe beyond. Gracie couldn't keep it in her head though; even
after he told her what made the Milky Way appear above them and
explained that the earth was part of the Milky Way, she didn't get
it. "How can we be in the Milky Way if the Milky Way is way up
there?" she asked.

This time she didn't ask. But she found herself getting out of
the car to get a better look. It was wondrous, she thought. The
wash of green across the sky, radiating like an electric light. That

rosy pink, like the petunias that grow in the stump by the corner of the porch at home, she thought.

Gracie walked along the road then, almost as if her steps might take her closer to the green and the pink. She passed the gas pump, headed beyond a couple of truck bodies Herbie was hoping to sell, past the trailer with the two ATV's on it, and then she saw it: An old Studebaker, probably made in the 40's, and again she spoke her thought aloud in order to beat Morris to it.

"Just like ours," she said. It caught her breath. Morris had bought a Studebaker the year they were married, 1948. It was a couple of years old then, but it had looked spanking new to Gracie. Purple, and it rode so smooth on the highway, the tires hummed like organ music. The seats were made of a soft velour, dark brown. The dash had buttons for everything; it had a radio too. Morris was as proud of that car as he was at the birth of his first son. Their four children fit comfortably in the back on the few occasions when they traveled together.

Gracie approached the Studebaker that rested in the moonlight. Clearly Herbie had retrieved it from the woods, had found it out behind someone's fields and had done that someone a favor in dragging it out. Now it had a sign with a price tag on it: As is: $375.00. Wouldn't this just be Morris' cup of tea, she thought. Just the sort of project for him. The car was stripped of its paint, its door handles, its windshield wipers; its tires were mere rubber shells, slashed by years of frost, and hanging in strips from the wheels. A single headlight had somehow made it through the years. Gracie peered in through a back window, carefully. The glass had been shattered long ago, leaving a few shards wedged in the base where the window had once rested. Inside, the back seat was ripped from its position; it lay tilted forward against the front seat which was scored with holes.

Morris would've loved this, she thought, and it sent a pang into her chest, a pang of missing him. He'd been gone these last two years, but maybe it was because of his all the time talking to her, she had actually come to think of him as a nuisance, she realized.

You live with a man that long, she thought, you get to know his quirks. And Morris had plenty. He was always noticing what she'd left undone; bills unpaid, boxes of cookies unwrapped, the bed unmade. Morris liked things done up right at all times. Another thing was the way Morris got when Gracie's sister Maxi and her husband Kirk came over; Morris would sink into a chair and watch the television the whole time, never giving Kirk the time of day. It was plain rudeness, Gracie figured. Oh, he had plenty of quirks, Gracie thought.

So when a person is gone, you sort of want him to stay gone, not keep coming back with advice and suggestions.

Gracie was surprised that Morris had had nothing to say about the Studebaker yet, but there was only the still night air around her as she reached in the front window and gingerly lifted the door handle. The door swung open. Gracie peered in. Instead of the ripped seat, the bent steering wheel, the naked dash, the gaping windshield, she saw the Studebaker she'd known when her children were young, when Morris used to drive them to town for ice-cream on Saturday afternoons.

Morris was different with the kids than other men; he took his time with each of them, throwing the ball with Richie, helping Teddy with his science, since Teddy took after Gracie and didn't understand a word of it. Even the girls; he admired every fish Francie caught with her brothers, didn't ever criticize her for being such a tomboy, didn't even ever use that word once. When Francie was injured in the eye with the baseball, Morris was more patient with her than most men would've been. He was the one told her she'd lost her sight permanently in that eye; he did it gently, and let her cry and wail all she needed.

Gracie felt something welling up inside her, a sense of something she'd left undone, something Morris had not once brought to her attention, but which suddenly seemed important. Had she ever told Morris what a good father he was? Had she ever—

In the dark to the right, from behind a shed, Gracie caught sight of three glowing lights. It only took Gracie a second to realize what they were: cigarettes. Within seconds three figures loomed in front of the Studebaker. Boys, she realized, but they were trying to look like men, dragging on their cigarettes like they were veteran smokers, their spines stiff.

One of the boys stepped up to the car, rested a foot on the hood, leaned a hand on his knee. "Hey, Granny, how's it goin'?" he asked. He grinned, then looked to the others for approval. His hand was wrapped around a beer can which he lifted to his mouth. He took a long swallow.

The other two chuckled. They leaned back and swigged their beers too.

Gracie felt those chuckles like arrows in her breast, menacing.

"It's kind'a late for an ol' bag like you, shouldn't you be home?" the one whose foot rested on the hood said, then guffawed. A boy's guffaw. One came round to the open door, placed his foot on the seat and leaned an elbow on his knee so he was only inches from her face, so she could smell his breath, a sour and damp breath that made Gracie think of things gone bad, like milk, or hamburg. He was having trouble keeping his balance, was swaying like a curtain in a breeze, gently. The other stood back, completely in shadow. "Come on, guys," he murmured, "she's just some old lady."

The one nearest her said, "She's some special old lady, is what she is," and in the shadows Gracie saw his teeth, white as a newly painted fence, and his eyes, glazed like frozen water.

"Where you boys from?" Gracie asked. It was the only thing she could think to say, the sort of thing her mother would have said to the occasional new faces of boys who sometimes gathered on the sidewalk by the Sunshine Grange when Gracie was a girl.

The one nearest her gave a snort of laughter, said, "You hear that? Boys, she's callin' us boys."

"I didn't mean—" she started, but stopped. The one at the front was rubbing his cigarette into the hood to put it out. "Oh, please," she said. "Don't do that, you don't want to hurt this car."

The one nearest her burst out. "This ol' piece 'a shit?" and then there was raucous laughter.

"In its day," she attempted, but it was no use. They were not listening; they were laughing, their shoulders shaking, their heads thrust back and Gracie thought about long ago, how Morris prized his Studebaker, how he trained them all to be careful with it, so it never was scratched and it always shined, oh, how it shined, to the point that sometimes Gracie thought he overdid and even once told him, This's just a car, for pity's sake, but Morris would hear none of it. And why were his eyes sorrowful, she wondered, when he looked at her that way? Did he think she should understand what she could not?

The boy out front started jumping around and singing words to some song Gracie did not know, slapping his thigh and holding his beer can like a trophy. He kicked at the grill, his boot making a *thwack* on impact.

"Stop, please don't—" Gracie started, but then she had an idea, she'd try one more thing. "This was Morris' car, he was the one bought it, you shouldn't—"

The boy out front stopped then; he became still and stared at her with a shadowed silvery face. The one with his foot on the seat looked to the others and mimicked, "This wa' Morris' car," the words slurring.

"It's true, it was 1948, the year we were married, and—"

"Ancient history, ol' lady," one barked. "You're talkin' ancient history."

"Forget it," the one standing off said. "She's an old bat. Let's get out'a here."

"This ain't yer car," the one nearest her challenged.

"Well," Gracie started, feeling a trembling in her throat, "it certainly is Morris' car."

Smash! The boy in the front kicked in the one remaining headlight.

"No," Gracie cried, and she tried to get out of the car, only the boy nearest her was so close, and though he did nothing to keep her where she was, Gracie was trapped. "Oh please, no," she moaned.

The boys started laughing again, an uproarious sort of laughter, shrieks of it, and they pointed. One said, "She's fuckin' nuts," and another dribbled the rest of his beer down the windshield.

Inside the car, Gracie felt a stiffening in her limbs; it swam into her chest, her face, so that all of her froze, so that she could not speak, could only see the shadowed forms and darkened faces against the green sky. The green sky! Oh, Morris, she cried in her head.

One was on top of the hood now, dancing, moving in an awful

way, shifting his hips left to right, forward to back, rocking the car, and Gracie felt herself drowning in that darkened rocking space, those boys' faces careening around her. She had never felt herself so alone, even in those days when she was swamped by the work of raising a family and keeping things right for Morris, days when she thought she couldn't do it, when she was always forgetting and he was always telling her, so sometimes it was as though she couldn't breathe, couldn't go on, and it became hard to—love him. But now it was different. Tell me what to do, were the words inside her head. Morris, she said over and over, all the while the boy was stamping across the hood, his hips going back and forth, and then one foot came down hard on the windshield and *sm-ack*. Surely the glass would break, Gracie thought, raising her hands to her face and twisting in her seat, trembling and moaning, "No, please, no," but the boy kept smacking his boot down against the glass, over and over, until suddenly it came, Morris' voice, "Bastids," it said just once, so the boy nearest her pulled back, removed his foot from the car, slurred, "Wha' w's tha'?"

"Wha' was what?" returned the one on the Studebaker's hood.

"Din't you hear it?" asked the boy nearest her, as he hurled his beer can over the roof and drifted back, back from the car.

"I heard the ol' lady, cryin' like a baby," said the one on the hood.

"What'd you hear?" the third asked.

"He's fuckin' trashed," the one on the hood said. "He's startin' to hear things. He's goin' fuckin' nuts," and he belched a laugh. "Like the ol' bat."

"I ain't," he said, "it were nothin'." But he stepped back up to the car, peered in the rear window, then withdrew. He turned to the others. "Din't you hear somethin'?" Then, "Jeez," he whistled. "Le's get goin'."

"Wha', you scared?" the one on the hood said. "Hey," he said to the other, "Clifford's fuckin' scared of an ol' bat, he thinks she's goin' to spread some wings or somethin', thinks—"

"I said, le's get outa here," and Clifford backed away from the Studebaker with hunched shoulders and hands stuffed in his pockets.

"Cliffy thinks the ol' bat is goin' to—"

"Forgit it," Clifford asserted.

"Awh, Cliffy, it's okay, guy, we'll protect you."

Clifford turned abruptly. He headed for the road and called over his shoulder. "I'm goin'."

Silence settled. The boy on the hood jumped down, stomped out his cigarette. The other one shook his beer can upside down, then pitched it under the car.

And then they were gone.

Once the boys were gone, Gracie uncovered her face with still trembling hands. Then she began. "Morris, there's so many things I forgot to say."

Gracie waited. She held to the steering wheel with one hand, a mooring. Above and around her was the night. No hint, even, of the Northern Lights, the pinks and the greens. There was only black, and on the ground was moonlight.

"The green lights in the sky. I never told you how much I liked goin' up to Height of Land to look at 'em," she said.

Silence.

"And Morris, I never told you what a good father you was." Tears were coming now. "You was right, Morris. I always forgot things."

More silence.

Gracie leaned forward to search for the moon. "Morris," she said, "I won't be short with you. Just tell me what to do now. Just please tell me."

The moon was behind the trees, lost to view. Gracie wiped her eyes. "Just tell me," she said again.

ROBERT M. CHUTE

The Bird Feeder

A dim December sun had hurried down
an afternoon behind a western wall
of cloud, cutting the narrow day off short,
so when Tom, driving back from town,
turned west on Long Swamp Road, he seemed to fall
into night, dark trees the night's bulwark.

Tom's place was the last: "Dead End
Farm," he called it. A weathered gray
center-chimney cape, the ell in shambles,
two walls of the barn still standing.
Barn roof fallen in on ancient, musty hay.
All but the front yard run to brambles.

In Tom's back yard stood three bird feeders
built from old barn wood. First snow until spring
there wasn't a day Tom failed to add some feed
or table scraps. From the swamp's alders and cedars
chick-a-dee, woodpecker, nut hatch, would bring
life that denies cold death to swap for seeds.

Two miles from home, as the road goes,
thickening night turned blinding white.
The leading edge of the Nor'easter struck,
a wall of cloying clots of snow.
Dark roadside trees withdrew from sight
and Tom's whole world was the blind pick-up.

The truck, without its eyes, drove slow and blind.
Seconds too late Tom braked to stop and wait

Robert M. Chute

but the road turned unseen beneath him, to the right,
and the front wheels found the snow-glazed incline,
a truck length down, as if seized by fate.
"Well, Truck," said Tom, "you're here for the night."

Ten pounds of wild-bird seed, six oranges, cheese,
two cans of beans in one bag, he forced the door against
the snow. It was two miles, or a little more,
by road. Straight through Long Swamp's shrouded trees,
a mile or less. Half-way, the old stone fence
would lead him straight to his back door.

Tom shifted the bag under his arm
and stumbled on. He should have reached the wall
by now, he knew, so he turned west, but he
was already west of it so he caromed
from thicket to stump to tree, like a ball
in a maze, every straight line blocked by a tree.

He struggled on in his random walk,
too stubborn to go back until he crossed his own track,
a line of depressions filling with snow.
He could barely see them, so he stopped. "Talk,"
he said. "Damned if I know which way's back!"
But the tracks were silent and filled with snow.

The bag grew heavy. He discarded the cans of beans.
There was no way to lighten leaden limbs.
His shins were bruised by dead-falls and snags.
He plunged ahead until he found a screen,
a thicket of spruce and forced his way in,
stamped the snow flat and set down his bag.

The spruce turned the edge of the wind. Tom broke
branches to build a mat of life beneath him,
sat and hunched himself thin. "Maybe
the cold won't find me in here." Tom spoke
to something he felt in the night. His limbs
said "sleep." Snow hissed. Snow lisped, seductively.

73

An insistent flutter of wings aroused him
to a clear sky, a half-moon, the flickering
of hundreds of birds settling in, clinging
around him—more and more. The light dimming.
A blanket of feathers, blood quickening.
Silence—but the night was singing.

The abandoned truck, empty house, cold stove,
told their story. Neighbors walked the road-bed,
then the woods, but it was because they heard
birds they found him. The seeds spilled, birds wove
all around him. "He did look peaceful," they said
"but he was always one to feed the birds."

No Night Life

Country towns have no night life. I like that. I like to find a village asleep if I happen to roll into it any time after nine P.M. And I roll into a lot of small towns at that hour and later. That's an inevitable condition of the trout fisherman's life. Say I drive up to the South Branch of the Dead River or somewhere north of The Forks for an afternoon and evening's fishing. I will, without fail, stay on the water until it is much too dark to see. It's too dark to tie on a new fly, too dark to see the water, too dark to see the trees in which I hang up my fly and therefore have to tie on a new fly that it is too dark to see. A headlamp would solve part of my problem, and one of these years—at the promptings of that voice in me that always says "Just one more cast, just one more cast"—I may take a head-lamp along. But the reason I probably don't take one with me now is that another voice urges obedience to the fading sun and the deepening shadows, and when they say it's time to quit, I quit.

So by the time I wallow out of the water and get back to the car, it's well after nine o'clock. Allow whatever travel time it takes to get to Rangeley or Bingham or wherever, and it's a cinch the place will not be booming. If you're hungry, you're out of luck. The restaurants, if there are any, are closed. The stores harbor only the dim illumination of their night lights and Coors signs. You may find a mom-and-pop store still open where you can pick up a Table Talk apple pie or a Devil Dog. Otherwise, it's back to the peanuts and apricots left over in your pack.

A rare car trundles slowly down the main, and just about only, street. Three kids on bikes whoosh silently by like earthbound bats. Some slightly older kids, male and female, squeak and squawk, running away from each other, running back together, bob-bing, weaving, punching, pulling, squeezing, wrestling, tickling, slathering for each other's flesh but not quite knowing how to go about it in earnest, or whether they dare to.

In Stratton, Cathy's Place is officially closed, but you may be able to kid and cajole a sandwich out of the crew cleaning up in the kitchen. The waitresses are sitting at the tables having a last smoke; the few customers still left have empty coffee cups or beer glasses in front of them and their NAPA caps pushed back on their heads. Business is over for today. You can't quite tell who is guest and who is help. This motel dining room isn't a commercial operation anymore. It's a place where a few folks have finished their day and are shooting the breeze together until somebody decides it's time to head home to bed.

You cannot buy gas. In larger towns downriver, like Skowhegan and Farmington, you can. They have been infiltrated by Seven-Eleven and Cumberland Farms and, worse yet, that most flagrant of the stay-up-all-night food-and-fuel hucksters, the Irving Big Stop. A Boeing 707 could land on that vast tarmac bathed in eye-splitting white light.

But in the small river towns and nonriver towns upcountry no gas flows. Just how tightly shut down the pumps can be I discovered a few years ago after a paddling companion and I finished an Allagash trip late in the afternoon. We were in Allagash Village. Our car was in Greenville. We had two options: We could camp overnight in the village and have Folsom's Air Service pick us up in the morning. Or we could find somebody in Allagash to drive us back to Greenville that night. I love camping in the bush, but I hate camping in or near towns, so we started looking for a driver, and we were lucky enough to find that broad-beamed and kindly Allagash guide, Wilmer Hafford.

After setting off in Wilmer's huge gas-guzzling van at six or six-thirty, we found the fuel gauge tilting toward low about the time we turned west off the Turnpike at Howland. We allowed as we would stop at the first gas station we saw.

I think our first stop was in or near LaGrange. I really don't remember the location, but I do remember the mute passivity of two gas pumps and a dark little storefront that would not come to life for any amount of knocking, even though the owners were clearly at home upstairs watching TV. They were absolutely right not to respond. Anybody driving around after dark shouldn't be encouraged.

"Well," Wilmer said, "we'll try it in Milo."

Milo is bigger, but as far as gas was concerned, it was no better. And the hour was later still, ten o'clock, ten-thirty maybe.

"Well," Wilmer said, "we'll try it in Dover."

How many more towns would we be able to reach on an empty gas tank? I don't like camping on roadsides much more than I like camping in town, but I was beginning to brace myself for it, particularly when the gas pumps of Dover-Foxcroft greeted us with the same lack of enthusiasm as their cousins in Milo and LaGrange had.

But before Wilmer's ever-optimistic nature could say, "Well, we'll try it in Guilford" or Abbot Village or Monson, I spotted a police car slowly cruising the streets, and I jumped out of the van to flag it down.

"Is there any way we can get a tankful of gas at this hour?"

There was. Because it would not do for the police cars ever to run dry, the town had a contract with a local station. The duty cruiser had the key and could fuel up at any time. We pumped our gas; the officer collected the proper amount of money and left it on the owner's desk in the station.

I've always liked Dover-Foxcroft, and that considerate policeman made me like it even more. We got to Greenville and, after two more hours driving, home to our beds in Temple. Wilmer got home to Allagash. If things had gone strictly by the rules, we all would have slept in the van or by the roadside, for the rules are that in country towns you are forbidden to buy gas after eight P.M. The rules are that you stop and rest when it gets dark. You don't keep running all night on fumes, hot air, adrenaline, and nerves. In the country, day is day and night is night; and if you insist on buying gas at midnight, that's a matter for the police.

Now I always make sure I have plenty of gas when I go fishing so that I can revel in the lack of night life when I roll into a small town. I may even park on the main drag, get out of the car, and bask in that lack. The few streetlights and what little activity there is cannot push back the night; and the town's single main street, overarched by darkness and stars, is awash in coolness and quiet.

If you walk to one end or the other of that street, you are back in the country again with the silhouettes of the hills black against the sky and the peepings, croakings, and rustlings of nocturnal creatures around you. Where there is no night life, the real life of the night can flood in on all your senses. The sky, the forest, and, where there is one, the river—the Kennebec, the Piscataquis, the Sandy, the Carrabassett—will reassert their hold over a small town, reminding us that it is we who are beholden to them, not they who are beholden to us.

THEODORE ENSLIN

Vespers

That time in the early evening,
a cold sunset gone—
colder than I remember
a year ago
            at apparently
the same time—
the time when cars
go by, one after another.
Purposeful, not speeding,
just to get home.
My neighbors are tired
and hungry.
            For what
do they hunger?
beyond a break in the day,
in from the cold?
            A warm dinner.
What more do they want?
Where do they turn?
Words fail.
They cannot tell me.
If they could
I would not hear them
going past
            down
this ordinarily quiet road.

JOHN THORNE

Maine Eats

We have a family oriented atmosphere. We
cater to the natives. We're always pleased
to see the tourists come, but it's the locals
who keep you in business.

—Lauralee Gilley

I.

Duffy's Restaurant is easy to miss. It lies about seven miles east
out of Bucksport on US Route 1—the stretch that locals call the
Ellsworth Road—tucked into the middle of a long, slow curve. Just
before it appears on the left, your eye is drawn in the opposite
direction as the sudden immensity of Toddy Pond flashes into view
for a few seconds through a break in the pine woods. Even if you
turn your head back fast enough to catch it, there's nothing much
about Duffy's to hold your attention, especially if, as is often the
case, a tractor-trailer has pulled up in the driveway directly in front
of the restaurant, completely hiding it from view. Otherwise, what
you see first is a line of green-painted posts topped with light bulbs
ensconced in up-ended jam jars. These border the driveway that
leads up to a small rambling cottage, painted white with green
trim, its window boxes filled in season with bright red geraniums.

When we lived in Castine, I drove past Duffy's often and,
strange as it now seems, at first took it for a roadhouse. This was
partly because of the neon Miller's sign that glowed in the front
window, partly because it had that slightly seclusive, clubby air of
a place frequented almost entirely by regulars, and partly because
the vehicles out front were that mix of Detroit behemoths with

beat-up, rusted-out bodies and noisy but still potent V-8 engines and pin-striped, high-sprung, Japanese-built pickups with over-sized tires and extra-long beds driven by male blue-collar Maine. However, I realized, passing by very early one bright fall morning, that the parking lot was fuller than I'd ever seen it. That crowd was there for breakfast, not booze. All of a sudden, Duffy's seemed to exude the aroma of fried eggs, flapjacks, and hot coffee.

You don't have to live in Maine long to learn to tell the differ-ence between the cheap-eat type places aimed at the summer and leaf-peeper trade and those that mainly solicit business from their neighbors. Both are housed in nondescript buildings and advertise plain home cooking, but the one makes a conspicuous effort to dress up Down East and the other, just as conspicuously, doesn't. If you want to eat with the locals, don't pull up at a joint, however down-home or just plain dumpy, draped with buoys and fronted with huge plywood cutouts of boiled lobsters. Especially avoid places with outdoor wood-fired lobster steamers smoking away or with names like Pop's Chowder House, Lucky's Lobster Land, Fisherman's Landing, or The Clamdigger.

Stop instead at the places without any tourist trappings. Their boardings, if there are any, should promise nothing more exciting than "Liver and Onions Today, $4.95," "Macaroni and Cheese," "Breakfast Special: Fried Tripe," or—both outside of Priscilla's Drive-In, also on Route 1 east of Bucksport—"Wicked Hot Chili" and "Priscilla makes the pies." Above all they should bear homey, insistently ordinary names without one hint of Vacationland: Just Barb's, Tall Barney's, Finally Mine, Hazel's Place, Gram's Place, Mary's Place, Rollie's Cafe, and, as I now realized, Duffy's.

It took us about a year to get around to stopping in at Duffy's, but late one hot summer afternoon, in the mood for some fried fish and a slice of blueberry pie, we finally turned up the driveway. At the time, you stepped onto a small enclosed porch and then into what felt like someone's house, or rather, for it's almost the same thing, into a house that had been turned into a restaurant. Even though it has become a public place, it still signals "home" with the proportion of its rooms, the size and placement of its doors and windows. In the summer, with these all open to catch the breeze, the smell of fried clams in the air, the random groups of casual eaters happily absorbed in their dinners, there was something immediately comforting and friendly about Duffy's. It was like a cabin in a Maine motor court: clean, cheerful, and individual, but also impersonal enough so that you don't feel an intruder in some stranger's home.

The food on the menu was equally unthreatening, a mixture of home cooking and old-fashioned fast food: pork chops with applesauce and baked ham with pineapple on the one hand, and cheeseburgers, clam rolls, and a variety of sandwich fillings heaped on "homemade bread" on the other. We settled into a table by an open window, checked out the specials on the board, and ended up ordering what we usually order in a Maine restaurant: fried seafood—on this night, clams—French fries, onion rings, coleslaw, and a couple of beers.

The menu also offered a little history. Duffy's was originally called Laura & Sadie's after its first two owners, the grandmother and great-aunt of Lauralee Gilley, who now runs the place with her husband, Richard. Laura and Sadie opened it in the 1940s, running it as a seasonal place for several years and then selling out to a Cape Cod man, William Tinney. He was the one who renamed it Duffy's, built it up into a year-round establishment, and ran it successfully until just that year, 1990, when Lauralee and Richard Gilley bought him out and brought the place back into the family.

Duffy's is, indeed, by any definition, a family restaurant. Not only were there families eating on every side of us, but Lauralee herself took our order, her husband was cooking in the kitchen, and her son Chad was busing the tables. Later we overheard them giggling about the family of raccoons that comes to beg for handouts at the kitchen door.

As mentioned earlier, there is something equally down-home about the place itself. Real pine paneling mingles cheerfully with fake pine wallboard; linen dish towels from Scotland decorate one corner, a vague gesture in the direction of the British Isles. The glass that tops the smaller tables (there are also some larger, oilcloth-covered, family-size ones) is mazed with cracks that have, from all evidence, been there for decades.

When, later, I asked Lauralee about this, she said that her grand-

father, who had made them, used plain window glass, not antic-
ipating the effect of years of stress—plates piled with food pressing
down from above, the wooden tabletop sagging away underneath.
They all cracked, but none actually broke. And, as the old Maine
saw has it—if it ain't broke, there's no point fixing it. The crazed
glass is so much a part of the decor now, she told me, that if they
tried to replace it the customers would protest.

Finally, the atmosphere here is also "family" in a way that other
places—however low-key and unpretentious—can't quite manage.
The very presence of professional waitresses, shiny red vinyl
booths, and uniform, Formica-covered tables signals the ultimate
indifference of an entirely public place. They may also be com-
fortable spots, but they aren't as vulnerable to your opinion.
Duffy's works hard to solicit your approval. Lauralee Gilley treats
you with the anxious friendliness of someone whose new neigh-
bors happened to have just stepped through the kitchen door. She
wants you to be happy here.

Of course, roughly speaking, many of her customers are neigh-
bors, and even the ones who are total strangers are still—or so it
seemed on that evening and those that followed—neighborly.
They are people, whether seasonal or year-round residents, young
or old, poor or reasonably affluent, who firmly associate them-
selves with the old, unfussy Maine, a place where people like to
think of themselves as making do, and making do well, with what
they have.

Maine is still full of such places, most of them geared, as
Duffy's is, to serving a local clientele, one that swells in the sum-
mer, but remains pretty much the same sort of folk. Intentionally,
then, others are kept away by the simple expedient of invisibility—
as Duffy's, for so long, was invisible to me.

The first thing to notice about these places, then, is how un-
noticeable they are. You may not feel like eating at the Colonel's,
but you certainly know when you drive by one. Restaurants, of all
classes, except at the very top and very bottom, are designed to
demand attention. Jasper's, The Hilltop House, The Mex, China
Hill, Jordan's, Maidee's, The Wok . . . I can name most of the
restaurants we regularly pass on our shopping trip to Ellsworth,
even though we've never been to any of them. They do everything

they can to stamp their names into your brain as you drive by. But the places I'm talking about seem to shyly duck their heads. In fact, one of them, Dick's, in Ellsworth, is in demeanor so retiring that a hand-lettered sign sits in one of the windows to say they're open. Otherwise, walking by, you can't really tell.

Duffy's also has a sign out front. It hangs, large and conspicuous, right beside the restaurant door:

> *Welcome to Duffy's—*
> *We here at Duffy's are a*
> *native oriented restaurant.*
> *We aren't fussy,*
> *and we're certainly not fancy . . .*
> *If you are,*
> *Ellsworth is 12 miles east,*
> *and*
> *Bucksport is 7 miles west.*
> *Yours truly,*
> *Duffy*

It was put there by the previous owner; it may express Maine sentiment, but posting it required Massachusetts nerve. Nevertheless, it's appreciated. T-shirts with the text printed on them are a popular item. It's a sign that—we've since discovered—has become legend with Maine folk up and down this part of the coast.

2.

Lauralee Gilley brought us our suppers. Fried seafood is often good in Maine eating places and, as we've previously written, so are French fries. The clams were sweet and fresh and fried whole, soft, succulent bellies and all, the way they are when eaters aren't put off by a clam's former life as a functioning bivalve. The beer was cold; the onion rings were great. The blueberry pie was awful.

Strangely, at first, I found its badness difficult to admit. This was partly because much of what had preceded this piece of pie had been so good, but mostly it was because the people around us were so plainly enjoying theirs—the couple at the next table even making loud exclamations of delight. I had gotten this far in the meal feeling a companionable kinship with my fellow eaters; then, unexpectedly, my dessert had exposed me as an interloper.

I knew that if those around me could have right then read my thoughts, they would have found them not only contrary to their own experience, but personally offensive. I was being too fussy. One bad piece of pie, of course, may mean nothing more than the luck of the draw. But you learn to recognize the difference between accidentally bad and chronically bad pie—and we had already encountered plenty of the latter at places boasting about their "home" baking. Now, eating this one, I finally began wondering what was going on.

Everyone—outside of the food world at least—knows that cooking that is better than you're prepared for can be as off-putting as cooking that is worse. Goodness in a meal is as much a matter of familiarity as it is of good taste, and familiarity is the specialty of places like Duffy's. Their pie was "good" because it was packed with real Maine blueberries, and because it had been baked right there in the restaurant kitchen.

That it had so much cinnamon in it that you couldn't taste the fruit didn't matter, nor did the fact that the crust was so tough that I needed a knife to saw through it. Topped with vanilla ice cream, it offered generous, mouth-filling, familiar flavors and the soothing if teeth-aching richness of sweet and fat. The pie was "good" not only because it didn't taste at all bad but because to the right eater there was something comforting in the fact that it wasn't all that good.

When we had come into Duffy's we'd read the sign outside and were amused by it but didn't particularly pause to think if it applied to ourselves. Us? Fussy? We were casually dressed; we didn't expect or want to find linen on the tables or stuffed lobster on the menu. But we weren't prepared for the fact that, for those who regularly eat at places like Duffy's, a certain imperfection in the food actually enhances rather than detracts from its flavor. The tangible anticipation we could see on the faces of these customers as they came through the door was prompted as much by the welcoming signals sent out by the place itself as by any good smells of cooking issuing from the kitchen.

This communication, tacit though it is, establishes immediate complicity—which is why even mentioning that piece of pie seems a betrayal of trust. Treating Duffy's in the language of a restaurant review is as meaningless and, really, as tactless as sending your neighbor a critique of her cooking the day after she's had you over for supper. To do the place justice, you need to call on the talents of an E. Annie Proulx or Carolyn Chute, not a Gael Greene or Mimi Sheraton. The writer's task is to flesh out the story of those fracture lines in the glass-topped tables, not to complain that the mashed potatoes arrive at the table cold or that the pieces of fried chicken aren't cooked all through.

At the very least, you have to get the signal. And, as best as I can decipher it, it breaks down into three complementary tones that I'm going to name particularity, generosity, and—the dominant of the triad—frugality. By "particularity" I mean simply what someone in Maine means when they say they're particular about something—that they don't like spices in their baked beans and do like buttermilk in their doughnuts. Maine people pride themselves on drinking Moxie instead of Coke and eating Jacob's cattle beans and cold-cellaring a hundred pounds of potatoes every fall. Unlike being fussy, being particular is a way of being thrifty without being mean.

Generosity is another of those ways. Whatever else you want to say about dinner at Duffy's, the portions are ample. They bring a whole small loaf of bread to you, even if you're eating alone, and they heap so many French fries on your plate that they spill off onto the table. Supper offerings like roast stuffed chicken with cranberry sauce speak of Sunday dinner, but they're priced only a little above a lunch at McDonald's.

Within these guidelines, there is much to like at Duffy's. The menu has a distinctly but completely unself-conscious regional feel, in the sense that "Italian" pasta—shells filled with meat sauce and cheese—served with a side of cole slaw is as much a Maine dish as the two kinds of chowder, fish and clam, that the menu also offers. (The fact that the fish chowder costs more than the clam chowder is another clue that this isn't a tourist place.) The vegetables, apart from the coleslaw, are—to the Maine taste—all out of a can, and include such favorites as boiled onions, pickled beets, and applesauce. The coleslaw is homemade and sprightly. The baked beans come from an old family recipe, and the seasons are marked with dishes like strawberry shortcake and apple crisp. Instead of generic fried "fish," Duffy's serves you a generous portion of good haddock. The mashed potatoes are the real thing. At breakfast you can get an omelet filled with genuine cheddar cheese or a plate of flapjacks: three big ones, crisp and brown without and fluffy and light within.

Despite all this, the cooking at Duffy's, like its tables, is shot through with fracture lines. Those flapjacks arrive at the table with a single-serving plastic container of Kraft syrup, a dull-flavored corn syrup blend without a drop of real maple stuff mixed in. The baked beans come with a slice of insipid ham cut from a daisy roll. The fried haddock is served with prepackaged Kraft tartar sauce. And when we moved up the coast and went to eat at Chase's, in Winter Harbor, we were served mini-loaves of "homemade" bread identical to those brought to our table at Duffy's. Obviously the same supplier of frozen bread dough, laced with dough conditioner, visits them both. All this in a place where local people still produce maple syrup, smoke and cure country hams, and raise organic vegetables, lamb, beef, and free-range chickens.

Duffy's customers know these things and many know their taste, but they also know that, today, none of them comes cheap. Things like maple syrup that were once free or near to it are now costly and hence not used. Maine vernacular restaurants zig and zag on this issue—many serve real butter with their biscuits and real cream with their coffee—but, while frugality and generosity are familiar constants, these places are now gun-shy about being thought too particular. If it's at all obtrusive, their customers are "agin" it.

Hence the absence of lobsters on the menu. Native Mainers—including lobstermen themselves—are, at best, ambivalent about the beast, symbol of the occupation army of out-of-staters, and rarely, if ever, eat it. "Too expensive," they say, capturing in that laconic phrase the fissure that cuts the state in two: the old Maine on one side, the rest of us on the other. Tourist boosters in the state government got the lobster on our license plate; public outcry got a law passed allowing objecting citizens to paint it out.

Duffy's customers aren't necessarily poor, but they do differentiate themselves from the newcomers who wear Eddie Bauer outfits, have their hair cut by a hair stylist and not a barber, and eat lunch at Blue Hill's Left Bank Café by an unease about money. And this unease means that the signal that Duffy's—and the many restaurants like Duffy's—sends out has a certain dissonance to it, a sharp edge that, if you're not careful, can cut. It usually isn't conspicuous but it's always there. You catch it in the tone of voice, the posture, the self-conscious restraint, the hint of bitterness, resentment even, masked by politeness and pride.

Like the people in any poor state, Mainers are in a fix regarding cash: they don't make much of it and they don't like what it does to people, but, more and more, lack of it is crimping their lives. Maine people, in our experience, work hard—very hard—but at jobs that make sense to them and in ways that feel right, neither of which has much to do with intensifying cash flow.

Once, when our old Honda Civic started running on three cylinders, I took it to Bim's Garage, located on a country road in Penobscot. Bim came out, discussed my problem, took the car into the garage, fiddled around in the engine, and discovered that one of the spark plugs wasn't firing. He was going to get me a new one when he remembered he had an "almost new one" in the garage attic that would do just as well. He went up the ladder, spent ten minutes rooting around through cans and boxes, found it, and installed it. All this took almost an hour. Bim charged me five dollars, giving me the spark plug for free, since it was used.

Again, the signal that this is the real Maine; again, the three familiar tones. The thrift: not throwing a good thing away; the generosity: not charging for it; the particularity: his determination to work at his speed, in his own way. At a city gas station, the attendant would have put in a new plug and charged me twenty dollars. He also would have taken about fifteen minutes to do it. Bim engaged me in a long conversation which wasn't finished when the car was, being interrupted both by his trip up attic and by two lengthy telephone calls. My payment was just enough to buy Bim breakfast someplace, with enough left over for the tip.

3.

Breakfast is a good meal to go out for in Maine. The local eating places take it seriously, as do the local eaters. Not only are portions generous but they include such specialties as expertly turned out corned beef hash, squash or molasses doughnuts, even genuine bean-hole beans. The reason I pictured Bim spending his fiver on it, however, is that—apart from tourists and summer people—the breakfasters at these places are predominantly men. We once watched three trucks pull into the parking lot of the Donut Hole in Winter Harbor, and fifteen men climb out to join the crowd inside a place not much larger than our living room. The resulting atmosphere is cramped, steamy, and, without being exactly convivial, friendly. Maine men, although always polite, rarely come across as social animals; a room full of them has a fascinating, slightly edgy feel to it, like attending a happy hour with a bunch of black bears.

Anywhere you drive in Maine in the early part of the day, you find these gatherings; breakfast is the male social hour. People who work outside get up early; one morning we got a misdialed wake-up call from a lobsterman at 5 A.M. Of course, lobstermen, except on stormy days, don't take their coffee breaks ashore, but construction workers, carpenters, linemen, and road crews—to name a few we've identified by their outfits or their trucks—do.

The smaller the town, the stronger the sense of community. Everyone in the room knows everyone else . . . everyone else, that is, except you. When we first moved to Steuben, I asked our UPS driver what he thought of the neighborhood eatery, the Rusty Anchor, since I'd noticed he ate lunch there every day. It wasn't until he had driven off that I realized that only thirty seconds of his description of the place had been devoted to the food. Clearly, what mattered most to him was that he was accepted there as a member of the club.

Despite its name, the Rusty Anchor, an old monster highway maintenance garage converted into an eating place by a local fisherman, has vernacular Maine written all over its weather-beaten facade. And it's never busier than around nine in the morning, when the front of the place is lined with cars. Regulars fill a special breakfast room called the Coffee Nook. If you happen in, there's a sudden hush while they size you up. After that, you are generally ignored, although conversational sallies are lobbed like softballs from one table to another, some right past your head. Whatever their content, the message is: you've intruded into a private place.

This sense of privacy is emphasized by design. In other parts of the country, the resolute disinclination of these eateries to connect to the outside world would signal a roadhouse or saloon. Earlier, when I first mistook Duffy's for one, I revealed how new I was to Maine, no matter the many summers I had already spent here. Outside of big cities like Portland, what distinguishes this state is the absence of drinking places. Maine took Prohibition seriously and in many ways is still markedly dry. Only recently has it begun to phase out the state-run liquor stores (or, in less densely populated areas, the designated "agency" groceries or drugstores) that controlled and limited the sale of hard liquor. Once you get away from the tourist trail, few restaurants offer mixed drinks, and a surprising number don't even offer beer. The traditional Maine beverage in a restaurant, whatever the meal, is a cup of coffee.★

Still, my reading was not altogether wrong. Maine's vernacular restaurants are places that offer a moment of rest and comfort from the pressures of the outside world. Like the traditional British pub—"pub" being short for "public house"—they are modeled on the room of the house in which customers will feel most at home. And, for Maine men, that room is the kitchen, especially if a woman is there on the other side of the counter to tease, cosset, and feed him.

★Not that drinking doesn't go on here, but it doesn't happen in bars . . . or, for that matter, all that much in homes. Instead, men hit the bottle in hunting shacks, back-lot sheds, gatherings of pick-up trucks, and other all-male enclaves, kept secluded and separate from women.

Maine is still a place where men are men and women get their traditional end of the stick. We have been in at least one tiny Maine eating place where a single woman ran the entire show—waitress, cashier, cook, dishwasher, and surrogate mom. She was trying to frost a sheet cake, cook a range of short-order breakfast dishes, and wait on the customers all at once. A woman came in to buy some doughnuts, took one look at the situation, and went back of the counter to pitch in. Recently, I overheard another woman at the post office tell how she had been invited by an old friend to the Rusty Anchor for supper. The friend was late and the Rusty Anchor short a waitress, so she picked up a tray, even though she had already spent the day at work somewhere else; by the time her friend arrived she had to go wake her husband for his night-shift job. No wonder that more and more Maine women prefer to take the kids to Pizza Hut or Burger Chef, and themselves to places that remind them as little of their kitchen as possible—and to go at a quiet time in the afternoon, when there is never any call to help out.

4.

When power-line, telephone, or road crews have been busy on our road, predominant in the litter they leave behind, next to disposable plastic coffee cups, are empty boxes of single-serving pies. Eaten as mid-morning snacks, these show—so far as such casually gathered evidence can show anything—the enduring power of pie over candy bars, jelly doughnuts, or Little Debbie Swiss Devil Dogs, as Maine male comfort food. It epitomizes a kind of home cooking that, we suspect, isn't cooked all that much at home anymore.

Pie is more than a mainstay on Maine menus: it's the Maine dessert. Mainers also like, and get, homey puddings—famously, Grape-Nut, but also bread and, sometimes, Indian. These are expected, but they're rarely featured. When a Maine restaurant boasts of its desserts, it's talking about its pies. The day we had the blueberry pie, we were offered a choice of six: banana cream, strawberry-rhubarb, pecan, apple, lemon meringue, and blueberry. Other days, different pies are on the list; the count, however, remains the same.

Still, Duffy's is a piker compared to Moody's, a diner on Route 1 in Waldoboro, midway up the coast, which may be Maine's most famous eating place, and is certainly its most famous diner. Moody's is a favorite with truckers and tourists but, whenever we've gone in, the majority of the customers are local. Mainers appreciate Moody's determination to be itself, neither a tourist attraction nor a self-consciously maintained antique. Visitors may see Moody's as Maine Past but regulars see it as Maine Present— or at least that part of today's Maine that still holds on as firmly as it can to its roots. The Moody family has fought hard to keep this connection alive, and no other Maine eating place speaks as directly to Maine taste. Moody's serves New England boiled dinner on Thursday, haddock with egg sauce on Friday, and baked beans on Saturday, with Indian pudding for dessert. And, any day, you can get fish cakes or fried tripe or liver and onions.

Moody's began as a lunch cart in the 1930s and, soon after, started adding: walls and a roof, a counter with stools, booths, bathrooms . . . until the place reached its current dimensions and ambiance in 1948. (Some Mainers are resolute in their belief that neither they nor Moody's has ever left that year; it's not uncommon, settling into a vacated booth, to find that the previous diners have left behind a fifty-cent tip.) Even so, here, too, holding to frugality and generosity (the fish cake dinner—three fish cakes, fries, coleslaw—is still an astonishing $2.75) has meant a gradual eroding in particularity. The fault lines run as deeply here as they do at Duffy's. Order the beef simmered in onions and you get something almost inedible; order the fried tripe and you get something near transcendental. Until you taste, there's no way to tell. Each time you wander from the dishes you know they do well, you put yourself at risk.

Moody's is famous for its pies. Ask the waitress what she has on hand, and she'll rattle off a baker's dozen: apple, custard, rhubarb, strawberry rhubarb, squash, raspberry, raspberry cream cheese, lemon cream cheese, chocolate banana, peanut butter, walnut cream—a breathless listing that seems the realization of a pie lover's dream. These pies can be very good. The rhubarb on a late spring visit had a filling of tangy-sweet fruit bound up in a simple, delicious egg custard and a crust prepared with a delicate hand.

But Moody's pies no longer carry the signature of a single cook. This means that, if you order wrong, you can end up with a slice where the filling is uninspired and the crust quite ordinary, and sometimes even stale. In the summer, when the pies pour out of the kitchen, they're always fresh; in the winter, however, they aren't. Once, when we asked, we found that only one pie out of the dozen offered had been made that day. And our waitress was clearly offended at our asking, treating the question as a shocking breach of good manners. Here we were, caught out being fussy again.

My father, who was born here, remembers when Maine pies all had their signature—a real one. Proud cooks worked their initials into the crust with the tines of a fork. That way, at the grange supper, you would know whose pie you were eating and, consequently, the baker would get due praise (or at least no credit would mistakenly be given a competitor). This was a time when those three strands of Maine character—frugality, generosity, particularity—were braided into a tight skein. The only pie ingredients not homegrown were the flour, the sugar, and the pinch of salt. The shortening was freshly rendered lard; the filling was custard contributed by the cow and the hens or fruit contributed by the orchard, the berry patch, or the monster rhubarb plant in the corner of the garden.

A pie was economical, filling, and good; it also allowed the maker to show her skills in the light touch required to make a tender, flaky crust. Home bakers opted for lard or butter or a mixture of the two, striving to balance flavor and tenderness and flake. They also had their tricks. Robert Tristram Coffin's mother, once a pie was ready for the oven, "calmly turned on the cold-water faucet and let the water run over the top crust. It came out of the oven with a top to it like French pastry, only more so."

Although few bakers cook with lard in Maine today and fewer still use their own, many still take advantage of the state's natural abundance of pie fillings—pie timber, they call it—from rhubarb in the spring right through to squash in the fall. Frugality is one strand that still holds true. So does generosity. These days, a piece of pie in Maine costs, in the sort of places we're writing about, under two dollars, and it's cut widely, with, if you want, a spoonful of real whipped cream set on top for no extra charge.

But the cost is in the particularity. Maine pies are fast losing their individuality. To bite into one is to risk encountering an indifferently concocted filling and a generic—and often stale—vegetable-shortening crust. Particularity is always the most volatile aspect of Maine character. If frugality is the red light and generosity the green, then particularity is the yellow or "caution" one—and, to an outsider's confusion, it means at once "slow down" and "speed up." With pies as with traffic lights, the wrong decision can get you into trouble—and an accusation of fussiness is the least of it.

Homemade blueberry pie! It isn't the gaping space between claim and reality that makes you think Maine cooking has gone seriously amiss; it's the determination not to notice it. The result is disturbingly like stumbling across a chronic family problem that everyone has decided to pretend does not exist. The husbands smack their lips. The wives, some of them, roll their eyes but mostly hold their peace. They, unlike their men, know the cost as well as the taste of a well-made piece of pie; the arrival of one on their table could be treated less as an occasion than a threat.

5.

When we moved here to the Maine coast, we had a fantasy of finding the "perfect" Maine eating place. It would be a small place—a cottage, actually, just like Duffy's—and it would serve only a few good things—nothing fancy—just fresh-dug, melt-in-your-mouth clams coated with cracker crumbs and fried up in a vat boiling with hot, sweet fat. In a companion vat, shoestring fries would be turning a golden brown. There would be a crisp coleslaw, hot-from-the-oven baking-powder biscuits, and, for dessert, a slice of homemade blueberry or green apple or raspberry rhubarb pie.

Instead, the best we have been able to do has been to piece this fantasy eatery together from fragments of the real places. The

Bagaduce Lunch in North Brooksville, a tiny take-out shack at Bagaduce Falls, provides the location—the rush of the tidal flow through the narrows, the bright blue sky and the deep green pines. Duffy's supplies the clams and the coleslaw; Chase's, the fries and onion rings; and Moody's, the biscuits and that rhubarb pie. The coffee we would bring from home.

Ironically, the closest we have come to finding the perfect Maine restaurant was when we celebrated my birthday last spring at Le Domaine, a French auberge-style restaurant on Route 1 in Hancock. Here, at first glance, "fussy" might seem the operative word. The tables are draped with white linen and set with handsome china. A fire blazes in a huge, walk-in fireplace; the room murmurs with quiet conversation and the clink of wine glasses.

The truth, however, is that the chef, Nicole Purslow, is rather courageous in her lack of fuss. Because she is particular about her ingredients, she keeps her menu short. The night we came there were only a half a dozen entrées, four on the menu and two specials. At the same time, she charges enough money to be able to select those ingredients with care. Our meal, with two glasses of wine each, came to about a hundred dollars.

The dining room at Le Domaine exudes relaxed elegance, and the food is prepared and served with finesse. This is not "fancy" dining in the Maine mode, which demands prime rib or rack of lamb or those cacophonous dishes that are today's symbol of gourmet opulence—lobster, sea scallops, and asparagus tossed together in pasta and dressed with lemon cream sauce, and the like. From choices that included grilled salmon, rabbit with prunes, and a beef filet, we had sautéed sweetbreads, served with wild rice and fiddleheads. The sweetbreads were perfectly prepared; the crusty rolls tasted only of flour, yeast, and salt; the after-dinner coffee was strong and good.

Like Duffy's, Le Domaine also presents a discreet road-front presence, just visible enough to alert those who are looking for it, without flagging the attention of those who aren't. Also, there are no lobsters either on the sign or on the menu. Those who come to Le Domaine—or, at least, come twice—come for the food, food they already know how to eat. In this, the customers and the cook understand and appreciate each other, and often know each other as well.

Some time ago, say when Duffy's was still Laura & Sadie's, this was the case at many plain Maine eateries. The food may not always have been as delicious, but at least it had the chance to be. It was built on real home cooking—the frying done in freshly rendered lard, the chickens taken from the hen house, the vegetables either brought in fresh from the garden or taken out of jars put up from it. As at Le Domaine today, the cook knew most of her ingredients personally. So did her customers. They knew the blueberries in the pie; they knew a good crust when they ate one. She knew they knew, and their pleasure pleased her. In Maine, praise may be rarely spoken but it is implicit in this kind of understanding.

Maine women know what their mothers did then and what they themselves do now. Many still keep kitchen gardens and put up for winter, but hardly any raise poultry or a family pig. When they have time, they pick wild berries and gather windfalls. Mostly, however, like everyone else, they buy their food at the supermarket. And that food, aisle after aisle of it, is cast—as it is everywhere—in the language of convenience, which is to say with contempt for those two pillars of old-fashioned Maine cooking: the taste of real food and the honest value of kitchen labor. Today, you must make a choice: you can have frugality and generosity or you can have particularity. Most cooks choose the former, and, even as they come to depend on the cheapness of out-of-state produce and meat, they get accustomed—or at least resign themselves—to its inferiority.

Maine cussedness may be a necessary luxury, but it is a luxury for all that, and it is the women who foot the bill. The men cling to familiar ways because they still find their identity in them; the women stay with them because they love their men—but at more cost to themselves, if not in effort, at least in pride . . . something the men do their best to ignore. This means a growing distance between Maine men and Maine women, a distance that doesn't get discussed. And that, if you like, is Maine cussedness, too.

One evening, sitting in Moody's over a plate of franks and beans, we heard a grandmother tell her grandson that Moody's served the best food in Maine. The sad thing is that if Moody's limited its menu to dishes it could imbue with genuine Maine character and plenty of good taste—if, in other words, Moody's really became a kind of vernacular Le Domaine—it's unlikely that couple would care to go there. It would just seem too fussy, which is to say, too threatening for them to enjoy their meal.

What she might have said is that Moody's serves the most comfortable food in Maine. In fact, comfortable is the problem with Moody's—the place is like a favorite pair of old shoes: impossible to replace, too comfortable to stop wearing out. The laces, heels, and soles can be perpetually renewed, but the shoe leather is worn and cracked and splitting at the stress points. Pretty soon, this particular pair is going to fall apart, and when it does it will be replaced, most likely, by an Irving Big Stop—a gas station plus convenience store plus eatery, the Moody's of the new poor Maine.

Maine food is shot through with cracks because the identity of the people who make it is similarly fissured . . . and parts keep breaking away. The landmarks of the old Maine that haven't been entirely covered by the encroaching tide are now rugged little islands poking out of a vast, bland bay . . . and so—though they don't often care to notice this—is the consciousness of those who look out over it. Like any holding action fighting inevitable defeat, there is a poignancy, even a pathos, to Down East cuisine. It is wounded and lives with its wounds like others in that situation, mostly making the best of it but sometimes giving way to hurt and anger or, worst of all, sheer denial that there is any problem there at all.

Living here in Maine, you come to respect this situation. You learn to look for places where the cook, out of conviction or habit, remains particular about some aspect of Maine food, or at least some aspect of a favorite Maine dish. The pie filling may be over-thickened and flavorless but is still encased in a deftly made, hand-rolled crust; the doughnuts may no longer be fried in lard but the batter is made fresh from a time-honored recipe, not some suppliers' mix; the seafood may be coated in a bland, generic batter and not fresh-crushed cracker crumbs, but was brought to the back door by a neighboring clammer or fisherman.

Hoping to find a place cooking only the old Maine foods in the old pure and simple ways is as much an outsider's fantasy as expecting to find a one-room schoolhouse with a schoolmarm still teaching readin', writin', and 'rithmetic. Today, such an eatery could only be opened by someone from out of state, or at least someone possessing an out-of-state sense of appropriate aesthetics. And people would gather there for the same reason that they come to an art gallery for an opening or a bookstore for a poetry reading: to share an aesthetic experience, that artful reproduction of neighborliness, the connection of shared taste.

However, the people who eat at Duffy's and the like are genuine, old-fashioned neighbors. Even if they don't happen to know each other personally, they're still cut of the same local cloth, still feel their fate is tied to the place in which they live. Few have the time these days to hang out at the hardware store; come winter, no circle of chairs rings a woodstove or cracker barrel at the IGA. As the grange dances and movie theaters and even church suppers fade away, these eateries have become the one remaining locus of casual public conviviality, where locals can share together the bittersweet feeling of common identity—of belonging.

Le Domaine versus Duffy's—here we have the two halves of America's wounded cuisine: real food on the one hand and real neighbors on the other. There are writers on each side of this divide who try to claim both these elements: that gastronomy is a form of neighborliness; that the eats at Moody's give unalloyed gastronomic pleasure. No . . . it's the longing for the closure that's the real thing, the yearning for real food and real neighbors . . . and for a national cuisine that can give us, as it ought to, both.

Meanwhile, there's the A-1 Diner in Gardiner, an idiosyncratic anomaly of an eatery where the two halves of modern-day Maine, old and new, sit down, if separately, to dine. A classic diner lifted by a dizzyingly high framework of steel girders to the level of the sidewalk on the Cobbossee Creek Bridge, its interior is a symphony of mahogany woodwork, blue and black tiles, and nostalgia items, with a pleasantly funky, Down East flea-market feel to it all that keeps it well this side of chic. The menu board offers such exotica as halibut with aioli, black bean chili, and Thai garlic soup, but there is also good plain Maine fare—flapjacks with real maple syrup, French fries with gravy, meatloaf, macaroni and cheese, a flawless fried tripe—all of it priced cheap. Desserts include Hummingbird cake, fresh raspberries and cream, and gingerbread with lemon sauce. The coffee, in the traditional Maine style, is weak, but, made from freshly roasted beans, it's also good.

Two young guys cook this food, a vintage Maine waitress dishes it out. The time we were there the booths were crowded with summer people and local yuppies immersed in happy conversation. For the duration of our lunch, however, an old Mainer sat on a counter stool, hunched over a cup of coffee, navigating the distances, a cigarette end smoldering between his fingers. It may not all add up to a marriage made in heaven—but this isn't heaven, just Vacationland, and you leave the A-1 feeling okay . . . about the place, the eats, the people, and, for a hopeful moment, the state of Maine.

CODA

This piece was over two years in the writing. During that time, the Gilleys have expanded Duffy's—tacking a large addition onto the front, which has erased the pleasing proportions of the original cottage; installing air conditioning, which has effectively eliminated its breezy, summery feel; and replacing the front porch with a handicap-access ramp and an entrance hall. They have taken on a staff of waitresses and gotten rid of almost all the crazed-glass-topped tables, diminishing much of the restaurant's original feckless character. There is no longer any sense of stepping into someone's house. The last time we ate at Duffy's was a Saturday, and the news from a waitress that they had stopped serving baked beans on Maine's traditional baked-bean day set the dining room abuzz. We drove by this summer and saw, attached to a post right beside the road, a three-foot-high cutout of a bright red lobster. The only good news is, come Labor Day, they took it down.   [1990–1992]

The Cornfield

My last day with them we'd spent fishing; coming home
I'd gotten in the back seat with the metal boxes, poles,
And wicker basket which had just two puny fish in it,
While up in front my aunt kept saying to my uncle,

Who was driving, that his shortcut notion was all wrong and
Simply wasn't going to get us home, and I was barely old enough
To know not to say oh yes it will because it did
Last year when you weren't with us.

Because my aunt's voice had a range from mean to mad
Most of the time, so I just sat still the way my uncle was,
Sort of staring at the more-than-sunburn redness of his neck,
And noticing us going a little faster all the time.

Next thing I knew the car was trying to go around
An L-shaped curve which suddenly came up, and which I
Suddenly remembered barely having made the year before,
And this time simply not being able to.

So off the road we went, straight through a single strand
Wire fence into a cleared and sunbaked cornfield where
My uncle brought the lurching car to a dead stop.
I'd closed my eyes tight, and my aunt had sort of gasped a scream,

And then, before she'd really found her tongue, my uncle,
Still without a word, switched the engine off, got out
And took a blanket and what was left of lunch
And walked a little way away and just sat down.

My aunt got out then too and I right after her
And just as she'd marched over to my uncle and opened up
Her mouth, he said composedly, chewing on a sandwich,
"Sit down here with me and watch this sunset for a while."

I think she gagged, but then she actually did.
And so they sat, and I did too; I don't remember how or when
We finally did get home, but I do know sitting there was the one time
I ever saw my aunt and uncle holding hands.

For Those in Peril on the Sea:
A Meditation

This is not a story about being caught in a storm at sea, swamped by a rogue wave, run into by a whale, sunk by an iceberg or even an enemy. But it is nevertheless a tale of fear and danger, of being frightened in a small boat on a big ocean.

It was a clear, calm day in Camden Harbor the June morning we arrived to move our 26-foot Ariel sloop, *Metaphor*, from winter storage to our summer mooring near Belfast at the head of Penobscot Bay. The sea looked flat and barely rippled, smoothed-out silver foil catching the light and throwing it off in dappled rainbow shapes that flitted over every surface like ghosts of butterflies. There didn't seem to be much wind at all, which was fine with me. Though I have sailed most of my life in one kind of boat or another, I was finding it difficult to make the transition from sailing on a nice little lake where you were never far from land and could always swim to shore if the boat tipped over, or the mast broke in half, or the rudder came loose, to being bounced around on a body of water so cold and vast and inhospitable that even in the height of summer the mean survival time for someone immersed in it, as Cowper's Castaway laments, "snatched far from all effectual aid," is somewhat less than eighteen minutes.

The irony of it all was that I was the one who had gotten us into this in the first place. Several years before, my husband had barely survived an operation for what turned out to be a very rare form of cancer, and though we had been assured that he was cured, his convalescence was long, and in the months following, he had been frail in both body and spirit, his faith shaken not only in himself but in life in general. A departing friend needed a place to store his small sailing dinghy, and since we lived on a lake, it seemed only natural that we should offer to keep the boat in return for a summer's use. One bright day we shoved off in the little boat, and after a few rudimentary instructions, I put the tiller and the mainsheet in Ed's hand, and that was that. It was clear from the beginning that he was the true sailor, intrepid, strong of mind and body, with an instinctive understanding of the relation between wind and water on which the art of sailing—and survival at sea—depends.

The Ariel was our third sailboat in almost as many years, but the first that was truly ocean-going. She was old but seaworthy, fast and steady on the wind, but low in the water, and also "somewhat crank," a sailor's term that I would soon translate as just plain "tippy." But here we were, my husband the captain confident and eager to be off, I the crew decidedly less enthusiastic but willing to give it a try. Still, the day was fine, the wind seemed light, no clouds or storms in sight, so we loaded our gear, motored out of the crowded inner harbor, raised the sails, trimmed them for a tight reach, and headed out to sea.

As soon as I saw the line of darker water at the mouth of the harbor I knew we were in for a rougher sail than I had bargained for. The wind was much stronger here, the water a dark navy blue fretted with white caps. As the boat began to heel sharply, I scrambled up onto the windward deck and sat there with my hands clenched, fervently wishing the voyage were over. Or better yet, had never begun.

"Hmm," said Ed, squinting down the bay at the white-caps, the 3-foot seas bearing down on us, the wind whistling in the rigging and feinting and pushing at our big mainsail. "Looks like more wind than the weather channel forecast said. We'll have to shorten sail. Can you reef the main? Or do you want me to do it?"

My heart sank. Could I reef the main? Of course I knew what he meant, it was just that I had never done it on this crank old boat before, and didn't especially want to start now. But I could see him wrestling with the tiller against the weather helm, and the last thing I wanted to do was try to hold the boat into the wind while he did the reefing. So I did the next to last thing I wanted to do. Picking my way carefully along the slanted, slippery deck, I went forward to reef the main.

The boat was already heeling sharply, and pitching over even more with each big wave. Being in a position halfway to horizontal is not a feeling I like under even the best of conditions, but I needed both hands to do the reef, so I leaned my belly against the mast on the upwind edge and, just to be on the safe side, hooked one leg around it. Ed headed the boat up into the wind—always a noisy business, but not particularly scary—then released the main sheet so the boom would swing free and take the wind pressure off the sail. I undid the main halyard and got ready to lower the sail.

Bang! A giant hand swept down and slammed the boat right over onto its side. In a split second we were heeled over almost flat, with the mast nearly in to the water, the lee rail buried, the hull of the boat virtually perpendicular to the waves, which were now crashing against the underside of the hull and welling up over the lee coaming, splashing over the deck, cascading into the boat from all sides.

I was still clutching the main halyard; only that and my legs—both of them now wrapped around the mast in a frozen parody of a firefighter sliding down the pole—kept me from going right overboard as my weight swung me around the mast to the downwind side. I grabbed for the mast with my free hand and hauled myself up, wrapping both arms, halyard and all, tightly around the mast, clinging to it for dear life as I hung there over the icy water.

I was transfixed with terror. Something had gone terribly wrong, and we were doomed. I started to cry. I hate this, I sobbed, I hate this boat, this sea, this wind, and most of all I hate sailing. It was all too much: wind, wave, water, cold, wild motion, the thunderous noise of sails and rigging flapping and flailing; every-thing—Everything!—out of control. Never before—or since—have I felt myself physically so overwhelmed and imperiled, in ac-tual danger of losing my life. Though I am not an overtly religious person, suddenly a poem by William Whiting, set to music and now known everywhere to sailors and landlubbers alike as the Navy Hymn—words and music both fixed forever in the memories of those of my generation during the terrible days following John F. Kennedy's assassination—started running through my mind: "Eternal Father, Strong to Save, whose arm hath bound the restless wave/Who bids the mighty ocean deep/Its own appointed limits keep/. . . O! Hear us when we cry to thee/For Those in peril on the sea."

But no one was listening; not this time. We were never going to make it back alive, the boat, with her ton-and-a-half lead keel, was going to founder and sink straight to the bottom, with us in it. Through the salt spray—hell, it was a deluge—I could see Ed, drenched and shivering, struggling with the tiller, trying to bring the boat back up into the wind. But the boat was not responding. Meanwhile we were scudding along at an impossible forty-degree angle of heel, with water still pouring in over the lee rail and waves banging and splashing against the hull on the other side. And all I could do was hang on.

But why were we still sailing in the first place, let alone at an angle nearly parallel to the surface of the water, a reach so tight it was ridiculous? I had seen Ed loosen the main sheet, and the line should be running free! Then I saw Ed reach behind him, pulling at a tangle of rope that seemed to be caught around the stern cleat. He yanked it free, the boom swung out, the main went slack, and as suddenly as the boat had gone over, she righted herself and came up into the wind. The main sheet, flailing loose in the strong wind, had looped around the dinghy cleat behind Ed's back, just out of his line of sight, in effect re-trimming the supposedly slackened main.

That's all. After I regained my breath and my nerve, I proceeded to reef the main with no trouble, and we sailed across the wind on an easy beam reach all the way up the bay to our safe harbor, on a glorious, sunlit day in which wind and water, boat and crew alike all came together in a harmonious balance of conflicting forces. It had not been a matter of bad weather, sea conditions, a failure of seamanship, of knowledge, or of will that had put me in terror for my life—only a sudden brief occurrence of the unforeseen.

I think that it is this ever-present possibility—being at the mercy of so many conditions all at once—wind, water, wave, cold—that gives to the sea, more than earth's other elements, our sense of its being so much like life itself. In the oncology unit of the local hospital where my husband and many others have gone to receive chemotherapy for life-threatening cancer—harsh and difficult treatments that extended his life for a number of years but ultimately could not save it—there is a sampler stitched by an unknown hand. I do not know where the saying comes from, nor have I been able to find anyone else who does, except to suggest it may be an ancient Irish proverb. It seems somehow appropriate that this brief saying should originate from an island nation both dependent on and threatened by the sea. It is not a prayer, or even an invocation; it is simply a statement of fact. But it is also a recognition of the sea as metaphor for life, with all its beauty and its danger. "Oh Lord, thy sea is so great, and my boat is so small."

This is what those who sail the sea have always known, a lesson we, earth's other voyagers, forgo only at our peril.

Handed Down

Raymond Hodgkins, his dragger last seen
in heavy seas off Schoodic, night falling
and still no word of him; and before him

Buddy Closson, Herb Damon, Ben Day,
Clyde Haskell, Larry Robbins senior,
Alan Thompson: the roll of the names

goes on and on, goes back thirty years
to Ray Dunbar, the day the *Lillian Mae*
broke up between the bar islands: back

to that scene, the men gathering, the women
waiting above the inlet, the skirts they still
wore in those days blowing out behind them

(a painterly embellishment handed down
by Grattan Condon) as one, unanimous
the way gulls are, heading into the wind.

Divers went searching, but found no body;
one of them tripped, fouled in a kelp bed,
came close to drowning. Days passed; nothing.

Then Vin Young—it was Vin, not Vic, his twin,
the way they remember—no more than thirteen,
but old enough to go out hauling, dreamed

one night, and woke up still afraid, of
finding Ray. He told only Vic, the two of them
dawdled and puttered until their father

said, "You kids better get out there
if you aim to earn your keep." So
they went out, and that day, sure enough

(the way they tell it), saw something floating,
a body, and it was Ray Dunbar. It's the names,
the roll call handed on and let down

in heavy seas, the visibility near zero,
the solitude total, night falling—it's the names
of the dead, kept alive, they still hold onto.

3,000 Dreams Explained

Early in the course of a night's dreaming
I smoke a cigarette
which may mean success
of one sort or another.
Later, around dawn, I ride
bareback alongside my brother
through water. Horses
imply independence in the future;
I don't recall their color,
but white and black can signify
a wedding and death,
respectively. At last
we stumble upon an island,
according to my handbook
loneliness to come.

I toss the text aside
to work my own interpretation.
Wasn't my brother
about to join me in a house
off the coast of Maine?
And wouldn't there be horses
in the ferry's engines
carrying us across?
Without Madame Aspasia's assistance
I relive the thrill
of last night's episodes:
a bad habit of the past

embraced again,
and my brother and I,
complete strangers to riding,
whipping our steeds
up out of the frigid waters.

Neighbors and Kin

Civil Defense

"I'm not going *anywhere*," Granny says, whenever the family so much as mentions an old people's home. For weeks now it's been the whispered topic of conversation among Mandy's mother and father and the countless aunts and uncles and older cousins who filter in and out of the house on Old Inn Road. Folks deciding Granny's future for her.

"You'll have to take me in a straight jacket," Granny threatens. She throws the mitten she's been knitting back into her basket. "You'll have to drug me first. Put sleeping pills in my tea like the nurses do in them homes. I ain't going on my own, that's one thing for sure."

Granny has gone to her room and slammed the door. Mandy hears her stomping about overhead, slapping all the doors shut on her dresser. She isn't really angry. She's just very hurt. Soon she'll come back downstairs and try to make up to Mandy's mother.

"It'd be different if she were my *own* mother," Rita is telling her husband. "But Clarence, she's about to drive me crazy. This morning she got out a scrub bucket and brush while I was upstairs making the beds. Now how many times have I told her to leave the housework to me? She just makes a mess of everything."

Mandy is half doing her homework and half listening. *Ponce de Leon searched for the Fountain of Youth and discovered Florida. The fountain was said to be on the island of Bimini and old men who bathed in its magic waters became young again. Ponce de Leon was governor of Puerto Rico.*

"By the time I come back downstairs she'd scrubbed all the little flowers off the linoleum by the kitchen door. Go look at it, Clare. I defy you to find a single flower anywhere near the door. I asked her why she did it and she said she thought they were boot marks. I don't know what in hell she used to scrape them off."

Mandy stares at the picture of Ponce de Leon and his men blazing a trail through the sand and palmettos. *It happened to be Easter, 1513, and Ponce de Leon named the country Florida from the Spanish name for that holy day, Pascua florida.* Mandy stares into the blue waves of the ocean in her book. Granny comes back down the stairs. She straightens a pillow on the sofa in the living room. Then she comes to the kitchen and asks Rita if she needs a hand with supper. Rita says no and bangs a pot into the sink. She's fixing macaroni with chunks of hamburg and stewed tomatoes. Granny goes over to Mandy's father and rubs his head. As if he's a little boy. He looks up at her and smiles sadly. Then he goes back to his papers in front of him. He's working on plans to build a bomb shelter in the backyard next summer. If the Commies bomb Maine, Mandy and her family will be safe from fallout. And it's a known fact that the first bomb will fall on Loring Air Force Base, only sixty miles away.

"Will you let me in, too?" Lois asked her one day last week, when Mandy excitedly told her friends at school. A real *bomb shelter* in their yard. She has thought about Lois's question all week. Something is bothering her about it, but she isn't sure what.

"How's it coming?" Granny asks, and then sits with her chin in her hands at the table, staring at her son. Mandy can see how they look alike. They have the same nice cheek bones, as if someone shaded them in with a pencil. And the darkest brown eyes. Mandy has these eyes too. And the deep cheek-lines. Sometimes she powders them with her mother's rouge to make them look like a movie star's.

"It's gonna be a corker," says Clarence, and folds up the plans. Granny goes over to the sink and leans against it and stares at Rita. Rita has fat arms and a big belly. She's pregnant right now, but she always has a big belly. And her legs are thick and round. Mandy has looked at her parent's wedding picture a long time. Rita's face still looks a little like the picture, but she's tiny and feminine in her wedding dress.

"I've got two perfectly good hands," Granny offers meekly to Rita.

"Thanks, Mrs. Burke," says Rita, snappily. "But I can manage just fine."

Granny hates it when Rita calls her *Mrs. Burke,* but Rita has never called her by anything else. Granny is distraught. Now she fidgets at the sink with her apron strings.

"You know I'd be perfectly happy to mash the potatoes. Clare loves my mashed potatoes, what with the extra margarine I put in."

"Mrs. Burke," Rita says. "You almost burned my kitchen down last week." She pushes past Granny and goes to the refrigerator. Granny looks helplessly at Clarence to see if he's listening. She wants desperately to prove, once and for all, to her son, that Rita is out to get her. To frame her. To set her up in front of everyone as old and incompetent. But he's studying the back yard, his eye tracing the layout of land beneath the snow near the old birch, where he plans to build his bomb shelter.

"A dish towel, that's all," says Granny, poo-pooing the incident. "Just the tip of a dish towel that got too close to the burner. I had it out in no time."

"Yes, you sure did," says Rita, mashing the potatoes herself and using less margarine than she ever has. "But while you were beating on the dish towel to put it out, you ignored the burning curtains behind you. *And* the frying pan which is a part of my good set and now has a hole burned completely through it."

"You can have my skillet I got packed away," says Granny. "I already told you that."

"It's heavy and old-fashioned and everything sticks to it," Rita snaps.

"Heavens, just grease it up real good and bake it a few times in the oven. That'll make it a no-stick," says Granny. She's worried that Clarence has heard this damaging evidence. She goes quickly to the back door and looks out into the yard.

"Where you gonna put it, Clare?" Granny asks. "Beneath the birch?" Clarence nods *yes* and goes back to his papers.

The arguments between the two women are not new to him. But lately they've come more often and with more intensity. There is rarely any peace in the house anymore. Rita is tense with the baby on its way. And Granny's mind isn't what it used to be. The truth is that she *isn't* capable of living alone. And there doesn't seem to be any way for her to coexist with Rita. But this house that is now in Clarence's name is the old homestead. Granny's father built it himself as an inn for tourists coming down the Mattagash River. Fishermen, and hunters, and sightseers from out of state were all greeted by the welcome sign. Mandy has read that Henry David Thoreau floated down the Mattagash in a canoe, right behind their very door!

Clarence is Granny's baby, born to her in her late years. She was forty-two and almost died. Clarence cannot forget this fact. "Granny won't let him forget it," Rita has told her friends, dozens of times. When Rita speaks to her friends, she never calls Granny *Mrs. Burke*. Rita is tired of hearing how Clare's father ran to get the midwife, leaving Granny alone, and how the cord was twisted around the baby's neck so that he couldn't breathe. But Granny kept her consciousness long enough to unwind that cord and slap Clarence's bottom. Then she passed out, but only *after* the midwife arrived to take over. "Granny was just afraid she'd miss something," Rita has said, of this feat.

"I remember when your father planted that old birch," Granny is saying now, and pointing. "Good Lord, that's almost sixty years now. We were still newlyweds then. That's the same year Grandpa give me the house and we took good care of him until he died. That was way back in 1902."

Rita bangs dishes onto the table. She knows why Granny is talking to Clarence about the old birch, and the house, and Clare's Grandpa giving it to her. She's saying, "This is really *my* house, not hers." But Rita knows that she and Clarence have put so many repairs into fixing the old house up that it's almost like a new house now. "Look at a picture of it way back then, and look at it now," she has told her friends, many times. "You'd swear it wasn't the same house."

They sit down to eat. Rita situates her bulges as best she can on her chair. Everyone is very happy that there will be another baby. Rita had to have a cesarean section to deliver Mandy. The doctor didn't think she could even *have* another baby. And she never lost all the weight she gained from carrying Mandy. Mandy knows this when she looks at the wedding picture. Now Rita *will* have another baby in two months. The only one who cares what it will be is Mandy's father. "I sure could use a boy around here," Mandy has heard him say. A lot of times. Rita tells her friends on the phone that as long as it's healthy, she'll be happy.

Granny has mostly forgotten the little details of her own babies. She remembers *some* things about them, but mostly now she talks about the days *before* her babies.

"When it goes all the way back," Granny says, "my memory is sharp as a tack." She tells Mandy about the old inn when it was *new*, when the road was called just Inn Road, instead of *Old* Inn Road, and how the colored canoes from exotic, far-away states scraped up onto the shore where the birch now stands.

As they eat, Mandy passes Granny what she needs. Granny takes the can of Carnation milk and pours it heavily into her cup of tea. She likes to say, "I put a little tea into my milk," when she does this.

"I like to put a little *tea* into my *milk*," Granny says again, with good humor. Rita frowns heavily. Mandy passes the salt and pepper. She butters a slice of Sunbeam bread for Granny and gives it to her. Rita is annoyed by this. She knows what Mandy is up to. Mandy stares at the little girl on the Sunbeam wrapper with the gold curls.

"Amanda, eat your *own* supper," Rita says sternly. Now Granny is on her own. Mandy hopes Granny will eat just one slice of bread. But she knows Granny always eats *two* slices with her supper. Granny is ready for her second slice now, and she drags it off the plate with her fork. Mandy is uncomfortable. Rita kicks Clarence under the table so that he'll watch. Granny takes her knife and licks the margarine off it, licks it good and clean. Then she sticks it into the margarine dish, fishes all around with it, and comes out with a big, yellow chunk. Mandy winces. Rita is glaring at Clarence with a look that asks *are you satisfied?* Just this morning Mandy heard her mother telling him again about Granny's eating habits.

"I've seen her *lick* the can of milk," Rita told him. "And the bathroom smells of pee. I don't know how she does it, but she gets pee all around the flush." Mandy knows this is true. She has smelled the pee too. Sometimes, when she's the first one in the bathroom on school mornings, she mops around the flush with toilet tissue and sprinkles some talcum powder.

Now Granny sticks her fork into a doughnut from the box Rita has put on the table. But the doughnut falls off the fork and back into the box. Granny spears a different one, then another, until one stays on her fork. What she can't finish of the doughnut, she puts back into the box. Granny believes in *Waste Not Want Not*.

"There's fork holes in everything," Rita has told Clarence. "And I find half-eaten food all through the cupboards and refrigerator. Last week, when I used paper plates for supper because I was too tired to do any dishes, she dug them out of the garbage and washed them. She said they were good enough to use again. They were all wrinkled up, Clare. You should have seen the mess."

Granny doesn't know she is being watched as she eats. She sucks down the last of her tea with the swilling sound she likes to make. Clarence has told Mandy's mother that the old-timers cooled their tea that way before they drank it. Clare even thinks it's supposed to be good manners to do that. "It sounds like *swilling*," Rita has told him.

Granny peers over her cup at Rita and Clarence. Clarence continues to eat. He says nothing. Rita has barely touched her food. She wants her husband to know that *it has come to this*. She twitches her big body around in her chair and grabs the teapot off the stove. She pours Clarence more tea. Granny holds out her cup and Rita pours it three-fourths full. She says nothing when Granny says, "Thank you, Rita." If Granny has a full cup, she will spill it on herself.

"Amanda, don't take that piece of doughnut. Take a fresh one." This is what Rita says instead of *you're welcome* to Granny. Granny only says *thank you* to Rita if Clarence is there, and Rita knows it. Mandy puts Granny's half-eaten doughnut back into the box and takes one with prong marks on it.

"No!" Rita says angrily, and Mandy takes a doughnut that Granny hasn't forked.

"I'm throwing away food all day long," Rita has told Clarence, just before they sat down to eat. Granny doesn't seem to notice all the fuss about the doughnuts. She has turned her empty cup of tea toward the kitchen window to catch the light. She stares into it for the longest time.

"A surprise visit, it looks like," Granny says, very scientifically, reading the tea leaves. She has stopped saying, "looks like I'm going on a little trip," ever since the trouble started about the old people's home. It used to be her favorite fortune, a hint to Clarence that he should drive her down to Bangor one day to visit her sister.

"She's in a nursing home there, poor dear," Granny has told Mandy. "And she doesn't recognize anyone, anymore." But Granny rewrites the tea leaves now. Reshapes the patterns. Now the tea leaves are very important.

"Looks like someone's coming for a long visit," Granny says, and plops her cup down on the table. It makes a big thud as if to say, *It's a fact. It's in the tea leaves. There's nothing we can do about it now.*

Rita takes the cup and looks at it.

"I thought a long line means you're going on a trip," she says. Mandy wishes her mother wouldn't do this to Granny.

"What long line?" Granny asks frantically. She grabs the cup. Rita has kicked Clarence again, and is smiling. Mandy's father is smiling behind his newspaper, and Mandy laughs too, then feels guilty.

"What line? Where?" Granny spurts, as she rearranges tea leaves with her fork.

There are banks of snow piled up to the eaves of the house, all white and cold and sparkly. Mandy has come home from skating on the swamp pond. The yellow lights of the house shoot out at her in the darkness. The sharp air pinches her nose as she breathes. Her hands are cold, her feet wet. She has stepped through the thin ice at the edge of the pond and now her boots are soaked. The walk home is a shivering one. But she knows that inside the house will be warm cocoa, and toast to dunk before bedtime. She stands outside the house, her skates tied together by the laces and slung over her shoulder. She looks up at the blanched sky and finds Orion overhead. And the Big Dipper. And the North Star. Her science class has been studying constellations, and all the myths that lie behind them. Mandy has the highest grades of all. Her teacher has told her that she is *insightful,* and she has looked this word up and written it down carefully in her notebook. Her teacher has also told her that the stars have moved only a foot in the sky since Jesus walked on the earth. Mandy looks up at the stars, shivering, and wonders what Jesus must have been thinking when *he* looked up at them. The weatherman in Bangor says it will snow before morning. Mandy loves the chunky flakes of snow. She loves to catch them on her tongue. No two are alike, her teacher has said.

In the kitchen, Mandy tells Granny about Jesus, and the mythical stars. Granny finds an empty coffee can, a hammer, and a nail. As Mandy watches, she pounds holes into the bottom of the can. She punches out the shape of Orion in the can. Rita is watching *The Beverly Hillbillies* in the living room, but she glances out now and then at Granny to keep an eye on her.

"Now you run get a flashlight and let's go down to the basement where it's dark," Granny says, and gives the can to Mandy.

"Mind she doesn't fall on them rickety steps," Rita whispers. "All I need now is for her to break them old bones."

Down in the basement Granny turns out the light. Mandy can see only her grandmother's silhouette, rounded like an old tree.

"Now put the flashlight in the can and flick it on," Granny says excitedly. "Point it at the wall."

As Mandy does this, Orion appears before her eyes, so close she can touch the belt if she wants to. Her mouth drops open.

"Oh, Granny!" she whispers.

Granny finds Mandy's shoulder in the dark, slides her rough hand down Mandy's arm in search of the warm, tiny fingers. She squeezes the hand.

"That's a trick my Daddy taught me," Granny says. Her words are shaky. Mandy feels a tremble rush down Granny's arm and into hers. It feels like electricity. "Granny can show you all kinds of tricks," she whispers. "Your old Granny'd be lots of fun to keep around."

Mandy looks up at the fake stars on the basement wall, imagines Orion's sword and belt. Orion, who was there for even *Jesus* to look up at.

"He was killed accidentally," Mandy tells Granny, "by someone who loved him."

"Your old Granny'd be loads of fun," Granny says again.

Mandy is at the breakfast table. The sky is swirling with snow, and the dooryard is fluffy white. The roads are filling up quickly. Heavy trucks inch by, loaded with snowy sticks of pulp. Only one or two cars are out and about.

"The snowplow just went by," Rita says, looking out her window. "I wish the town hadn't hired Edwin. He's so old, it takes him forever."

Mandy is happy that school has been canceled. It has to snow hard in northern Maine before that happens. And it is. It's snowing *very* hard. And drifting. The wind is picking up flakes and spraying them about the roads. That's the worst part of a bad snowstorm, the wind getting involved. Later, when Edwin makes his return trip, Mandy will go out in her snowsuit and let the plow spray her as it passes. She'll let the snow cover her, as if it's a big white wave from the ocean.

Mandy's father comes in and stomps his boots onto the rug by the front door.

"I need some new thermal underwear," he says. "These are worn too thin."

"That birthday set is *already* worn?" Rita asks.

"We used to *knit* full suits of long johns in my day," says Granny. "And they worked miracles keeping our men warm."

"I don't have time to sit around and knit all day," Rita says sharply, and narrows her eyes at Granny.

"Nowadays, young women can barely knit a mitten," Granny continues. She pretends not to notice Rita as she takes up her skeins of gray yarn. Mandy holds her arms out straight so Granny can loop the skeins around them. Now Granny takes an end of the yarn and rolls it until she has a small ball. She keeps rolling as Mandy moves her arms to help ease the yarn off. Mandy likes to help Granny ball her yarn. It comes from Canada, and is what Granny calls *real* yarn.

"My daddy used to wear his woolen underwear all through the

heat of summer," says Granny, and Mandy laughs at this. Rita holds up her right hand and makes it talk like it's a mouth.

"All day long," she says softly to Clarence.

But Mandy loves Granny's old stories of lumberjacks who've accidentally chopped off all their fingers. Granny has told her a million times about the old log drives, and lumber camps full to the rafters with hard-working men. The lumberjacks went off to those camps in the autumn to cut the huge pines which would go all the way to England. They didn't come home until they brought those logs out in the spring, when the river was high and running. Granny's own father came home one April to find that his bride had died in childbirth. She and her baby had been in the cold ground for two months, and he didn't even know it! But he'd married again.

"His next wife was a rugged woman," Granny says to Mandy, telling her the story one more time. Mandy can almost *feel* the weight of snow pressing down on the roof, blanketing the words to the old stories. "She weren't *fat,* or anything like that," Granny says, and looks quickly at Rita. "Just strong enough to handle things."

"And then he had *you,* Granny?" Mandy asks, and Granny nods happily.

"Me and a whole wagonload of brothers and sisters," she says.

Mandy's father hauls pulp for a living with his big green Mack. But the engine won't turn over. It's twenty-five below zero. With the wind chill factor, it's sixty-five below. Clarence *had* covered the hood of the truck with an old quilt, but this morning it still won't start. A garage would help to keep it warm. But few people in Mattagash have a garage.

"I'm just standing here watching money go down the drain," Clarence says hopelessly. His cold is worse and he coughs loudly. "When Bobby goes by with a load, I'll stop him for a boost," he says. He takes off the hand-knit mittens Granny has made for him and blows on the ends of his fingers.

"Let the dog in," Rita says. "He's about to freeze to death on the porch."

Clarence opens the door and Smokey lopes into the kitchen, ice matted to the fur on his stomach.

"Don't let him near *me,*" Granny says. The skein of yarn is now a big gray ball. "I won't be cruel to an animal, but I don't like them near me."

Smokey hears Granny and drops his ears. He runs up to Mandy's bedroom and crawls under her bed. Even Rita laughs. Smokey is afraid of Granny. She says dogs and cats *draw* lightning. Bring it right into the house. During a lightning storm Granny covers the telephone with a towel so lightning can't come out. And she grabs Smokey by the scruff of his neck and scoots him out into the storm, when she can catch him. Now Smokey runs and hides the minute he hears the first thunder, or Granny raise her voice.

The snow keeps falling all day. Mandy's father has finally gone to work. Rita is making whoopie pies in the kitchen. Granny is telling Mandy about the days when the inn was brand new. People came from everywhere, and everyone was welcome there. It cost a quarter to spend the night when Granny was a little girl. And that included a breakfast of moose meat and biscuits and hot tea. And mincemeat pies. Once, a lawyer from Boston named Lucius L. Hubbard spent the night. He wrote a book called *The Woods and Lakes of Maine*. He even mentions the inn in that book, and how Granny's mother tended the fire with *baby in arms, pipe in mouth*.

"That baby in arms was me," Granny says proudly. Sometimes she shows Mandy the book, and the worn page which is no longer stuck to its binding.

"My Daddy could stop blood," Granny says now.

"That's nonsense," Rita says.

"I've seen an injured workhorse drop to its knees, that's how fast that blood would stop. You ask people who's seen it. Clarence has seen it." But Rita goes on making whoopie pies.

Mandy watches *Bozo the Clown* on TV. She has sent her name and her birth date to Bozo. On January 27th, Bozo is going to read her name out of his big birthday book.

"Ain't that something," Granny says, when Mandy tells her for the millionth time. "I remember when I never would've believed there'd *be* such a thing as a television set. Now one of mine is gonna be mentioned on it. Imagine that!" And Mandy blushes with pride. She can hardly wait for January 27th, when she'll be ten, and hear Bozo read her name on TV.

After supper Clarence tells Rita that they'll have to wait until the snow stops. Mandy knows she shouldn't be eavesdropping, but she does so, quietly, at the kitchen door.

"You said to wait until Christmas come and went, for Mandy's sake, and I done that," Rita is saying. "It's in your hands now. They ain't gonna hold that space open for her forever." Mandy's father sounds very tired and unhappy.

"At least wait until the snow stops," he says again, and washes the grease from his hands into the sink. His truck has broken again and he's been working on it himself. He can't afford a mechanic. Or a new truck. And his cold never seems to leave him. He hacks loudly and his eyes water.

Granny is sleeping in the recliner in front of the TV. She has dozed off while watching *The Donna Reed Show,* unaware that the weather determines how many more nights she will sleep in her own bed. Her hair is packed nicely inside a hairnet, and in the glow of the television screen it looks bluer than ever. Like a chunk of sky in the middle of cold January. When she hears Clarence cough, it wakes her. She worries, still, about her children like that. Intuitively. When Clarence coughs again Granny sits up in the blue light, with her head of blue hair, and for a minute she doesn't know where she is. As if Rita might have moved her into an old folks home while she was sleeping. While *The Donna Reed Show* was happily going on.

"Clare, you still got that cough?" Granny wonders, vaguely, as if asking no one in particular. As if it's an old, motherly instinct that's asking.

"I can't seem to shake it, Mum," says Clarence, and comes into the living room. "It's turned into a kind of croup." Granny wrestles to get out of her chair, pulling on the arms of it and waving her legs like she's a spider.

"A good mustard poultice," Granny is saying. "I need to make you a nice hot poultice. That's the best thing in the world to break up the croup." And Granny strains again to get up.

"No, Mama, you stay in your chair and watch your show. I'll be okay," Clarence says. He pats Granny's hand sadly. "You just sit still, Mum," he says.

"Are you sure?" Granny asks. She puts her glasses back on and squints at the TV.

"If she made a mustard poultice every time she threatens to, we'd be up to our necks in mustard," Rita says, when Clarence comes back into the kitchen. Mandy sits at the table, waiting for her cocoa and toast before bed.

"For Chrissakes, Rita." Clarence sounds so tired that Mandy is afraid he will fall asleep on his feet. But he slumps into a chair and rubs his eyes. "Will you get off that old woman's back?" he asks Rita. "She's almost eighty-three. What do you want from her?"

Now Rita is angry. She jumps up from the table so fast her big belly seems to stay in the chair at first. Then it follows her. She's banging dishes in the sink as she washes them.

"You always side up with *her*," Rita says. "She does no wrong in your eyes. Well, *you* stay cooped up in the house with her all day long and see how long you can stand it!"

Mandy tries to swallow her toast, but it scratches her throat and stays there. *The Donna Reed Show* is over and Granny has come into the kitchen.

"That's one happy family, that Reed family," says Granny, and takes off her apron. Rita hates Granny's apron. She has no reason to wear it, Rita has said, because she does no work.

"She *parades* it in front of visitors," Rita has told her friends, "to make it look like I work her to death."

Granny takes off her apron and folds it. She holds it tightly in her hands, kneads it like it's bread. If she puts it down, Rita will hide it from her.

"You sure you don't want me to make you a poultice, Clare, for that croup?" Rita throws the dish towel into the sink and goes on up to her bedroom. Granny pretends not to notice, but she lays her apron on the counter. Clarence has taken out his designs for the bomb shelter and spread them on the table. He isn't really looking at them. He just wants something to stare at. Granny leans over his shoulder and stares too. She has heard about his civil defense class, two nights a month at the Watertown high school.

"I don't like the look of things," he's been saying, each night after Walter Cronkite. "Kennedy can keep a lid on things just so long, but when it blows, well, it's really gonna blow." Mandy wonders if Ponce de Leon looked in Cuba, too, when he searched for his wonderful fountain. At school, Lois has said she doesn't care if Mandy lets her into the bomb shelter. Lois's father has told her *Better Red Than Dead.*

"He'll never get up the money for that *thing,*" Rita is always laughing to her friend Lorette on the phone. "He just needs something to keep his mind off his *big* problems. He gets cabin fever every winter."

Granny is tired of looking at the plans for the bomb shelter. She takes her apron and goes to bed. Clarence rolls up his charts and puts them back on the top shelf of the cupboard.

"Come to bed, honey," he says to Mandy. He holds her hand tightly as they climb the black stairs.

Before Mandy falls asleep, she hears Granny saying her beads in the bedroom across the hall. She can't make out the words, but she likes the soft litany that floats across the hall to her. And she imagines the ancient rosary in Granny's old hands as she handles it slowly, bead by bead, like it's a necklace. Like it's a fine piece of jewelry that Granny strung years ago, back when she was a little girl herself and the old inn was new. Mandy looks out her window at the mythical sky. She can't find her blessed stars because it's still snowing. But Mandy doesn't mind that the stars are gone. When she says her own prayers, she prays it will never stop snowing.

Mandy opens her eyes and is alarmed at how bright it is outside. It's Saturday. Her mother didn't wake her because there is no school. She hadn't intended to sleep late, but it's eleven o'clock. She sees the fat yellow sun, on its way to *noon* in the sky, and knows that the storm is over. Because she has overslept, she has a funny feeling of being *left out.* She pulls jeans on quickly. With each step of the stairs, she buttons a button on her blouse.

In the kitchen, Granny is knitting by the radio, listening to country music from Watertown. Mandy feels a tremendous relief to see her there, in her chair by the stove. Granny's needles are clicking softly, like her rosary beads, and Rita is making a salmon loaf for lunch. Her big belly rubs along the counter as she works.

"Hi, Sleepyhead," she says, and kisses Mandy. Mandy's father comes in for lunch. He's still coughing and has dark circles under his eyes, as if he hasn't slept. Rita pushes her body against him and gives him a big kiss. She takes his hand and puts it on her swollen stomach.

"Tell Clarence Burke Junior *good morning,*" she says. Clarence smiles faintly and pats the belly before him. Mandy knows by all this that they have made up, and that her mother has won. Rita buzzes about the kitchen like a huge hornet, setting the table, stirring the peas, arranging things on plates. Granny puts down her knitting.

"Can I lend you a hand?" she asks Rita. "I've got two perfectly good ones."

"Thanks," says Rita. "But no." She's very polite to Granny. Mandy looks out at the yard full of bright sunshine.

"What's the temperature?" Rita asks Clarence, who is washing up.

"Twenty-five above," he says. "The cold spell is breaking up."

"I remember one winter," Granny says, sitting in her chair at the table. "It was way back before you was born, Clare. I got snowed in all alone with four little children. And I had one on the way, about as far along as Rita is. Your daddy had gone to Watertown for supplies. There was only horses and sleighs then. That snow come down on us like it was a mountain waiting to fall on something."

"What year was that?" Clarence asks, and gives Mandy a peck on the cheek before he takes his place at the head of the table. Rita puts the salmon loaf down and sits in her chair.

"Oh Lordy me," says Granny, rolling her eyes up at the ceiling. "Now let's see. Wallace was the baby, so that would've been 1912. And I was stuck here for four days. Couldn't even get my front door open. So I fanned out the food, I tell you. We ate potato soup more than we wanted to. And melted down pans of snow to drink. I was lucky we had the cellar full of plenty of hardwood to burn. Your daddy saw to that. You had to think ahead in them days."

Everyone is having a nice lunch. But Mandy is wondering why. And even Granny is starting to get suspicious. She's eyeing Rita with little, round eyes. Rita doesn't seem to mind that Granny has licked her knife and thrust it into the margarine.

"Here, Granny," says Rita. "Have some more salmon loaf."

Granny is *very* cautious now. Rita has called her *Granny*. Mandy twiddles her fork and kicks a foot against her chair. Granny has continued her story in a tiny whisper. She glances over her shoulder as though she expects someone to reach out and grab her.

"Just me and my babies," she's saying. "Alone here in this house. And there were wolves, you know. And black bears." Granny is beside herself now. "And I sat up all night long, every night, with a shotgun leaning against my chair, and the moon so bright the whole house was like daylight. Protecting my babies."

"Have another slice of bread," Rita says. Granny is crying now. She pushes her chair back and takes off her apron.

"In this very house!" Granny cries, as she flings her apron at Rita.

Aunt Maggie has come, and Aunt Rachel, and Rachel's daughter Millie, who's divorced and living at home again. They sit around the table like undertakers, holding their black woolen gloves in their hands, squeezing them as if they're wringing them out. Their purses are fat and bulging on the table before them. They keep their coats on. They're always in a hurry.

Rita is wearing a dress, and has pinned up her thick hair. She had made a stack of bologna and cheese sandwiches. All the aunts are having one, except Millie, who prefers the whoopie pies.

"It's like I was telling Lorette this morning," Rita says sadly. Her hair has come loose, and she dabs at the wispy strands about her face. "The baby will be here soon and I'll have my hands full with him." Mandy wonders why everyone is so *sure* it'll be a boy. And so what if it isn't? She remembers her teacher telling the class that baby girls were once drowned in China. A chill runs through her, cold as January, when she thinks of it. She's sitting on a chair by the kitchen window, as she waits for her father to come back from the store. He's taken the day off because his truck is broken. But Mandy suspects some other reason. And she has something to ask him.

Rita pours each of the relatives a cup of tea as she rattles on. Her tone is confidential.

"To tell you the truth," she says, "me and Clarence is on pretty rough ground right now. The money problems alone are about to drive us up the wall. I think that's the reason we've been arguing so much. And Granny just makes it worse." The aunts nod in agreement, their mouths too full to speak.

Mandy is still waiting for her father to get back from the store. He's gone to gas up the car, but he's wearing his good suit. Mandy kicks her feet together and waits.

"I come upon her teeth in the strangest places," Rita is saying. "She takes them out wherever she naps and just leaves them." Both Aunt Rachel and Aunt Maggie nod knowingly. Millie sucks on her cigarette and is disgusted at the notion of stumbling upon fake teeth.

"Well, look at *me*." Aunt Rachel is done eating now, and ready to talk. "The only spare room I got is jammed full of junk," she informs them. "Even if it wasn't, it's too small, really, for a bed."

They sit around the table in their heavy black coats. They are stiff and somber as judges. Mandy plays with the curtains behind her and watches down the road for her father.

"God knows I'm lucky to get my new Singer stuffed into the sewing room," says Aunt Maggie. "I can't imagine turning *that* into a bedroom."

"She's afraid of the washer-dryer," says Rita. "She thinks it's gonna blow up. And I'll have it running all the time after the baby gets here."

Mandy remembers Granny's fear of things electrical.

"It makes such a big noise," Granny has said of the dryer, once, when it woke her from a nap. "Like a big old bear pawing to get in. If it was up to me," Granny has said, "I'd vote for the sound of a sheet flapping in the wind."

Mandy gives up on her father and goes up to Granny's room. Granny is packing only a few of her things. Rita and Aunt Maggie will pack the big stuff later. They want to make it as easy on Granny as possible. Granny is crying now.

"Oh," she says to Mandy, and pulls at her worn wedding band. "Oh, what I'd give for a little house somewhere. Where I could go and fend for myself." Granny packs her big scrapbook, the one with the wedding pictures, snapshots of babies, line drawings of ancestors long gone back to their maker. Mandy has started to cry

now, too. Aunt Rachel and Aunt Maggie come into the room. Rita
is with them. They stand stiffly and stare at Granny. Mandy won-
ders if this is how the Commies will stand.

"I *can* fend for myself," Granny is telling Rita. "And I'd be two
extra hands for when the baby comes." She holds up her purply
hands so that everyone with eyes can see that she does, indeed,
have *two*.

"Oh Granny, sweetheart," says Rita. "I couldn't leave you with
a little newborn baby."

"Don't you sweetheart me!" shouts Granny. "What do you
think: I'm gonna jump on it like a cat and suck up all its breath?
I've had more babies than you can count! And I had all of them
here in this very house! Not in one of your shiny, fancy hospitals!"
Granny is crying so hard that she has to sit down on the bed.
"These are two of them babies," she's saying, and pointing at
Maggie and Rachel. Her teeth seem to drop in her mouth. She
sucks in both sides of her face to pull them back in place. Rita tries
to lift Mandy up off the floor, but Mandy hits out at her mother's
fat arms. Rita leaves her there to cry it out.

"Janice just placed *her* mother there," Aunt Maggie says calmly.
"And she dearly loves it. There's always something to do. There's
folks *paid* just to think up things for you to do. Mrs. Finley just
loves it."

"Grace Finley should've been in a home when she was *young!*"
Granny is screaming. "She was *always* off her rocker! I got plenty
to do right here!"

"I wash my hands of it," Aunt Maggie whispers to the others,
and stands up.

Clarence is back from gassing up the car and announces that
it's all warmed up. It's cold out, but the roads are clear. He'll drive
slowly. Granny has stopped crying, and is wearing her coat and
boots and scarf and gloves. Granny has stopped crying so as not
to give them any further satisfaction. Her face is puffy and pink,
like it's made of taffy. She has taken off her glasses. She no longer
cares to see the faces around her, she tells Clarence, whose own
face is red and swollen. Granny has told Mandy not to worry. She'll
be ok. And Mandy has promised that when she grows up, and
has a house of her own, she'll come to the home and get Granny

out, and they'll poke holes in cans to see the stars, and fend for themselves.

Now Mandy pulls her father down and puts her mouth to his ear. Her father just smiles a little when she asks him, and squeezes her. She wants to know if it's possible, if there's any way, in case he really *does* build it, can Granny live in the bomb shelter? And be no bother to anyone? But her father laughs all he can and pats her head.

Now Granny is holding her chin up high, and pulling her coat about her like it's new.

"If your father was still alive, he'd take the whole bunch of you across his knee," says Granny, and her voice trembles. She looks down at Mandy.

"Granny's ok," she says softly.

Rita is at the door, with her belly full of a baby everyone is sure will be a boy. A boy coming to save a marriage. To be company for Mandy. To take up a spare room.

"This'll happen to you, too," Granny hisses at Rita as she passes. She refuses to let Clarence hold her arm, and goes down the icy steps alone. Mandy has stopped crying to watch the car drive away. Granny's little frame is in the back seat between Millie, who is still smoking, and Aunt Rachel. Aunt Maggie is in the front with Mandy's father. If Mandy didn't know better, they could be going to the drive-in. Just five people in a car, on a cold sunny day, with nothing but clear roads ahead of them.

Mandy writes two letters to Granny that very night. One is to assure her of the promise of a little house to live in when Mandy is older. The second is to remind her to watch *Bozo the Clown,* three days away, on January 27th, when she can tell everyone at the home that it's one of *her own* whose name is being mentioned. But the letters will collect dust with the days that pass so slowly to the young. Yet Mandy is *insightful.* She knows some things. She knows Granny will forget her. Will forget *everyone,* like Granny's own sister has. Granny will move inside her body like it's a bomb shelter and never come back out. Mandy knows the house will never be the same with Granny gone because she cannot remember Granny not being there. When she came into the world, Granny was in the house. As if Granny *was* the house. And Mandy knows that when January 27th comes, she will not go downstairs and sit in front of the television to listen as Bozo reads her name from his big birthday book. And for weeks she will dream of Commies, and baby brothers, and bombs, and large, fake stars spread across an artificial sky. She will dream of those glorious fountains of water that can make you young again.

A. POULIN, JR.

The Front Parlor

Whenever someone in our family
died, the wake was in our house,
downstairs, in the front parlor.

It was a spare room, really, and,
except for a few extra folding chairs,
empty and unheated. The shades were

always drawn, the best lace curtains
hung. And in that constant cool
twilight, the wallpaper damp

as banks of carnations, when we
dared to go in, forbidden to,
we played like shadows under

the great cross, the enormous
suffering, dying or dead Christ,
the room's only constant ornament.

It never was a living room.

*

I've slept above the dead before,
my bed in the same far corner
as their caskets. Assured their lips

were sewn, their arms clamped,
I've fallen asleep to the rhythm
of hummed rosaries. My grandfather,

choosing to die on New Year's day.
His wife, big-boned and stubborn,
paralyzed for fifteen years,

bedridden five, decaying three,
gangrene growing on her back
like some warm carnivorous herb.

An uncle who never spoke a word
until the week he died, insane,
babbling the poison of his liver.

I've slept above the dead enough.
Whole generations of a tribe. Still,
in the middle of the night, I hear

the prayers of the living and the dead,
a crescendo through the floorboards,
filling my room like an ancestral chorus:

Que les âmes des défunts reposent
en paix par la miséricorde
de Dieu. They have burned

the seams of their eyes, chewed
the nylon cord threaded through
their lips. They have cast off

their clamps. They stand at my
bedside every night moaning my name
off endless strings of beads, burning.

A. Poulin, Jr.

She plants a growing kiss on my forehead.
With her green hand, moist as moss,
wide as my skull and, forever free,

she strokes my back and thigh.

from "The Saltwater Farm and the Spleeny Yowun"

I don't remember ever using the actual front door to enter my grandparents' farmhouse. The door must have been open sometimes in the summers, as the enclosed porch door was; but year-round, everyone used the back sidedoor in the ell of the house. The main structure was a classic Cape Cod farmhouse, which downstairs featured the living room, master bedroom, a smaller bedroom, and part of the kitchen. The rest of the kitchen was in the ell along with the main shed, the wood shed, and the two-holer. Up over the sheds was an attic area used for storage and which also featured a playroom where my mother and her eleven brothers and sisters once played; and in my generation where my cousins and I also played.

The cow barn was not connected to the house. It stood a few yards from the back of the ell, and beside the barn were two more outbuildings, one in which Papa made barrels and one which served as a combination livery stable and horse barn. Nearer the house was the ice house and the milk room in which my grandfather and uncles stored the milk and eggs from their dairy and chicken operations. There were pig pens, hen houses, the smokehouse; and the largest building, which was a multi-door long garage where the tractor, truck, hay wagons, and other farm equipment were stored. Halfway down the backfield was the saw mill and way down the field was the ice pond where we used to go skating in the winters. Part of the back field was fenced in for the cows and bull. There were vegetable and strawberry gardens; and across from the enclosed porch, or southern side of the house, one could see the tops of the Mount Desert Island hills. Across

the road from the farm proper was an old road that led down to
the family property on the shore where we had our picnics and
clambakes.

I was a little five-year-old towhead staying with my grandpar-
ents one winter day when Grammie chopped the head off a chicken
right in front of me, and because of my horror at this incident, she
started calling me spleeny.

I used to love to curl up on the old couch in the kitchen by the
stove and be looking at the *Saturday Evening Post, Life,* or assorted
farm journals while Grammie was washing dishes, rinsing out
milk bottles, or cooking. On that particular winter day, she told
me, "We've got to go out to the hen house and get a chicken for
dinner." I followed along behind her over the snow. She was
carrying a pail of boiling water and a hatchet. I didn't know what
was going to happen, but she made it seem, as usual, like fun.

Until the killing. She was struggling to hold the hen down on
the chopping block with one hand while raising the hatchet high
with the other. Being an expert, Grammie took off the head with
one quick blow. And the headless chicken ran right at me, blood
spewing all over the snow. I must have either cried out or just stood
there looking shocked, for Grammie laughed at me.

"Don't be so spleeny, An-day!"

Finally, the chicken flopped down in the snow, Grammie re-
trieved the body and dumped it in the pail of boiling water. I'll
never forget that sharp smell, or the sight of the bloody chicken's
head lying in the snow.

To me, the farm was full of such scenes: sudden, violent, bloody
death; the messy but beautiful birth of a calf; casual but also vio-
lent sex among the animals; manure and chicken shit underlying
all. It was lively, earthy, and real. As a child growing up in such
surroundings, I was alternately frightened and fascinated, never
bored.

By 1950, Papa Warren was nearly eighty and Grammie was in
her late sixties; and so the farm was in the control of two of my
uncles, Oliver and Owen, then both divorced and living home.
Oliver handled the milk business and Owen was in charge of the
wood mill. The vegetable gardens were greatly reduced. Oliver
and Owen did business with Jake Kaplan, a Jewish cattle dealer

from Bangor, who seemed part of our family. Jake would drive down to the farm on Sunday afternoons in his Plymouth sedan. My uncles would sit out in the car with Jake, all of them with hats on, smoking and talking over their deals. Grammie would always bake Jake an apple pie, which he loved. There was a great deal of trust, respect, and affection between Jake and our family. We always benefited from his deals. In fact, it was Jake, years later, who tipped off Uncle Oliver about the good caretaking job the other side of Ellsworth that Oliver took, closing down the farm for good.

"Jake's smart, and a good man," Uncle Oliver told me.

One time Jake was carting away Buddy, an old sway-backed horse that I loved. I ran screaming down the driveway after Jake's old green Chevy truck that day until Jake stopped, rolled down the window, and looked down at me. He seemed miles up.

"Jake! Where are ya taking Bud-day?" I asked, tears welling in my eyes.

"To the glue factory, kid!" he said and drove off.

As a youngster I remember gathering eggs, picking berries, picking string beans, picking and shelling peas, digging up dandelion greens, plucking feathers off the just-boiled chickens while squatting on the saw dust piles in the ice house, gathering lady slippers from the woods and violets and forget-me-nots from the fields, and generally helping out my elders. "You be available now, and don't run off," my relatives would say.

My first big adult job was cleaning out the barn. I was about eleven and it was on summer mornings before The Milk Drive got underway. That was what my relatives called the daily delivery of milk, cream, and eggs about town in the old International pickup.

I'd step into the cow barn those mornings and there'd hang that hot, heavy smell in the close and dusty air that would hit me strong in the face. Even with the windows open, with the low ceilings, the piles of hay, and the dozen or more fat bossy bodies, it was a stifling and oppressive place. Nice and warm in the winter, however.

The walls were whitewashed and there would be thousands of flies everywhere. Uncle Oliver had rigged up an old radio, as well as a couple of electric lights in the barn, and it's a wonder none of us ever got electrocuted, standing around in the wet troughs, trying to turn up the radio so we could hear Johnny Desmond or Vaughn Monroe singing while we did the chores. If we didn't have our rubber boots on, we were always getting little shocks from both the radio and the lights, and every switch snapped and popped.

Papa named the cows after fairy tale characters like Rapunzel, Snow White, and Rose Red. One of the bulls, I remember, he called Grimm. They'd be there all in their row, penned in their stalls with their huge, sad eyes looking at you, their ears and tails flapping at the flies, their bumpy heads bobbing up and down, their lower jaws and mouths chomping and chewing away at their continuous cud. And from behind, where I got to know them best, there was manure everywhere: caked on their legs and tails, on the water and milk pails, tools, floors, and walls. You couldn't even see out of the windows. All I had to do was to take a square-shaped shovel and scrape down the troughs behind the cows and pile the manure into a wheelbarrow and dump it out a back door, adding to the ever-growing pile half as high as the barn itself.

Grimm used to scare me when I was cleaning out the barn. I had to keep treading quietly by his pen to dump the manure; and it seemed as if he'd always be on the verge of escape, snorting, raging, and butting against the wooden confines of his cage. My uncles had nailed reinforcement boards around and about the locked door, but it always seemed to me that the nails were loose and getting looser. I pictured the wild, red-eyed beast breaking out and butting me headfirst into the manure pile. As a small child, I once caught the bull and one of the cows when they were out in the pasture "doing the dirt," and I ran fast to tell Uncle Owen down in the saw mill that the cows were fighting. He looked out and laughed, saying, "You look again, An-day! They ain't fightin'; they're propagatin'."

There were a number of mice and rats that used to live in the barn; but I didn't know who was scarier—the rodents or the wild cats that my uncles kept to keep down the rat population. The cats were gray and beautiful with yellow eyes and we yowuns used to try and capture them, but they were always too wild and would bite, scratch, and dig us whenever we tried to catch and pet them.

Of course, just as soon as I got done scraping the troughs, Rapunzel, Rose Red, Cinderella and Company would start plopping, drizzling, and exploding all over again. When I first started this job, I couldn't drink any milk for a week or so, for I would picture the milk all mixed together with the plop and pee and flies from the manure piles. I never did much milking of the cows either. They and their teats nauseated me.

By the time I had the barn cleaned out, it would be time to go on The Milk Drive. Uncle Oliver and Ricky Rowe, a neighborhood boy two years my senior, would have the back of the International pickup all filled with crates of milk, eggs, and cream. the "homo" milk bottles had green cellophane tops, the pasteurized red, and the raw milk, which Uncle Oliver bottled himself from our cows, had just plain caps. The milk was in bottles then, but the cream came in half-pint cardboard conical-shaped containers and the eggs were in cardboard boxes.

"Did ya scrape that shit off the eggs?" Uncle Oliver would ask Ricky, his job while I scraped the barn. "They gotta look clean, ya know, for the summer people."

Uncle Oliver would fling a heavy canvas sheet over the back of the pickup—for there was no refrigeration—and off we'd go, jouncing along with the clank and jangle of the milk bottles in their metal crates, up one side of Taunton Peninsula and down the other, stopping at almost every house; for by the time I was growing up, Papa's dairy farm had little competition. Our milk carried the Hancock County Creamery labels and every afternoon Oliver would take the milk cans of our cows' milk to the Ellsworth creamery and return with the processed, bottled milk for the next day which he'd store overnight in the "Milk Room," a small building with a few ice boxes in it connected to the ice house.

The Milk Drive was kind of fun. After a few trips I had memorized almost what everyone had or wanted each time. If they wanted more or something different, they'd usually leave a note in one of the empty bottles. Some customers would pay each time while others would run up bills. According to Uncle Oliver, some never paid, including a few of the most prominent folks in town. But still Uncle Oliver delivered to them. All he'd say in explanation was "folks gotta have milk."

Summer people's places scared me the most. They were really foreign territory, even though I had been in many of them and had helped my relatives clean and care for them; but they weren't empty houses during the summer season. People were living in them and they were people I didn't know. And there was that difference between their cedar-shingled rusticity and the natives' year-round plain frame domiciles. There was a more worldly atmosphere and a certain classiness to these coastal retreats. Down around the bay, with that beautiful, constant view of the Mount Desert Hills, they felt and smelled different. They were built rather close to one another, but inside the rooms facing the water seemed more open than our rooms at home without a view. Summer people's cars were apt to be foreign makes with foreign license plates. These people grew ferns and planted pretty gardens about their front doors and porches, and some of the more elaborate cottages sported water fountains, Japanese gardens, and statuary. There were tennis racquets, golf clubs, and sailboat equipment stacked in their sheds, garages, and entryways, items not readily found in my relatives' and neighbors' homes. These people were my betters and my parents' betters, or so I thought I understood. I wasn't to have a scene with them. They were our bread and butter, as we were their milk and eggs. I tried on every Milk Drive to catch a glimpse of some of them, and their kids, but most of them were asleep that early in the morning. If one ever did come face-to-face with them, one was to be pleasant, say little, always agree with them, act the dutiful servant. One could disagree and complain behind their backs and make fun of their strange ways and ideas, but never to their faces. This was the old established practice.

As the morning would wear on, Uncle Oliver tried to hurry Ricky and me up. "Goddamn it, boys. The milk's gonna turn sour," he'd say; or "Let's get the hell out of here before someone comes out and tries to talk to us."

All of my Warren aunts and uncles, and Sid, too, have this wild-eyed look. All twelve of them with their wounded and yet determined-looking faces with their red, horsey-faced, English-Irish features. They always seemed to be looking beyond the here and now, never completely absorbed by the present or the task at hand. Most always good-humored, resigned to their fate, busy rushing about, they competed with each other, trying to top each other with the latest joke, a new purchase, a new job, new trip, new child. It got very irritating after a while, especially to all of us cousins, my brother and me. And yet, we, too, compete. Whenever the Warrens get together, they all talk at once.

Uncle Oliver and Aunt Eller were especially wild-eyed. They looked like they were always on the verge of running away from home or looked as if some monstrous eruption was beginning to evolve just beyond the person they were facing and they could only express their fear and excitement through their eyes. But while Oliver was very shy and quiet, never wanting to be noticed in his clandestine comings and goings, Aunt Eller was much more gregarious, liked having people around to dance, laugh, and drink with. Years after I worked for Uncle Oliver on the Milk Drive, he took the job as caretaker that Jake Kaplan had told him about; and when he left the farm for that job, Aunt Eller took over the Milk Drive.

One memorable time when I was home from college during the January break between semesters, I was with my lifelong pal Russell Barclay, who was also a student at the University of Maine, and we went on The Drive with Aunt Eller. The same International pickup, ten years older, and the same canvas sheet were still in use but the atmosphere inside the cab was totally transformed thanks to Aunt Eller's ebullient spirit, especially in the company of young men. She had names for all the customers. One old lady living alone she mysteriously termed "The Prostitute," while an old couple who had been married for many years she called "The Honeymooners," and a lady who had a number of children by various men she termed "The United Nations." A couple who never bought more than one quart of milk or a half-pint of cream or a half-dozen eggs she called "The Misers."

That wintry day on The Drive, it was cold and icy, but still there were barking dogs with which to contend. At one stop Aunt Eller whipped off her slipper—she was wearing Uncle Fod's slippers—and waving it out the window on her side of the truck, yelled, "Hurry up, An-day! Run in that quart of skim to The Prostitute while I keep Rover busy!"

By noon time, Aunt Eller stopped at the store and bought a six-pack of Narragansett for lunch. "You boys, being college men, don't want any milk to drink now, do ya? This is a cold day in January, and milk won't warm ya up as good as a beer."

Near the end of the day's Drive, we were feeling no pain, jouncing along in the broken-down seat of the rusted-out truck, when we came to the steep driveway to old Ida Purdy's house. It was all icy.

As soon as we started up the incline, the back tires began to spin around. "Christ! Hold on, boys! Ya might have to get out and push! Old Ida's gotta git her cream. But I don't know . . . I'll wind 'er up and shift 'er down. Here goes nothin'!"

We jerked about, inching our way up the driveway, the back wheels spinning about eighty miles an hour, when all of a sudden, Aunt Eller really floored her. The tailgate fell open, and about three or four crates of milk cartons and bottles went flying out the back and rolled down and splattered all over the driveway. A few dozen of them smashed or were crushed. The ice was covered with milk and eggs.

"Shit! There go the profits!" Eller said.

At least we had made it to Ida's front door. She came out, a little, old, white-haired lady in a housecoat; and Eller hollered at her. "Whataya want, Ida? One-a-milk and one-a-eggs? Same as usual?"

"Nothing today," Ida said.

"How do ya like that, boys? The old bag's gone on the wagon just when we lost ours!"

It took a while for the three of us to pick up the bottles, cartons, and pieces of glass, with old Ida tsk-tsking from her front door, clucking to herself, and saying things like, "Oh, isn't that too bad; that's too bad, dear, dear."

"I'll tell ya what, Ida," Eller said, "for the rest of the winter we gotta work out a signal system. When ya see me coming, a white hanky means come on up—unless it's icy like this again—and a red bandana or something equally flashy means go on by—O.K.?"

"Well, I guess so . . ."

"*I guess probably!*" Eller said. "I can't afford too many more stops like this one!"

As it turned out, there weren't many more stops left for The Milk Drive itself; for a few months after that icy incident, the old International pickup broke down for the last time. No one in the family wanted to invest in a new truck; and the county creamery had already taken over most of the routes with its own delivery trucks. So, after driving the milk for over forty years by both horse and wagon and truck around Taunton, the Warren family was no longer in the dairy business. Aunt Eller went to work in a fish factory where she cut the heads off sardines and threw them at the tourists.

The saw mill was the only money-making operation still going down on the farm during the late '60s. I only worked there for Uncle Owen a little bit, when he needed me. The whir of that old rickety saw ripping and whining through the wood scared me even more than the summer people. It was like Robert Frost's poem, "Out, Out . . ." in which a boy working with such a saw gets his hand cut off and dies. My mother had once pointed out to me a man in Ellsworth with only one arm. She told me he was the only survivor from a grisly mill accident in which the saw blade got loose and cut through the men standing around. A couple of men were cut in two, or lost a few limbs, while the man she pointed out was lucky only to have lost the one arm. Every time that blade hit a knot in the wood, which I was helping to steady, I thought of that incident and the Frost poem. While I trusted Owen, I could see the blade flying loose and cutting my head off. I quit Uncle Owen and "The Woodbutchers," which is what my uncles had named the mill, for it just didn't seem safe.

Today, in Taunton Ferry, where there used to be a half-dozen busy farms like my grandparents', there are none. One doesn't wake up any more to the sound of wood being sawed, of roosters crowing and hens clucking, or any of the other farm noises of old. Fields have grown up, or been sold as house-lots. When it used to be unique for anyone to commute to Ellsworth or Bangor for work, now it's unique for anyone to have any kind of job in Taunton Ferry.

Many of the old-time summer people have told me how years ago how much they enjoyed driving up to my grandparents' farm. They'd make the excuse that they were going to get an extra quart of milk, more cream or eggs; but they really loved visiting my grandparents, their children, and the farm.

"A remarkable family," one lady told me. "They were always so warm and welcoming, full of fun and good stories. It was like what we imagined farm life in Maine to be, only more so." What impressed this one woman especially was the story of how my grandparents finally had water put in the house.

"The cows got sick," she said, "and it was decided to put running water in the barn for them; and only after that, did they decide to put running water in the house, too, and that was only for a pump in the kitchen sink. Your grandparents thought of their animals before they thought of themselves. That fact made a great impression on me."

By the mid-sixties, Uncle Oliver had sold off most of the dairy and chicken business; and while still living in the family farmhouse, he was commuting to work in Ellsworth. By the late 1960s, when he was promised a place to stay at his work, he decided to close up the house and move. I was home from teaching at Christmas when I went down one night to see Uncle Oliver and take him a gift. It was only about four P.M., but dark; and when I knocked on the old side door in the ell of the house, I found it locked.

"Uncle Oliver?" I called.

"Who is it?" he called back.

"Andy."

"Just a minute." I heard him coming and then opening the locks, for there wasn't just one.

Entering the shed, I was momentarily surprised by the sight of about twenty-five cats, the wild barn cats, lapping out of dishes on the floor, their tails up in the air and their yellow eyes glowing in the half-light from the kitchen door. I followed my uncle into the kitchen where he had about four cauldrons of oatmeal bubbling on the stove.

"What are you doing, Uncle Oliver?"

"Tryin' to make friends with the cats so I can kill 'em!"

"Why?"

"I can't just leave 'em around here. There's nothing for 'em to eat any more. The milk's gone and the mice and rats are gone, too. And now I'm going. They're too wild for pets."

Poem

I remember an old house in
Lille, Maine—
                unlikely place
and naming—
                  an unlikely house
Leaning like an old man
up too early after
a lifetime of work—
                possibly
not much,
          but enough
to sag and bend.
                Likely
not there now.

Cold Spring Nights in Maine, Smelts, and the Language of Love

"Gettin' any?"

"Nope."

"Checked out the other end yet?"

"Nope."

"Aren't goin' through Flying Pond are they?"

"How about Four Corners?"

"Nope. Nothin'. Might not be tonight."

"Christ Almighty, my feet are freezing already," says Hilde, our friend.

Hilde is tall for a woman but she also weighs more than she would like to. She is thinking of going on the Zen Macrobiotic rice and vegetables diet because eating Weight Watchers is too expensive, but right now she's sucking a Tootsie-Roll lollipop to which she is lately addicted. It's a night in late April. The snow is still deep in places but spring is here. We have parked on a back road, which at this point skirts a large black pond, to talk to some other fishermen; but now she and my husband and I are headed down a path into the woods alongside the pond. It's ten o'clock at night; we are carrying a Coleman lantern, a net on a long stick, and a bucket. We are following, between snow banks and down a muddy path, an invisible, rushing, splashing stream to the point where it feeds into the larger waters. We are after smelts.

We—my husband and I—have never caught or eaten a smelt and when, weeks later, we finally do, there isn't much to them. They're too small to gut or bone. Cut off the heads, dip them in egg then corn meal, fry them fast, and the little bones crunch right up like potato chips. We've been smelting every night for a week, under a full navy sky, a foam of stars, a small white hard moon, cold hard winds, and all around us every night the freeway roar of invisible, just released water. It's that invisible roar that we hunt.

We've been ice-locked since November, not a sound in our world but wind and cold birds, not a movement visible but wind and birds, bare trees, cars, and chimney smoke. But now it's spring and melting, all heaved up, and we're out in it, the nightly chase of the elusive smelts which don't swim, but "run." But when? If we're at the right place the right night, we'll get enough fish for breakfast the next day.

We have never eaten fried fish for breakfast, but are willing to go along with most anything these days, any new rules or news, because we're "from away," fresh from fifteen years lived in Midwestern faculty ghettoes where, by and large, people tended not to go fishing with buckets and nets at ten o'clock at night. Anything now seems possible. Every night all the possible places must be checked.

These smelts run through at small water mouths, where one lake feeds into another or a stream narrows into a pond. A bridge makes a good spot. The mouth funnels all the smelts together so that if you're there when they come through that spot, all of a sudden the cold water is replaced by what looks like one shivering silver animal, oily with life, thousands of smelts, each no longer than a small hand, all running through at once, headed out, no slackers.

You can't smelt in the daytime because you can't see them. Lantern, in this case, is a stronger beam than sun. Like so much other lore about living in the country, this turns out to be true. The sap won't run when the wind blows, either, and the sap stops running at night. Birch logs burn good. My first batch of maple sap turns into sludge on the stove. The second batch turns to lumps that would crush healthy molars. I want so much to be here. I bottle up jars of each, take them to town for advice. The first person I ask, Carl, looks at the jars, shakes them, holds them up to the light, shakes his head, hands them back to me, says, "well, I think you must of tapped a hog." The thing about lore is that there's so much of it, and you don't know any of it because you never needed it before, and then you hear a piece of it and it happens. Or, you do it.

As we stumble through the woods, my husband going ahead with the lantern, me in the middle, Hilde behind, the person of Bart Stone figures in the general air of spawning, breaking up. Hilde, watching in the lantern's erratic swing for deep mud, and sucking the lollipop, confesses, and cheerfully so, to "going almost all the way" with Bart Stone, "several times."

"When?" I scream back. "How? Where?"

"In a dark corner," shouts Hilde, pulling the sucker from her mouth with a pop. "At the party after Town Meeting!"

"*That's* why you didn't want to leave!"

"At your party last week, too!"

"Where?"

"By the front room door!"

"Does that unnerve you?" I yell. (Her husband Everett is out of town, taking his parents someplace. Otherwise, Everett would be with us tonight.)

"Nope!" Hilde yells. "Should it?"

Voices, clank of lantern handles and buckets, slog and suck of mud, lights ahead through the trees. Roar of wind and water, moonlight, the fish. Where are they plotting up? What rush of blood or signal do they obey, and how do they know it? One night, a week ago, all of a sudden, the frogs are back—spring peepers. It doesn't begin with one or two peeps a night, then several more the next, building to a chorus, but all at once, all peepers where there was nothing but silence, wind, snow. When we walk outside the kitchen door that night to smell the new wind, there the peeps are, coming from the swamp down the dirt road. "Listen to that," someone says, "the frogs thawed out." Is that lore? Have they? I would have thought they had just been born.

"What I'd do if I was doin' it, is, I'd glue her in the joints first. But do it in the back. If you don't she's not gonna take the stain even and wherever she's got that glue on her is gonna show up like a sore thumb when you stain 'er."

"How'm I gonna keep 'er stain from gettin' on the wall then, get somebody else to do it?"

The old gent looks around the hardware store to see if we'll all laugh at this witticism. We all do.

"Stain her first," says the hardware clerk, "stain 'er first, then nail 'er together. She goes right up. Looks real good."

I can't resist. "I wonder," I say softly, "how come men talk about boats and cars and engines and stuff, projects, I guess, as 'she,' 'her,' do you think?"

"Never noticed," says the old gent, "just do I guess."

"Women don't, at least I don't think so," I say.

"Maybe," he winks at the clerk, "may be 'cause women don't have no projects!"

I haven't learned how to boil syrup but I've learned a little something about keeping my mouth shut. Women, I think, refer to projects as "the," or "it," or "my," as in "I take my material and lay it this way on the bias," or as "your" as in "first you take your flour then work your lard into it until your dough is real fine crumbed." I have not yet heard a woman refer to an engine or to a pie as having any particular sex at all. "Gimme a quarter-inch drill bit, please," I say, wanting to add, "she broke yesterday while I was tapping a hog," but I don't.

If I'm willing to believe I'll behead fish to fry them for breakfast, I'm willing to sit at the feet of nearly any lore. "Yes-ma'm's, he had some trouble drivin' over the yes-ma'ms," says a man about his son who's just home from the hospital, his back, industrial accident, been operated on. Out the first day, coming home a hundred miles in the car, he had trouble when his wife, driving, hit the "Yes-ma'ms."

"What did you say?"

"The . . . ups and downs, the, what do you call it the potholes, the little dips and such, you know. Always called them the 'yes-ma'ms' but don't have any idea why."

Lore makes cosmic sense, I'm sure of it. And it makes visions, and the vision of this nightly smelting event is one of overlapping nets: the fish spread, submerged, invisible, dog-paddling probably, waiting, unfocused, ungathered, just thawed out, maybe. About to gather, about to pour and tumble together through chutes of stream and creek mouths, about to become a net. But now they're lying, patternless, in a net of lakes and ponds. We wait. The water, thawed out, now everywhere, makes a net; threading and pouring from one lake into another, from new mud to trickle to creek to pond to river to the mighty ocean, all the water connected and spreading out under the net of blowing black naked trees, under the net of the sky, the stars at steady random, a million sparkling fish above us.

Between these nets we creep, us fisherfolk, following lore and the once a year craving for this spring tonic, this rank, oily, bony titbit of a fish; crossing paths, moving up back roads, across bridges, stopping out on broken docks, on mushy ice floes, driving to the next spot, getting out of the car, walking, lantern-lit, lantern bobbing, checking, peering, waiting, not talking much, moving off again, back into the car, all with our dots of light like fireflies in late June. A patient, eager dance of lights, tying the knots of nightly movement across and around the net of lakes, in and out of the sound of breaking creeks. From very far above, it would be a net of nets, in pursuit, and spring causing them all.

"You think I'm stupid, don't ya?" yells Hilde.

"Oh no," I yell back. "I just wanted to know how you feel about feeling this way."

She slides in the mud but catches herself against a wet tree. My husband's gotten too far ahead with the lantern for us to see the path.

"God-damnit. God-damn mud. I thought you were trying to tell me I was crazy."

"Oh no, I don't think you are!"

Our world has not had any smell but chimney smoke since October and the first hard frost then which deadened the air. Actually what the first hard frost did was freeze up the last things of the year that smelled—mashed apples on the ground, rotting leaves, rotting marigolds, deer droppings, rain-soaked cabbages left in the garden. Hard frost has no smell, neither does snow. Though it's true that you can smell snow coming.

"I don't love him," Hilde continues, "but I sure like him. I couldn't feel this way about somebody I didn't like. And Everett knows how I feel. I think."

"Well, it's hard to avoid those feelings in this town," I say, a little grimly, feeling a little grim, trying to imply that one is taxed by these eternally rambunctious circumstances.

"That's for sure," she says.

She's gotten far behind me. "What?" I scream.

"I say, *that's* for sure."

And this seems to tie up the subject. It hasn't happened but it almost did. Maybe it will still happen. There's another dance next week for someone's birthday. We'll all go. We slosh on, after the bobbing light. Where is the creek mouth?

I think, sidestepping a bog, of the intricacy of language that rightly ought to form the details of this investigation into the facts and feelings of wanting Bart Stone. Bart Stone, currently unmarried again, is about thirty, has hundreds of white teeth, white as a wolf's, rubs musk oil in his hair for parties in emptied sheds, or garages, and after the first dance has stripped down to his thermal underwear shirt which, in cut and charm and cling, is curiously like Calvin Klein's cashmere sweatshirt style sweaters. Bart Stone gets sweaty at dances because he dances with all four limbs and dances every dance. In between records, he goes outside and stands in his sweat in the snow, drinks whatever's at hand, someone else's hand, and yells several times at the sky. How far ought Hilde and I to go with this language? "I went almost all the way," intended to be a confessional delicacy, despite the wind and water noise, really sounds brutal if you think about it. Like a car wreck; totaled, "all the way." I want to start netting the subject with some details.

They can't have met in private because there's no place to go in private up here. Is necking in a dark, late, but public corner— the Town Meeting dance in the wooden Grange Hall—called an "affair"? We have only naked space here in the country, against which no one's car or truck is anonymous. And otherwise, only these sweaty public events. "Affairs" are urban. They take place in good clothes in small, tasteful, dim, empty bars on late afternoons after your last seminar, in a part of the city not your own; and affairs are largely composed of talk. Whatever it is that takes place with your head against a splintery upright, in a large damp crowd smelling of wet wool and felt-packs (a crowd which sometimes includes your own children, as children also come to the town dances and dance), while wearing a thermal undershirt, while holding a can of warm beer stiffly, politely off to one side during the kiss, while overhearing bits of argument still hot about the further outrage perpetrated at today's Town Meeting over using revenue-sharing funds for filling spring road potholes or the unwarranted and totally unnecessary and undeserved raise in the dogcatcher's salary, whatever it is that happens during all this seems to need a word other than "affair." But then I'm not sure that Hilde would care that much right now about figuring this out, and exploration in this case seems finished, anyway. It's too noisy to talk. Nature makes too much noise for talk. At least we've understood each other.

"And I just want you to know, I don't care if you think I am crazy. I think I would've gone all the way if he'd've wanted to."

To this, I attempt no reply. "Wait!" I yell at the lantern, my husband, who's dancing ahead down the muddy path. He dances back.

"Wow, we live here! this is not a vacation! I went to work today!"

"That's just what Everett and me were saying last night," says Hilde. "Ten minutes from your back door, and all this beauty."

The next afternoon, the children are home from school. It's the week off called "mud vacation," and truly, the school buses can't get down the country roads. Together, Hilde and I have seven children. They're all here at my house. She and I are sitting at the kitchen table drinking tea. We have propped the kitchen door open to let the sunshine in, sun shines on the melting snow and mud, little insects—snow fleas—play in the bar of light. Things outside hiss and trickle. Maple sap burbles on the wood stove, two canning kettles and one turkey roaster full. Everything is sticky and muddy. We've stopped cleaning anything for the duration: the tops of things, the floor, the kids.

The thawing mud is so deep that nobody can drive anywhere near to the house, so we can't hear cars. That's a loss, because hearing cars is always an event out here where we live, and sends the dog to one kitchen window and the children to another. There's

no place for cars to be going but to this house. In winter the snow
plow stops at the edge of our yard and turns back. So in winter,
even the oil man coming is fun.

But now, with the mud, we can't hear the cars they have to park
so far up the road, and so suddenly there's a great spawn of men
on foot: Bart Stone, Marshall, P.D., Spider, Timmy Coffin, Fred-
die Ferber, and an unknown friend in a red hunting hat—filing
largely into the afternoon through the spillway of the sunny door.
They are muddy and tolerably drunk, in good spirits, each one
carefully wrapped around a 16-oz. beer. They fill up the kitchen
with an energy beyond their number and literal size. The dog leaps
up and down. Hilde and I move our chairs together, offer tea. They
don't want tea. "Tea! tea! oh yes Jeesus, tea!"

They have been out visiting all day, here and there, house to
house. They are full of plans, and have come to engage whoever
they found at home. It's Patriots' Day, but no one knows what that
signifies except that none of them is at work. "I thought Patriots'
Day was in November, man!" "No man, that's *War* Day in
November."

First they talk about Freddie Ferber's troubles with Mrs. Mar-
melot, an elderly foreign lady from whom he's rented space for a
lunch counter, the only one in the village, up front in the building
in which she also lives, out back. She has lately retired from run-
ning the lunch counter and has given Freddie the lease. He is cook,
manager, and the sole waiter and dishwasher. He's been running
it for three weeks. It's housed in an old airy studio built and then
abandoned by a taxidermist sometime in the 1930s.

"He rents her place, pays rent, he pays, man, to be her fuckin'
manager. Do you know what he *makes* a week? Take-home? About
one fuckin' quarter!"

"I can't put up with it much longer," says Freddie, shaking his
head, with an early Beatles haircut, and looking down into his
empty beer can.

"You know why she's so fuckin' crazy and tough? She was in
the War, man, that's why, she was a fuckin' Chesso-sov-lakian go-
rilla, man, that's why!" Much play on "go-rilla." Bart Stone im-
itates a gorilla, scratching his ribs, showing his teeth, and falls off
a stool laughing.

154

Freddie looks up, happily, inspired, forgets about his empty can. "That's what I'll tell the customers I got out back! a go-rilla! But ah, man, she's gonna ruin the breakfast crowd comin' in in her nightgown at 7:30 in the morning. 'Don't mind me boys, I'm just getting myself some coffee!'" Freddie mincingly imitates Mrs. Marmelot's Hungarian voice, her lordly girth, her ladylike demeanor. "You know what she says to me yesterday? She says 'I guess I'm going to have to give you your marching papers!'"

"Oh man *why* do you *take* it?"

A fight, Freddie now explains, has taken place with Mrs. Marmelot over the proper way to make a beef stew. Freddie is frying each piece "separate, with onions." But Mrs. Marmelot objects, wants him to add "lima beans and vinegar and all kinds of shit."

"Man, how can you let her do that, it's supposed to be your fuckin' place, she's got no fuckin' business bein' out there at all telling you what to do!"

"That's right! that's right!" says Freddie, now properly outraged. "When she ran it, would anybody with any brains even eat in there? You don't see me fixin' coffee in a frying pan, warming up that old crap from the morning, using two-day-old bread and five-day-old hamburg."

They've forgotten that Hilde and I are there. Much loud advice, head nodding, commiseration: "I'd kick her fat Russian ass right to Russia, Freddie, right back to Russia." "Let's hog-tie 'er and have a party in there tonight and then you can fuckin' quit Freddie." Netted with all this, talk of the coming Saturday night's birthday party, the beer supply for today, the adventures of today. "Let's liberate the bridge in Chesterville for Patriots' Day!" "Let's liberate Camp Bearspaw and have a party in that fuckin' big lodge of theirs." "Yeah man, let's do that, but what about them people up the head of their road in the chicken farm there though?" "Fuck it, man, we'll park way down and walk in." "Who can fuckin' walk, man?"

The stub of an already used joint passes back and forth, burning fingers and lips. The kids swarm through the room out into the mud and back in again. Some of the men are standing, some on stools and chairs, one in the open doorjamb, two on the edge of the lit woodstove. All of them talk at once. And sex, it runs like the major thread. "How about Faith Coffin, she's about what do you think eighty-five? Eighty-six now?" "That don't make no difference, I can go for a hot old lady anytime." "How old's *she* now?" They point their beers at and tease Hilde about Patty, her nimble blond ten-year-old, whose, face, blank and friendly as a school slate, pops into instant grin at this incomprehensible but adult attention. "*She's* old enough. When did you start Hilde? Thirteen? Fourteen? Fifteen?" "I was married when I was seventeen," says Hilde, primly. "Ah, man, twelve, then!" They wave their empty cans, pound the furniture, fall backwards with laughing. The kids have no idea what's going on—does anyone?—except that it's exciting, better than the oil man.

"When you gonna teach me t'dance?" asks Marshall, turning my way.

"You have to come to a party first, don't ya?"

"He's been on the wagon since New Year's Eve," says Hilde in a loud *sotto voce*. But I knew that. Marshall "goes overboard" everyone says. He's married to his high school sweetheart. He's avoiding the temptation of parties. His wife has already gone home several times to her mother, home being almost next door, and Marshall is not drinking, won't dance, and watches TV every night. Now he's so drunk his eyes roll, his eyelids are transparent lavender. He keeps rubbing his thick beard, forgetting that he has a lit cigarette in his hand.

One of them, Bart Stone, being a bachelor these days, has been invited out to supper. He asks to borrow the phone and calls the woman who invited him to tell her to expect fourteen. Then they all get up to leave. Marshall gives one rub to the top of my head while going through the door and groans with ritually acknowledged frustration. They're leaving because they've run out of beer and we don't have any. Of course, no one says this. It wouldn't be polite. Hilde and I stand in the sunny doorway and watch them go and we talk a little of what we'll now fix for our respective suppers. And we know, though we do not say so to each other in the quiet, that they'll get back in the one crowded car and talk about us sexually. Not intricately, nor much, but with sighs and brief agreements. They won't use our Christian names: "she," "her," "the big one," "that little blond kid."

They'll talk about us, and some of our children, as "lays." The raucous, elaborate flirtations of the kitchen like mere spray on the larger creek of their deeper feelings, and those, they share only with each other, not with women. At least, not with women that they don't know. And not much with each other, and never in mixed company. Their deepest feelings may not be known.

They will squeeze and settle into the car, and in the lull of opening new beers, looking out the rear window and slowly backing out the quarter mile of still passable road to the tarred road, they'll talk. "A little to the left, a little to the left! Watch it!" Not hard to imagine their heavy, gloomy insinuations, the language of their serious formulas: "Yeah, I could sure go for that." "Oh yeah man, couldn't you though." The afternoon is over. It's time for everyone's supper at home. Hilde begins to gather up her children. "I'll have to hose you bunch down," she says.

Next day, seen singly in the village store, buying gas, bread, screws, stain, baby cereal, each man is subdued, circumspect, stiff, polite, perfunctory, eyes kept down, parsimonious, shy, Yankee. This is store decorum, and lore that I don't know yet controls it. It is as much ritualized, however, this decorum, and as much agreed-upon as are the protected ceremonies of abandon, to which we all move in and out the days as to an invisible music, a minuet, that calls the spring dance.

The Solemn Son

"It's his." They'll weigh it out behind the store.
Harry Nason writes the boy's name, Steve
Burnell. The boy looks solemnly at the floor,
Trying to work it out. It's hard to believe
That in one deafening moment in the woods,
At daybreak, as he shivered from the cold,
So much could change. He overhears his dad's
Words as Harry has the story told.
"Two shots . . . the heart." He'd hardly time to see
The buck before the crashing blasts that killed
Him rang in his ears so overpoweringly
That just when he was sure he'd be fulfilled
He felt dazed and deserted. Now the son
Hears Harry's voice from miles away. "Well done."

Bob Ward (1955)

Two nights a week Bob Ward the insurance man
Whose office stood beside the hardware store
Got in his car and drove to other rooms
In other towns to meet another man.
They loved—and held a joy that terrified
The sickly light of day. The words that seemed
To probe his every moment fell away.
The hell of every shame and fear, each nod
And smile, the famous business handshake
Unplumed in the cock's hard grace. He prayed
For himself later in the clockbound dark.
He prayed for the soul that seemed unreal
But must be there. He cried peculiar tears
And watched the sun come up: the slightest pink
Flame simmered on the horizon. He chose a tie
To match his suit then headed to the cafe
Where each morning he took his determined place.

Bent Reeds

Funny, Grace thought, as she approached the crest of Spindle Hill and saw seven or eight cars parked higgledy-piggledy on the left-hand shoulder of the road, as if the drivers had dropped everything to respond to some emergency. Wonder what's going on at Millard's? She didn't stop to find out, though; she didn't want the milk to turn or the eggs to poach right in her knapsack. Instead she headed for the house across the road, wheeling her bicycle over the crushed stone that had recently been dumped in Owen's driveway. She leaned the bike against a popple tree and wiped her forehead in the crook of her arm. Maybe I'm getting a little long in the tooth for this form of transportation, she thought. From the rear of Owen's house came the sound of steady tapping. Finally getting those last shingles up. Two hammers at work, she judged. She went on into the house.

When she'd unpacked the groceries she climbed the stairs to the back bedroom and poked her head through a window. "What's transpiring over at Millard's?" she asked.

Below her, balanced on some rickety scaffolding, nails sprouting from his mouth, stood Owen. Also Perley Pinkham, one of the deacons. Owen didn't look so good. His face seemed kind of pinched. Oughtn't to be outside in this heat, on that bad leg all day, but just try to keep him from working on his house. Perley shifted his weight to hammer a nail and the scaffolding swayed. "Garage sale," he said.

"What did he do, clean out his attic?" Grace asked.

"Guess so," Perley said.

"Whoever heard of doing spring cleaning in August?"

The two of them looked so uncomfortable she thought it must be more than the cockeyed plank they were perched on or the heat.

Perley spoke. "You know Millard don't do things by other people's calendars."

Owen took the nails from his mouth and said, "Did you remember to pick up that extension cord, Grace?"

"Course I remembered. Got you some eggs, too; I saw yesterday you were almost out. Owen, why did Millard clean his attic?"

"Reamed the whole house out," Perley said. "Stem to stern."

"Why don't you go on over there and take a look?" Owen said, rummaging in the pocket of his carpenter's apron. "I bet he's got some great bargains."

"If you fancy old junk," Perley said.

"Owen, I want to know what's going on."

Owen positioned a nail and focused busily on the shingle in front of him. Tap tap *tap*. "He's moving," he said, not looking up.

"What do you mean, moving? Where to?"

Perley took out his handkerchief. He lifted his feed cap and mopped the crown of his head. "Going to live," Perley said, "with his married son. Over to Aurora."

"I don't believe it. Millard always says the only way they'll get him out of that house will be in a pine box."

Perley glanced sideways at Owen. "I reckon his boys want him where they can keep an eye on him," Perley said finally, "on account of his ticker."

Then she got it. *Owen* was the one supposed to keep an eye on old Millard; that had been the unspoken agreement when Millard sold Owen the parcel of land across the road at a price well below its market value. But since Owen's operation . . . "Maybe Millard's jumping the gun a little," she said. "Plenty of life left in the old geezer, seems to me."

Perley shook his head. "Nobody tells Millard what to do."

Including his boys, Grace thought, though his "boys" must be pushing sixty. Funny Millard would knuckle under without a fight.

"Any red tomatoes yet out at your place?" Owen asked.

"Tom says next week."

"If it don't turn cold and rainy on us." Perley stuffed his handkerchief into a rear pocket of his overalls and resumed hammering.

She could stand a break in the weather, she thought, as she drew her head back into the bedroom. The room still smelled of paint, a dazzling yellow, picked out by Owen himself. Whichever parishioner painted it had left a handful of brushes soaking in a coffee can full of turps, figuring women's work: let one of the women come along and do the tidying up after. With a sigh Grace stooped and lifted the can. She wasn't in much of a mood to do somebody else's scut work, but she'd better get it out of the way so Owen wouldn't go stumbling over it in the middle of the night. She had an idea he didn't sleep much. Spent a lot of time wandering in his house after everybody'd gone home. Thinking over ideas for sermons, maybe. Or just thinking.

Down cellar, she found some rags and drenched them in turps and began to clean the brushes. Fumes made her remember the hours she'd spent down here late in the winter, February it must have been, when Owen was still in the hospital. She'd volunteered to dip the shingles that Owen wanted on his house in that preservative stuff. Quite a job it turned out to be, clipping the wire on the bundles, discarding the split ones, dousing the shingles one by one in Cuprinol and standing them in rows in a piece of plastic gutter she rigged so the excess would run back into an empty can. Splinters. And small cuts the Cuprinol would find and work its way into, in spite of her rubber gloves. And the fumes, enough to knock you out, nearly.

Tom had said she was nuts to do the job in February, no way would that bunch of arthritic old-timers and assorted do-gooders the Reverend had building his house get around to shingling until well into the summer, if then. She'd freeze down in that cellar. No, she told him, she'd collect that old kerosene heater from Grammy's house. Right, he said, blow yourself up, then. Be my guest. People who perish doing God's work go straight to heaven, that the deal?

Naturally Tom missed the point. She couldn't explain it to him, didn't even try. She thought—no, it was more she *felt,* deep in her bone marrow—that if she took pain and danger on herself, even in a small way, she could force God to take away some of Owen's. Owen would have scolded her, if he'd known, for entertaining such a sacrilegious notion. But Owen made his home in the New Testament. Her experience and intuition drove her to dwell in the Old.

Dipping those shingles had been something like dipping sheep, she thought now, that spring ritual they performed on the farm when she was a girl. *He shall feed his flocks like a shepherd,* she began to hum, *and carry the young lambs in his bosom.* . . .

It was shepherds that got saved in that avalanche, she remembered. A couple of weeks after Owen came back from his stay in the hospital, around the middle of March, she heard on the radio there had been an avalanche in Turkey or somewhere, tons of snow loosened by a thaw slid down a mountain onto a village, and hundreds of people were buried, and the ones who survived were those who were at prayer and the shepherds out in the fields. A perfect idea for a sermon, she'd thought, and she'd given Owen a call, but there wasn't any answer, and he hadn't turned on that fool answering machine of his, which wasn't like him. Must have forgot, she supposed.

Well when Tom got home from work she took the car to do one or two errands and came back the long way through town, figuring she'd stop at Owen's and tell him about the sermon idea in person. He still rented that shabby apartment over the Bargain Box then, waiting for his house to be finished. But he didn't answer her knock, and she didn't see his van in the place he always parked it. She had to start supper in a hurry because Monday was Tom's lodge night and he had to be there early to polish the swords or something, and then after supper that woman from the recycling committee dropped by with the envelopes she'd mousetrapped Grace into addressing and stayed on to unburden herself on hazardous wastes and seepage. So with one thing and another Grace didn't get around to calling Owen again until after eight. Still no answer. She began to have kind of a shivery feeling, and Tom wasn't around to reason her out of it, so she decided to give Millard a call even though she risked dragging the old grouch out of bed. But if anyone would know where Owen was, he would.

Those two had grown so close after Millard's wife died and Owen's wife, seized by some women's liberation fancy, took it into her head to toss him out of the house and sue for divorce. An odd friendship, everybody said so: the dig-in-your-heels chair of the deacons, whose family had lived in town for six generations, and who wouldn't water his garden because God knew best—and the easy-going doctor of divinity, who'd happened into town one July on vacation from the community college where he taught philosophy, and never left because the parish needed a preacher. The two of them, thick as thieves, making the rounds of public suppers and fish-fry nights from one end of the county to the other, more night life than they'd had in their two lives combined up until then, Grace guessed.

So she dialed Millard's number. "Haven't seen him," Millard said.

"What about the Monday meat loaf luncheon special at Uncle Nippy's? You two never miss that."

"Told me he couldn't make it this week."

"Why not? Did he give you a reason?"

"Nope."

Damn the man. "Millard, Owen doesn't answer his phone. Or his door. His van's not in the lot by the Bargain Box. It's not like him just to disappear."

"Van's here."

"What?"

"Across the road. Parked in the driveway."

"But he can't be staying there."

"Course not. Wood stove ain't been installed yet."

"Well where is he, then?"

Grace could hear the old man's sinuses reverberating as he mulled all this over. Maybe he'd turned off his hearing aid.

"Millard," she shouted, "did he tell you anything about what . . . the doctors said?"

"Doctors?"

"After the operation. Do you know anything about Owen the rest of us don't?"

"Can't say."

She recognized the intonation. It was the same way he said "Blest be the reading of God's word" every Sunday morning at the end of the scripture lesson. Trying to drag any more out of him would be futile.

She was about to hang up when he muttered, "Grace?"

"Yes?"

She listened to him breathe some more. Then he said, "He don't have a gun. Not that I know of."

Grace flew into her coat and boots and out to the drive before she remembered that Tom had taken the car. She ran up the Strouts' porch steps, nearly falling on the ice, and grabbed their car keys off the hook inside the kitchen door. "Explain later," she shouted.

She maneuvered the old boat of a car across the bridge, braked at Spindle Road, cut the corner, and floored the accelerator, which raised the Oldsmobile's speed from 15 to 17 mph. "Damn. Damn. Damn." With each explosion of breath the windshield clouded over more. *Just like a Maine man . . .* Furiously she rubbed at the fog with the heel of her hand—her gloves were still on the floor of the mud room—creating a smear that furred house lights along the road. . . . *to think the only way you can kill yourself is with a gun.*

At the top of the hill she found, sure enough, the van squatting in the drive, an inch of snow on it. Snow that had fallen the night before. He must have preached his sermon, shaken the hand of each of his parishioners, and then driven here and . . .

With a start Grace recalled the text of the sermon. *Lo, thou trustest in the staff of this broken reed.* One of the prophets. Isaiah. But what had Owen preached on the text? Rummage through her brain though she might, Grace knew she'd never be able to reconstruct it. She must have woolgathered, as she often did during Owen's meandering conversations with the text and with God, allowed her thoughts to turn toward some such question as whether she should make new slipcovers for the chairs in the sitting room, and if so, what color? Floral? Stripes? Grace cursed herself for failing to pay attention.

Owen's house would be locked, but Grace knew the whereabouts of a cellar door key; she'd used it all those days she dipped shingles. Hard going under foot: beneath the layer of new snow that slipped like quilt batting was mud frozen into ruts. She hugged the side of the house as she made her way, tarpaper snagging her coat. The penlight on the Strouts' key chain flashed a feeble dime of illumination on the snow.

At last she got to the bulkhead. The toe of her boot nudged the section of clay drainpipe where the key lay hidden. With fingers

so numb she could scarcely move them she groped inside and found
it. Now to open the bulkhead door. Tough enough to manage in
daylight, the key stiff in the new lock, the heavy metal doors slop-
ing at an awkward angle. Knees braced against the bulkhead, she
brushed snow off the door with her coat sleeve, directed the pen-
light at the keyhole, and tried to poke the key into it. No luck. She
backed off, pocketed the key, and rubbed her hands together to get
some circulation into them. Try again. She leaned forward, key in
hand, and as she bent to kneel on the door one foot slipped out
from under her and she landed flat on her belly. The key skittered
against metal and fell somewhere in the snow.

"All right, if that's the way you're going to be!" she yelled at
the sky, or the chink of it she could see, a leg or something of
Orion's. "Let somebody else find him! I quit!"

She didn't, though. She found the key, got the door open, and
searched the house, every cranny, with the penlight. He wasn't
there, of course.

How could she have imagined he'd give up on life so easily? It
must have been her own chicken heart made her react that way.
She returned the car keys to the Strouts with some lame excuse,
never mentioned to Tom she'd gone out, never confessed to Owen
that she'd tried to break into his house, expecting to find a corpse.
Even after she found out where Owen *was*—had a few things to
talk over with his ex-wife, he said; left the van in the driveway on
Spindle Road and went on foot the mile and a half to her house
because he didn't want people to see the van parked there and jump
to the wrong conclusions—Grace didn't say a word.

Only Millard—sleepless, maybe, gazing across the road, won-
dering about guns—might have seen the car entering the driveway,
seen her bundled stubby figure groping its way toward the house,
and guessed what she'd done.

Now Grace laid the brushes out on newspaper to dry, disposed
of the turps-soaked rags, and left the house. Wonder what the old
goat's got for sale? she said to herself as she unhitched her bicycle
handlebars from the popple trunk.

Behind her, on the crushed stone, she heard Owen's footsteps.
Unmistakable, his gait, ever since they cut the muscle in his thigh

to get at the tumor lodged against his pelvic bone. She turned and let him catch up.

"Do you really think he'll do it—move to Aurora?"

Owen's face opened into its grin, which only made her realize how slack his jaw had become. "You know Millard when he makes up his mind about something."

"But he built that house with his own hands." The bike wobbled as she steered it over the gully at the foot of the drive. "His kids grew up there. His wife died there."

Owen waved at the driver of a pickup that passed in the road and then said, "We all do what we have to do, Grace."

She leaned her bike against Millard's mailbox post and they walked across the grass, dry blades crunching under their feet, past the jungle of raspberry bushes that year by year ate up a little more of Millard's lawn. The crop hadn't been good this year; she'd heard that for the first time in living memory Millard had neglected to fertilize them. Must be getting past it, somebody'd said. Beyond the raspberries lay a vegetable garden—pumpkins the size of boulders sprawled on the tough clay—and beyond that his acreage gradually sloped down to the rock-strewn river. Cattails and reeds by the riverbank looked dry enough that the next tide might snap them off. No rain to speak of had fallen since June.

"Garden sure is parched," she said. "I have half a mind to sneak out here some night with a hose and water those poor desiccated beans myself."

"He'd probably take after you with a baseball bat if he caught you. The way he does with porcupines."

"He wouldn't catch me." She rolled up the cuffs of her dungarees. "Thick skulls, porkies. Funny how they keep coming back for more."

"He claims all he does is stun them a little."

They turned and began to walk toward the garage, where five or six customers stood pawing through Millard's goods and chattels. "You in the market for anything?" Grace asked him.

"He mentioned he was putting his boys' old bunk beds in the sale."

"What would you do with those?"

"Set them up in the back bedroom for when Celia and the kids come to visit."

Celia, Owen's daughter, lived in Cincinnati and was married to some kind of engineer. She'd made herself pretty scarce all those months Owen was in Bangor under the knife and being pumped full of poisonous chemicals. Of course, she had a job and those kids, and airline tickets cost money. Still, Grace wondered if Celia would ever stay in his house, bunk beds or no.

Millard had moved his pickup and tractor-mower out of the garage and set up boards and sawhorses inside. On the planks, in heaps and stacks, was all manner of old rubbish. Dozens of those canning jars, the kind with glass lids that clamp on. His wife, Aldina, had been noted for the quality of her preserves, and she'd apparently assembled quite a stock of jars. Pairs of rubberized boots in various sizes and stages of decay. Primitive-looking power tools. At one time Millard used them to make toys to sell at the church fairs, trains and pull-toys and such. The toys hadn't gone over very well lately, except to the summer people; kids nowadays went for bright plastic, not wood. Cords on the tools looked dangerously frayed. A pair of bedroom dresser lamps, milk glass painted with roses, their ruffly shades on crooked so it appeared their necks were twisted out of whack. Everything musty-smelling and strung with cobwebs. At the back of the garage, in a lawn chair, presiding over the dispersal of the earthly remains of his whole past life, sat Millard, glowering.

"Well Millard," Grace said, "this is a surprise."

"Guess you don't read the paper."

"Not the yard sale ads." She picked up a dented aluminum six-cup percolator and peered underneath. "You didn't put prices on, Millard?"

He grunted. "Make me an offer."

Oh no, she wasn't going to play that game. Offer too much and he'd think you a fool. Offer too little and he'd take it as an insult. She set down the coffee pot and began to examine some Christmas tree ornaments in a flimsy box stamped *Made in Occupied Japan*. "I'm surprised you decided to move," she said. Meanwhile, Owen had put on a pair of hunting boots and was stomping around in them. He spotted someone he knew on the lawn and went traipsing out of the garage, rawhide laces trailing behind. "Aurora, is it? The *real* sticks."

"Those're antique," Millard told her.

1946? Well if that's antique so am I. She had to admit the ornaments did have a certain something about them, though. Maybe the forty-odd years of grime. "How much do you want for them?"

"How much are they worth to you?"

Oh well, why not let him think her a fool? "How does seven dollars sound?" she said, figuring that was the absolute tops he could expect for them in his garage.

"Eight," Millard said.

"Seven-fifty."

"Done," he said. He hefted himself out of the lawn chair and moved over to the plank that displayed the Christmas decorations. "What about Rudolph?" he asked, pointing to a plastic reindeer with one missing hoof. Millard's plump hand squeezed the tail and a bulb at the end of Rudolph's nose flickered. "Fella from the realty told me confidentially this here's a collector's item. Probably worth upwards of a hundred, fella said, but I could let you have him for seventy-five, keep him here in town."

"I appreciate that, Millard, but I think just the ornaments will do me." As she was counting singles out of her wallet to pay for them, Owen came limping back into the garage, the rawhide laces dragging on the concrete. They'd collected some twigs and a shriveled leaf.

"Those boots suit you?" Millard asked. He was back in his lawn chair.

"A little snug," Owen said.

"That's because they're stiff. Nobody's been wearing them lately."

Forty years or so, Grace thought.

"You walk around in them, they loosen right up."

Or he could always lop his toes off.

The bunk bed parts, boards of varying widths and lengths, leaned against a wall of the garage. If it hadn't been for the scuffed blue paint on them, you'd probably have thought they were just a bunch of old planks stacked together for no particular reason. Millard noticed Owen eyeing them and said, "You interested in those beds?"

Right away Grace saw that Owen wasn't going to play games with Millard; in fact, the idea would never enter his mind. They were friends, buddies. Eating companions. Companions in misery. Those are the kind of people you're above-board with. "Sure am," Owen said.

From the depths of the lawn chair Millard said, "Make me an offer." It was so dim in that garage you couldn't see the expression on his face.

Grace stopped breathing. She sensed that something awful was about to happen.

"Fifty dollars," Owen said heartily. Generously, or so he must have believed.

Millard scrunched down farther into the lawn chair. "Made those bunk beds," he said in a voice you could hardly hear. Nevertheless, a summer person inspecting one of the frilly-shaded lamps swiveled her head to catch what he was saying. "For my boys."

"I know," Owen said, his face bright and cheery. "It's good they'll be put to use again."

"I don't accept your offer," Millard said, dropping each word like a wad of biscuit dough.

"Fifty dollars, and not a penny less."

Oh my God, Grace thought. Owen must think Millard's angry because he offered too much! How could Owen be so numb, even if he is from away? Grace wanted to sprint over and drag Owen out of the garage, but three long planks balanced on sawhorses and loaded with possessions intervened.

Slowly Millard rose out of the lawn chair, like a backhoe out of a bog. The inner corners of his eyes almost met and his wattles quivered. "I do not. Accept. Your offer," he said.

Grace gripped the box stamped *Made in Occupied Japan*. One or two ornaments crunched sickeningly in the box.

The following day, for the first time since the weekend his wife died, Millard did not appear in church. As the choir was filing in singing the processional, someone grabbed Perley Pinkham, shoved him into the aisle, and pointed him toward the pulpit. Poor Perley stumbled over so many words in the scripture lesson it was agonizing. The text: Ecclesiastes 3:1–8. *To every thing there is a season* . . .

At Grace's prodding, on Monday and then again on Tuesday Owen limped over to Millard's to make a higher offer on the bunk beds. But both days Millard had risen at dawn to drive his pickup loaded with furniture the hundred-and-twenty-mile round trip to Aurora and back. Damned if he'd pay a moving company to do what he could perfectly well do himself, he explained to Vi Leighton in the post office, when she ventured to inquire why his pickup was idling out front, crammed to the gunnels with bed frames and kitchen chairs and supermarket boxes. Just asking for another heart attack, Vi said on the phone to Grace, stubborn old skinflint.

Quarter to six Wednesday night Owen drove across the road to pick up Millard, just as he'd done very Wednesday night since the fall of 1989, except when he was in the hospital. But Millard said, from behind the screen door, no he didn't think he'd be going to the all-you-can-eat fish-fry tonight, Uncle Nippy's haddock just hadn't been settin well on his stomach lately. He was sorry, but Owen should go on without him.

Very well, Owen replied, why don't you let me know when your stomach *is* up for haddock? Briskly he got in his van and drove back across the road and microwaved one of the frozen pot-pies Marvella Look had baked for him.

That was Owen's version, as he reported it, a mite sheepishly, to Grace—men of the cloth were expected to turn the other cheek, after all. Nobody knew Millard's side of the story. Millard wasn't talking.

It went on that way for weeks: Owen mad at Millard for abandoning him by fixing to move to Aurora, and Millard mad at Owen for abandoning him by fixing to die. After the first week nobody could summon the courage to mention the name of one to the other. Spindle Road became like a moat between the two houses, which were in fact almost within spitting distance of one another.

Millard's Ellsworth Realtor erected a big sign next to the mailbox and took out ads in the county newspaper and, buckling under pressure from Millard, in the *Boston Globe*. Of course nobody bought the property because Millard had put way too high a price on it. The trailer on his son's land in Aurora was all spiffed up, ready for him to move in, but Millard lingered on in his house, camping out with just a few sticks of furniture and a pot or two. If you'd run into him in town he'd confide that a couple from Boston, professional couple, had made an offer on the house and were waiting to hear on their mortgage—but nobody believed him. Every once in a while, Owen told Grace, he'd look out his kitchen window and spot Millard propping up the Realtor's sign, which had blown to the lawn in the wind.

Meanwhile, Owen's sermons were becoming even more disorganized than usual. Truth was, you couldn't make head or tail of them. And he looked strained, his hands gripping the lectern, almost as if he'd keel over if it weren't there. He'd forget to show up for church council meetings or Bible study. One Sunday morning Grace went into the bathroom in the church basement right after Own had used it and found blood on the linoleum. She decided just to mop it up and not say anything, since Owen had made it clear that a possible recurrence of the tumor was not a topic open for discussion. He was cured, and that was that.

October arrived. The maple in Grace's front yard shrank into itself and discarded its leaves like so many sandwich wrappers. Grace stood on the porch steps, broom in hand, and noticed Owen's van bumping over the bridge. Off to that meeting of the people trying to organize a soup kitchen, Grace thought. When the van turned below her house and chugged up the drive she figured he had in mind roping her into yet one more save-the-world rescue operation. Definitely not, she thought. This time I'm going to say no and make it stick. She waited for him to burst out of the van and yell hello, how are ya, Grace, but he just sat there in the driver's seat. She leaned the broom against the railing and walked over to the window. He'd rolled it part way down.

God, he looked awful. Cheesy yellow patches under his eyes. She sucked her breath in.

"Grace, do you think you could drive me to Ellsworth in this thing?"

"I don't know, Owen. It doesn't look very reliable," she said, but when he didn't smile, she said, "Sure. I'll just get my jacket."

"I set out, but I realized I wasn't going to make it without help."

"I'll only be a minute."

As she was grabbing her jacket off the hook in the mud room she realized that before the silly squabble over the bunk beds, Millard would have been the one he'd have asked. He wouldn't even have *had* to ask. Somehow Millard would have known and had the pickup all gassed up for the journey.

At the hospital in Ellsworth they didn't bother to admit him; instead they sent him on to EMMC in Bangor in an ambulance. CAT scans and other complicated tests were performed and the deacons scrambled to find a substitute minister. While Owen was in EMMC Millard finally locked his doors, loaded the last items of furniture into his pickup, and moved to Aurora.

The following day, when Grace and Lizzie Pinkham went over to Owen's to clean out the refrigerator, they found, neatly stacked against the bulkhead, a number of planks of various shapes and sizes, freshly painted blue.

MARY PETERSON

Crazy Lady

She had a Ph.D. in philosophy and two master's degrees, but they didn't stop her from being the town's crazy lady. Maybe they even helped. She was smart enough to be inventively crazy, and she always knew when they were going to commit her to the state hospital again. Perhaps there was a line she knew about, and she crossed it when she decided to.

She lived in a small white clapboard house with green shutters, on Main Street, tucked neatly between two larger colonial houses and directly down from Flo's Steamed Hot Dogs and Arnie's Real Italian Pizza. The house had a rickety rose trellis over the door. The houses staunchly on either side were really lawyers' offices.

Even with the bushes, and although her house was set back some distance from the road, people could still see the things she did to the lawn. She left the front door and back door wide open in any weather. She dressed the elm tree with a toga of sheet. She hung politicians' signs upside down in rows next to the front door. She found a blue sign that read "Bernie's Feeds" and nailed it over her window. She took the television set out to the side lawn and tried to bury it with a shovel, but there were too many roots and she couldn't dig deeply enough. So she left it there, antenna askew, the shovel stuck into the dirt upright.

Early in the summer, when she went bad crazy, her lawn was positively garlanded with toilet paper fluttering wildly from the tree branches, and balanced in one tree was a startling pink umbrella. People said, "What's the umbrella for?" But nobody knew. Then somebody said at Jimmy's Store that she was talking about the Viet Cong, and maybe she put things around her house for protection. But nobody knew what protection a pink umbrella would provide.

174

Townspeople saw her out walking every day, always heading in a new direction, and they avoided her when they could. If she saw a person she would stop and talk, and nothing she said made sense. Sometimes she chattered in Latin, or French. Sometimes she left notes for people on their doors, but even the town doctor—who understood Latin—could make no sense of the notes.

She usually wore a scarf and a trench coat, sometimes a long grey sweater. She was perhaps fifty-eight or sixty, but from behind she looked like a slim-hipped girl. Her walk had the forward urgency of someone on important business. She thrust her head and clenched her fists. She clenched her face within the babushka scarf, too; her face was lined and tight, tense with the pressure of whatever went on in her mind. A thin face, and old-looking. You could almost guess her age when you looked at her head-on. Perhaps she could have been beautiful. She had astonishing, insistent bones. Perhaps she could have been striking. She looked rather like an artist. Like a weaver. Her little thin legs had ropy muscles, and so did her arms.

The people who were most afraid of her were probably of two types: those who were so proper-polite they couldn't tell her to go away when she stopped them on the street; and the artists. There weren't many good artists in town—three writers, a sculptor, and only two good painters (the rest of the painters, and there were many, weren't good at all, and they were most outspoken about being artists, and they showed their work every summer in an open outdoor festival on the Meeting House lawn). The real artists were bothered by her in different ways that may have added up to the same way:

Perhaps the writers were reminded of their dreams. The dreams they couldn't shake when they woke first thing in the morning—when the house grew a tiller and set sail out of the harbor; when the tower spurted flames around the screaming family; when the swarthy rapist pursued from behind and clutched like a dog on the gravelly shopping center parking lot.

Perhaps the sculptor was reminded of the draped sheet of the covered object in his studio. It was unfinished. He was a practical worker and always finished everything, but that one tugged and nagged at him even when he had dinner with his kind, patient wife and his quiet, intelligent children. If he could only get the shape behind the drape to take form, then something very important would be finished. Formlessness was terrifying to him.

Perhaps the painters were uneasy about letting the public see their work, perhaps they were angry with poor attention that made people shake their heads and scratch their jaws and leave without noticing the quality of color in the foreground, the careful details that brought a subject coherently together in a frame. The crazy lady's lawn was like details without order; the eye skidded all over the place and never found a home. It was unbearable.

The artists in town were not very good friends, and probably never spoke to each other about it. They all had astonishing egos and bitter little insecurities, and they were loath to confess anything to anybody.

As for the proper-polite people, they let her stop and talk her gibberish while they looked around helplessly for rescue. Sooner or later somebody would come along and say to the crazy lady, "Harriet, knock it off. You're bothering people." Like magic she would shake her head and pull her grubby trench coat closer around her little bird body and shuffle off, muttering, down the street.

People in town had seen her do almost everything: walk into a restaurant and come quickly out again within a minute, as though somebody had thrown her out. Stand in the post office for three hours filling out change of address cards. Sneak home the back way through overgrown vacant property. Pick up things along the road and shove them into her pockets.

And everybody knew she smelled terrible. They were sure of that.

Her daughter, who lived in town but refused to try to do anything with her mother, said, "She's always been crazy, but worse the last few years. She has pills—just one in the morning and she's fine. But she won't take them. I don't know why. Maybe she likes being the town's crazy lady."

Somebody said, *A person ought to be careful of what they wish for, because of course it will come true.*

Her daughter said she hadn't known her father well either, and when he shot himself in that very little house five years ago, while her mother was institutionalized upstate, she wasn't even sad. "How could I be?" she said. "I didn't speak to him for years. He was a stranger." She said her brother felt guilty but was a weakling and wouldn't have anything to do with his mother. "He just pretends she doesn't exist," the daughter said.

Earlier in the summer, when the crazy lady was getting worse, she made friends with a halfwit in town and spent hours a day with her. But the halfwit finally couldn't stand her either, and threw her out. After that she took to wandering around town in her trench coat and finally she did not put on clothing under the trench coat, and walked into Jimmy's Store and the Economy Gas Station and the Mariner Bar and opened the coat and was picked up by the police within a day for "indecent exposure."

Later in the summer, when she was back from the state hospital, she was good for a while. Children stopped, for a while, calling her the witch. Mothers forgot to warn their children to avoid her house. But sure as the weather, in September she started to go off her nut again and began to redecorate the front lawn. And threatened a respectable woman in town with burning. And in a day was found on that woman's spacious front porch lighting little fires and smiling to herself. She was trucked off again by the police, who spoke afterward of the smell of her, and that she probably hadn't had a bath all summer.

Her daughter, who meant to leave town for California, stayed a while to clean up the house. She saw the television on the lawn and the shovel next to it. She put them inside. Also the sheet around the tree and the upside-down political signs and the boxes set on end and the gatherings of tindery sticks and rotten vegetables. She took the knives out of the trees. She told people her mother must have known she was going away soon, because the kitchen was cleaned spotless, although the other rooms were a disaster.

Maybe when the artists drove past they noticed that the house was orderly again, and they felt something relax inside. They would never have to speak of it.

Maybe the polite people could finish a cup of coffee at Jimmy's in the morning, and walk on errands, since she wouldn't tag along embarrassing them. They were safe, too.

Somebody said, *Even a true story has a moral now and then.*

When the daughter was cleaning outside, she noticed a powerful and rancid smell. It took a long time to locate. Finally she saw a decayed cat's head—mostly bone, a little fur—lying in the bird feeder.

She threw it in the trash.

And made a mental note to tell her mother, if she saw her again, one should never feed cats to birds if one lives on Main Street.

Bird Lady

You think I don't work for the Feds? What do you know,
you're only here once a week and can't even get it straight
who takes black, who wants the sugars. I'm 91 years and 4 days.
If you don't believe it, I hope you live longer on less.
Just last week, with two lousy dimes and a used Handi Wipe
over the phone, I did a 9-1-1, and those chrome studs
have gunned through this street for the last time.

You like my glasses?
I wear them so you can't see nothing
but your self looking at me. That gets the little punks
with their stolen skateboards knocking up the sides
of the fountain. I flap bird shrieks in their faces,
and they drop my bags real quick.

I have mystical powers,
which the pigeons who picket this square reciting
Longfellow have revealed to me. When they single out
an individual to surround, namely myself, of which I have
photographic proof, they are making a statement of substance.

I sold antiques. I testified to Congress.
I could dump this bag of used crumbs right here
on your scuffed up floor, make them spell out your
pitiful future.

Any back room I want I enter. Swine, I tell them,
stupefied by your own desires. And they zip up,
they drop the dice. My face is contagious. I spit,

and they're out on the street, dazed, lice-raving birds,
stuck in their own throats.

And I want you to know, Miss-Dish-It-Out-So-Politely,
I did not always eat what was offered. I did not just take
what was put in my face, cooked in big pots, mashed down
for the toothless, of which I am not one,
but don't get so close.

KENNETH ROSEN

Stormy Night

That night I looked out from our front room,
Warm, safe, with its piano and the violins,
And watched the poor people from the house
Across the street kicking at a snow drift,

A gang of demented gremlins, five of them,
Needing to get their cars put away
Before the parking ban at 11:30,
Batting at snow with rags and bare hands.

A woman with limp leather for hair
Sought to scoop it away with a dish towel.
Later I could see it was a toy, a plastic
Fireman's helmet, and the refugee Cambodians,

Who seemed to be wearing bathhouse turbans,
Were actually wearing knit caps. To care
So much about clothes and tools I must be scared,
And because I was scared I hated their scared,

Hoarse voices, their noisy stereos and rusted
Mufflers, constantly revving their engines
To test an adjustment or repair, drying their wash
On the street. I wanted their cars towed forever,

I wanted winter to destroy them. I wanted them
Living in boxes under the bridge or in some
Government preserve, the way the scared Israelis
Tried to warehouse the Palestinians they hated

And feared, which was not my point when I
Took my shovels, and crossed the street to help
Out for the first time ever, to push their cars
Through the drifts, shovel through a plowed bank,

And when they asked me, the moonfaced wife
With the dull hair, man with the Uncle Sam
Goatee—what a pair, Popeye and Olive Oil—
Did I need any help myself, was I all right

Over here, their faces became so complicated
When I said no, so human when it was clear
I had come to help them for no reason, for
Sympathy or something I didn't know was there.

MONICA WOOD

Wish

My first song went like this:

> *Gray squirrel, gray squirrel*
> *Whisk your bushy tail.*

I sang it several times, along with my new classmates, as I stood in a holding-hands line before the awesome height and beauty of my first teacher. But on the way home my splendid song disappeared into a pinwheel of other splendids; by the time I sang the song for my mother I was in my pajamas and the second line had become "*Wish* your *wishy* tail." My mother summoned my father from his blue chair in front of the TV and I sang it once more.

My mother believed in wishes-come-true as miracles: childbirth, physical beauty, good weather on special days. On this special day of my first song and first teacher came a new cat to our house, hardly a first, one my mother had discovered behind the grocery store a few days before and had finally brought home. It was a gray tabby with a regal, pointed face, full-grown but spindly, with a sad thin tail no bigger than a shoelace. Each cat in our house had its own song, and now, with a day not quite gone, the new cat had his. My mother changed the first line to "Gray *Tabby,* Gray *Tabby,*" and my rewritten second line became my mother's dearest wish for this creature to flourish under her care, to become, like the others, a handsome animal with a filled-out coat and a true cat's tail: full and bushy, the sign of a happy home.

Each of my mother's cats knew its song and at the sound of her voice would sit upright, its grand tail curling like a hem around its forepaws. Other animals responded in the same way: there were nights when we'd wake to the strains of my mother's soft cooing on the back porch, and find her hand-feeding a raccoon that sat hunched on her lap, or once a possumlike animal that stretched its length to her on tiptoe to sniff her outstretched hand. My mother had a communion with animals that appeared—to my sister and me at least—to have something to do with God, and we were secure in the knowledge that we had been born into a home of greatness.

❋

At the time of my first weeks of school and Gray Tabby's arrival, other, subtler changes pulsed around us. My parents talked in low urgent voices in the kitchen at night when we were supposed to be asleep. They pointed out newspaper articles to each other before dinner, their exchanged glances grim and meaningful. And the man with the collie moved in across the road.

Besides Gray Tabby we had only four other cats then, plus Joe, our parakeet, who roosted on top of his gateless cage, and a newly acquired rabbit in a pen outside. The rabbit had come to the door and hopped through my mother's legs into the hall and that had been that. We weren't equipped for rabbits, but my father relented as he always did, and built the pen as my mother wished. He was a little cranky about this. "The damn rabbit'll be in the house most of the time, anyway," he told my mother when she came out to inspect.

My father had been working long hours at the mill, work that he had done for many years, hard work that had begun to make him tired. He was often short of breath and his famous appetite had given in to attacks of indigestion.

"That new man wants to know why we have too many pets," my sister said to no one in particular, watching my father staple chicken wire to a post.

We all looked across the road to the new man's porch, where the collie sat tied to the steps, as he had every day, all day, since the man had moved in.

"What did you tell him?" my mother asked, her gaze lingering on the dog.

My sister looked at me. I was the one in school.

"Because we love them?" I ventured.

"Next time he asks," she said, "you tell him this is how we learn to be kind."

❋

"I don't think I can take another day of watching that poor thing," my mother said to my father. He was out sick for the first time we could remember, and my sister and I were so thrilled to have him home in the daytime that we made a holiday of it. We convinced him to take a lawn chair into the front yard and sit in the sun.

"It's none of our business, Lily," he said, watching my mother watch the dog.

"Well I just can't stand it," she said, flopping on the grass next to my father's chair. My sister and I flopped down next to her, imitating her distress, and after a while I began to feel it too, an aching in my throat for the tethered chestnut-and-white collie staring at us from its empty yard.

"Do you feel better, Daddy?" my sister asked.

"Yep."

"Are you going to work tomorrow?"

He grimaced. "Yep."

He looked at my mother. Something was awry.

"You *like* the mill, Daddy!" I said, certain I'd heard him say so, many times.

"It's not the mill anymore, honey," my mother said. "It's nothing but a big company."

A big company sounded very bad. We sat in silence, my sister and I trying to decipher this, sensing that the man across the road was somehow to blame.

"What if the girls went and untied him for a while, John?" my mother said. "We could all take him for a walk."

"Yaaaaay!" my sister and I yelled, on our feet and halfway out of the yard already.

"Back here, right now," my father said, and we stopped dead as he looked at us with what I remember now as a troubled, hollowed-out face under his characteristic ruddiness.

"I'm tired, Lily. We don't need problems with the neighbors, especially this one."

My mother said nothing, just turned her eyes from the collie across the road to my father next to her, as if devising a way to free them both.

✳

My first day of school was followed by more special days, and each of those days brought a song or a picture or a sheet filled with large imperfect letters. The brown rabbit—Brownie—had made a liar of my father by preferring the grassy pen to the kitchen linoleum, and Gray Tabby pleased us all by becoming a fine cat: affectionate, bushy-tailed, and smart. Like the four other cats—Pinky, Chum, Fluffy, Oscar—he purred loudly, sat up when he was sung to, and stayed away from Joe.

My father had been home sick twice more, once for three days in a row, but my sister and I could no longer coax him to do anything but lie down and rest. My mother took on a quiet that was unlike her, and the animals in the house responded in similar fashion, huddling in the kitchen while my mother did her work.

"Why is Daddy sick?" we asked my mother.

"He's not sick, he's tired."

"Why?"

"He works too hard."

"He always works too hard," my sister said. And it was true; my mother had always said this.

"It's different now. It's not the same kind of work."

"What's different?"

"A lot of things. Pride and joy, mainly."

"Oh," I said, not understanding. Then I put my mother's words in my pocket to save for later, along with the mica, marbles, Canadian nickels, and other shiny things I kept there.

✳

During the week of Columbus Day I came home with a popsicle-stick ship, colored green and midnight-blue, thinking nothing

186

could be more wonderful, when to my delight the collie from across the road greeted me at the door. I was speechless. My sister was squealing and hopping, and my marvelous ship went almost unnoticed in the great excitement of a new animal in the house.

"We got him dog biscuits, look!" my sister shouted, dragging a box from the counter next to the stove.

The collie, who seemed enormous in our tiny kitchen, pranced on his delicate snowy paws, his ears fluffed forward, a friendly groan at the back of his throat.

"No, he's had enough now," my mother said. "You can't just stuff them like that. Animals don't know what's best for them; they expect *us* to know."

The collie was an impressive creature, moist deep eyes that seemed a mix of brown and gold, a sweet thin face, a fine sheen of fur that covered him in waves of dark auburn. He sat primly on the floor at my mother's feet, leaning against her legs.

"Oh, Mum!" was all I could say, my arms hugging the splendor of my green-and-blue ship, the snap of winter already wafting through our drafty windows, and a wondrous beautiful dog a guest in our house.

✳

The cats were wary at first but soon became as nonchalant with the collie as they were with each other, and the collie was waiting for me with my mother and sister most days when I came home from school. We called him "Brother." The man worked from early morning until after our suppertime, so my mother untied Brother from the porch rail just after she saw me off to school, and returned him before my father got home. Our house was small but Brother seemed to enjoy the space, trailing my mother from room to room, allowing my sister and me to dress him in hats and scarves, rolling on his back for us to stroke his belly.

Soon after Thanksgiving, winter began in earnest. Our house, with its many drafts and weak spots, began the hissing and creaking it expressed only in winter. Boots and snow pants and flannel nightgowns were taken up from the basement, and my father abandoned the blue chair to huddle with us under the afghan on the living-room couch. Winter was the best season.

The man across the road moved Brother from the porch to the open garage. At the end of a long rope Brother lay on the concrete floor, lifting his head at the least sign of activity at our house. The man came and went, apparently intent only on his job at the mill, managing the very section in which my father worked.

Brother's new cell posed a dilemma for my mother. Though she had talked herself into the propriety of untying a dog from a stranger's porch rail, once it involved entering the garage it became trespassing. My mother tried several times to convince the man to let us take Brother for a walk, but the man was large and brusque and rigid and always said no. My mother was shy and tiny; she would turn without a word and herd us back home. But as my father got sicker and Christmas got closer she took on a boldness with the man across the street that surprised us.

"My dog is well cared for, Ma'am," the man said on one of these occasions as my sister and I ran our mittens over Brother's shiny pelt.

"'Care' is an interesting word," my mother said, drawing her coat closer around her. It was a cold day after a hard snow and the wind was blowing the top layer like fine sand in our faces. "We feed our cats, don't we, girls? We feed Brownie and Joe."

"Yuh, we do," my sister and I said, assuming my mother's new air of authority. She had a trump card someplace; the suspense was exquisite.

"We brush their coats. We sing to them, don't we? We let them sleep where it's warm."

"Does this have a point?" the man said. He looked miserably cold.

"Yes," my mother said. "As much as we do for *our* pets, a dog is a different story altogether. A dog needs affection more than food. A dog doesn't have the intelligence of a cat or the independence of a bird." She turned to Brother, who had fixed on her an adoring expression, his tongue hanging out as if it were melting. "A dog like this will die without affection. This dog is dying, sir."

My sister and I stood with our mouths open, gazing with Brother at my mother's bright-eyed, unflinching face. The man was too mean-spirited and small to understand that he was in the presence of a woman with special powers.

"Thank you very much, Ma'am. Now I have work to do, and you have a zoo to tend to."

He turned his back and left us staring at the messy spot where he'd stood in the fresh snow.

"I don't think he liked it that dogs are dumber than cats," my sister said when we were back in our own yard. We were careful not to look back at Brother, who was undoubtedly sitting at the door of the bare garage with his nose quivering.

"I don't know why people like that keep dogs in the first place," my mother said.

"It's for a watchdog," my sister said knowingly.

"A watchdog?" My mother laughed. "He doesn't even bark. He lets strangers untie him. Oh, that pathetic man. He just said that to scare you."

"I'm not scared of Brother," I said.

"Of course not," my mother said. "We don't *fear* animals, do we? We *respect* them."

❆

By Christmas week the rabbit had turned white and the boundaries of his pen had disappeared under the snow and he had not run away. We renamed him Whitey and made a bed of sticks and hay in the garage and he came to the door for food at night from wherever he had spent the day. We trimmed the tree, adding an ornament for the rabbit and Gray Tabby and one for Brother, whom we had not laid our hands on for several weeks. On Christmas Eve we went to Mass and had dinner at my aunt's and walked home together in the silent blue snow. Our one streetlight showed us Brother's silhouette as we passed the open garage set back from the road. "Merry Christmas, Brother," my sister said, her voice barely carrying across Brother's yard. The dog stayed still, but in his darkened outline we could see he'd heard, and we in turn heard his wish for my mother to come and untie him again.

At home we lit candles and said our Christmas prayers and, except for my father, ate sinful portions of plum pudding with hard sauce. We sang "The Friendly Beasts," the carol about the animals in the Nativity, and my mother made up a verse for Brother and wished for our neighbor to learn about the dignity of God's lesser creatures.

There was a sadness about this Christmas Eve, even as we opened our presents and passed each one among us with careful fingers. As was our tradition, all the animals got a present: catnip for the cats, a seed-bell for Joe, and we left extra carrots in the garage for the rabbit, who wouldn't come inside. My sister and I sang more carols, the cats lolled in clouds of catnip, and my mother started to cry. My father, who had known all along about Brother's clandestine visits, stood up and said: "All right."

"Yaaaay!" my sister and I yelled as he went to get his coat.

We pressed ourselves against the glass of the living-room window and watched my father trudge across the road to free Brother. It was snowing again; in the dimness of the streetlight we saw the dark imprints of my father's boots trailing his form as he neared the other house.

"Is the man home?" my sister asked, pushing me out of the way for a better look.

"I don't think so," my mother said. She rubbed the steam of our rapid breaths from the window. "He's probably having Christmas Eve with one of the other managers."

"I don't see any lights," I murmured. My father's progress was very slow.

"We didn't get Brother a present!" my sister shouted, turning from the window with a stricken look.

"Come on," my mother said. "You can each wrap a biscuit for him."

We were waiting in the back hall with the wrapped biscuits when Brother appeared. He charged through the door and darted in circles around the kitchen, whining and yipping.

"He's happy," my sister said, her face shining. We showed him the biscuits and caressed his cool fur but he would not stop yipping and darting.

"Where's Dad?" my mother asked the dog. There was a sudden cold change. Everything stopped.

"Stay here," she told us, turning without a coat to the back porch. We heard her soft steps and a sudden horrid cry.

I have forgotten much, but this I remember: my sister and I in our nightgowns and bare feet in the blowing snow, Brother's pink tongue licking my father's face, my mother's heaving body thrown over my father where he lay on his back in our blue-white yard, his arms swept back as though he had been out there making angels. And I remember this: like the friendly beasts of our favorite carol, the cats came, drawn by my mother's grief. They appeared at the open door and scattered themselves around her, staring like owls as the lights of a large car swept across us and then into the driveway across the road.

His steps were swift and he had not bothered to shut off his headlights. His shadow came over us in the shimmering dark as he lifted my mother from my father's body and carried my father into the house. He laid my father on the couch and covered him with the afghan and picked up the phone. As he spoke into the receiver his eyes roved over the room, coming to rest on my sister and me in our damp nightgowns, each still holding a dog biscuit tied with a red ribbon.

My mother pressed her reddened fingers into the color-drained flesh of my father's cheek. Her gulping breaths escaped into the room as if by accident, and for the first time I knew there were no miracles, that what you wished for had nothing to do with what you got.

❊

In the end, after the colored lights were put down and the rest of the pudding eaten by relatives we didn't know and the tree stripped and thrown and my father laid in the vault at the cemetery, the man across the road gave us his dog. My mother accepted this as a miracle, as if the gift of Brother would have been bestowed upon us no matter what, as if it had nothing to do with the man's presence at my father's dying. The gift of Brother was a miracle, because on that sixth day after the most terrible Christmas she needed one.

"Thank you," my mother said to the man. "You have no idea."

Her eyes held the man in a powerful grip, but her grief was heavy and she did not stand. She sat in my father's chair, my sister and I standing at either side of her, one of the cats dozing in her lap. Brother curled himself up at her feet when the man released him.

The man did not seem to know what to do. He was big and tall like my father but could not fill a room the way my father had. His expression kept changing. Even then I recognized his discomfort, his struggle for clarity.

"What will you do?" he asked, finally.

My mother looked at him as though he had asked something rhetorical. "I'll love my children and care for my animals and remember my husband." She extended her hand to him and smiled, her first in many days. "You've been kind."

The man made his way out of our kitchen to the back door. Brother raised his head, understood, and stayed.

Not everyone believes that wild birds came to my mother's hands, that each cat recognized its own song, that the animals never stalked each other or fought among themselves. They say that my sister and I remember from a child's view, that we were in love with my mother and therefore everything seemed magnified, truer than it really was. They are both dead now, my mother and father, and except for my sister I am the only one to say that the stories are true. And I tell you this: the cats and birds and rabbits and dogs that my sister and I have divided between us are extraordinary animals; people comment on their beauty and intelligence and capacity for affection. These are my mother's animals, and my sister and I love them, and there are still times when I believe we learn to be kind through our care of them, just as my mother wished it.

A State of Mind

❄

Fog-Talk

Walking the heaved cement sidewalk down Main Street,
I end up where the town bottoms out: a parking lot
thick with sea-fog. There's Wister, my boyhood friend,

parked on the passenger side of his old Dodge pick-up.
He's waiting for Lucia, the girl who drives him around
and feeds him, the one who takes care of him at home.

Wister got married late. Wifeless now, no kids, he's near
sixty-eight. Like me. Watching the ebb, looking out into
the fog. Fog so thick that if you got shingling your roof

you'd shingle three or four courses out onto
the fog before you fell off or sun came. Wister knows
that old joke. Not much else, not any more. His mind drifts

every whichway. When I start over to his old pick-up,
he waves to my wave coming toward him, his window half up,
half down. He forgets how to work it. I put my head

up close. *Wister,* I say, *you got your compass with you
to steer her home through the fog?* Wister smiles at me with
all sorts of joy, nodding yes. He says *I don't know.*

On the Island

On the first Sunday in September there was a storm, and the following morning the carcass of a seal washed up on the short, sandy beach below Minot Point. When the Kennett boys found it—and ran back to the house telling about it—it was shapeless and bloated, a pale, puffed-up sac of poisons rolling and tumbling in the yellow water. Someone had shot it; a small hole, clean and bloodless, showed above its tiny, glazed eyes. It had been dead for a week, said one of the boys. No, said the other, older boy, only three or four days; there was no stench of decay to drive you back from the beach.

By midmorning all of Pine Cove had been told. Some of the men and most of the children came down to the water's edge and stood in a ragged half-circle around the swollen flesh—not mourning, any of them, but still and respectful. A few gulls, black against the sun but silver circling away, called nervously over the heads of the people as over a picnic.

Long before dusk only the children remained on the beach, and most of them were boys. They squatted on the sand and sat on the black rocks and made a chorus with the rising and falling water. As the seal rolled up the beach, their voices pitched upward in unison; as it lolled back, their voices trailed downward. Over and over they sang the senseless dirge; it was like slow wind in the sparse pines that stood above the point. Old lobstermen who had long ago given up hauling traps heard the treble chant, and they shuddered without knowing why.

Lyle Kennett heard it and lifted his hands to his ears to shut out the sound. It was a slow movement of some delicacy, for he was an old main in pain who passed the long afternoons in motionless remembering, seated on an open porch overlooking the sea. What remained of his world lay eastward; it included the narrow channel of green water separating the mainland from Needle Island, the island itself with its overgrowth of hightopped pines and evergreen scrub, and, in transparent weather, the remote low shadow of Monhegan beyond the southern and most slender tip of the Needle.

Often Lyle noticed activity on the island, for several years earlier a man from a city had built a small brick cottage on the weather side where the strip of ledge and sand was broadest. The cottage was half-hidden, but in the evening stubs of short firs stood out in silhouette against lighted windows. When the breeze was onshore Lyle heard the closing of doors and, rarely, the murmur of voices. The builder's eldest son spent vacation summers on the island. Lyle had never seen him; he knew only that the young man owned a rifle, for day after day the noise of sharp firing reached him across the channel. It was the gravest and loudest of all interruptions, and was by itself the reason that Lyle had asked no more than the first question when Martha, his son's wife, came out of the kitchen after putting away the noon dishes.

"What's that devilish whining?" he had said, lowering his thin hands to his lap.

"The children," she answered. "There's a seal dead, down on the beach."

"I should go down there," he said.

Lyle had never heard such a sound. Now, trying to think above the voices of the children, he could not have said how many days had passed since he last saw seals on the gray layers of rock at the end of the Needle and in the dark water at the channel's mouth, but he knew he had missed them in the way men miss all easy pleasures. There were many seals in the cove—Lyle had seen nine and ten at once—and their antics were the single delight of his inactive days. They wriggled ponderously over the rocks, rolling and toppling one another into the sea; once in the water they vanished beneath the choppy surface, then reappeared a hundred feet away, their slick snouts and gray heads bobbing foolishly into the light.

When he was much younger and taking a charter fishing party out of Pine Cove, Lyle thought he had seen a rare white seal sun-ning itself on a ledge; the next day he saw it again, but when he steered close to shore he discovered only the outline of a seal made with whitewash on an upright face of rock. The matter-of-fact seals in the cove provoked that memory; he told stories about the white seal, but he had never told the truth. All his life the fact had seemed less important than the wonderful pretense.

Abruptly, the unison voices stopped. A few minutes later the children—Lyle's two grandsons among them—appeared on the ridge overlooking the beach. They turned away from the Kennett house and ran laughing, under shadow, in the grove of pines. When he could no longer see them, Lyle stood up and shuffled unsteadily across the porch. As he started fumbling along the pipe-iron railing beside the steps, Martha came to the door.

"Where are you going now?"

"Down to see for myself," he said.

"Supper's in a half-hour," she said, "and be careful climbing down that hill."

He reached the foot of the steps and began walking deliberately toward the ridge. Without looking around he was aware of Martha watching him with embarrassing concern, and he made an impatient, backward gesture with his hand. He was pleased to hear the screen door of the kitchen swing shut.

Lyle went stiffly down the narrow footpath toward the sea, where left and right beside the path were small white wildflowers trampled under the dry stalks of grass by children's feet. The dirt path wound through the grass, around and among gray rocks sparkling pink with mica in the rays of the late sun. At intervals its course was broken by ledges of roots and pebbles, and at these interruptions the old man stepped slowly, reaching to the earth for support, so that his journey was like that of a man descending a rotten staircase. In time the path gave way to a waste of black scrub and flat black stones swept smooth by tides; here Lyle stopped for a moment resting with his hands on his hips, at the head of the beach.

The dead hulk of the seal lay echoing with the throb of the water; the dark sand was wet and clean around it. Approaching the carcass, Lyle knew what had driven the children away. Tired of the game of their voices, they had gathered stones and sticks from the beach and hillside, and then, circling the seal like dancers, they had pelted it with the stones and poked at it with the sticks. Out of a score of gashes and tears had burst the stench and corrupt matter of decay, repelling the celebrants in a scurry of astonished cries. They would not come back. Some of the stones were still embedded in the dead creature's flesh; nearby, two or three short driftwood sticks turned in the shallow water.

The stench was powerful; it caught in Lyle's throat and woke a sharp agony below his chest. He stepped back and away. Then he moved across the beach and stood, looking at the seal, with his hands in the pockets of his overalls. He thought it was like standing over an open grave.

The sun by now was behind the grove of pines on the hill, and the shade was cold on the back of Lyle's neck. As he turned, intending to climb back up the path to the house, he saw two men coming down the slope toward him.

"What you doing, Lyle? Saying a prayer on the poor bugger?"

Squinting, he recognized Chris Simpson, a near neighbor and one of the cove's councilmen. The man following wore a uniform; Lyle did not know him.

"She's starting to stink," Lyle said. "The kids poked holes in her hide."

Simpson walked past him, halted, and came back holding his nose. "Makes a man want to puke," he said. "This is Daniels, warden over from Damariscotta. Lyle Kennett."

Lyle shook hands. The game warden was a young man, his face smooth and tanned, and he wore his uniform stiffly.

"Somebody shot her," Lyle said.

"I don't suppose there's any way to find out who it was," Daniels mused. "You people swim off this beach?"

"Kids do, some," Simpson told him. "We ought to get rid of this thing soon as we can."

"Won't be no more seals in the cove till we do," Lyle said. He watched the young man closely. "Might be they'll never come back at all."

Daniels was studying the dead seal, scratching his nose. Simpson scuffed his feet in the sand as if he were impatient. Finally the young warden coughed and made a clucking noise with his tongue.

"I don't suppose there's much chance it'd burn," he said, "all waterlogged like it is."

"We could bury it," Simpson suggested.

"She don't belong ashore," Lyle said. "I could take her out to sea."

"You let the State of Maine worry about disposing of this mess," Daniels said briskly. "That's not a bad idea, though," he added. "You got a boat?"

"I got one," Simpson said, "with a good little five-horse outboard. Wouldn't take me ten minutes to fetch her around."

"Of course I got a boat," Lyle said peevishly.

"You go get yours," the game warden told Simpson. "Bring some rope and we'll clean off this beach before dark."

"You bet," Simpson said. "Won't take me ten minutes."

Lyle watched the man scramble up the embankment to the road. Left alone with Daniels, he felt more strongly a personal irritation at the young man's way.

"What do you figure on doing?" he asked.

"Tow it out and cut it loose," Daniels said. "Simple as that."

"She'll come back."

"Not if we tow it far enough."

"How far?"

"Three, maybe four miles out."

Lyle shook his head. "She'll come back on the next tide, or the next one after that."

"We'll wait and see," said the young man.

When Simpson arrived with his boat, a shiny aluminum skiff powered by a new outboard, the two men had been standing silently for a quarter of an hour. Lyle stood back from the shore and watched them go about their work, the warden tying a wet handkerchief over his nose and mouth before he waded into the water to wind several lengths of line around the bloated seal. Daniels was scrupulously careful not to touch the creature more than he had to in binding it, and he took pains to carry easy extra loops around the seal's useless flippers. When he had finished, he secured one end of the line in a slipknot and threw the other end into the boat. During this performance Simpson knelt in the beached skiff, holding tightly to the sides and looking off in the direction of the ocean horizon. As he made the line fast to a seat, his lips were compressed and colorless.

At last they were ready. Daniels pushed the skiff into deeper water and vaulted aboard. Simpson lowered the screw of the outboard and yanked life into it. Then the skiff edged away from the shore, Simpson steering, Daniels holding out the rope to keep it from fouling. The rope tightened; the great dead beast slid noiselessly into the small surf and followed the silver skiff away from the beach.

For nearly twenty minutes Lyle traced the progress of Simpson's boat, seeing Daniels remove the handkerchief and drop it over the side, Simpson move his head as though he were talking at last. Once they had cleared the tip of Needle Island they held to a southeasterly course. Before long Lyle could not see the men, only the metal boat shining on the sea and the dun-colored seal bobbing behind it in the choppy water. The tide was running toward the full, and when Lyle looked down at his feet the dark traces of the seal's track had been softened by the waves and nearly obliterated.

When he returned to the house, Martha had put supper on the table. He sat at his place—the eldest grandson to the left of him, the youngest at the right—bowing his head not for grace but to recover his breath after the climb from the beach. When he looked up he met the questioning of his son's eyes from across the table. Lyle managed a gray smile.

"Frank," he said faintly, "the old man's a little winded."

"You quit running up and down that hill," Frank said. "That's plain foolish at your age."

"He went down to look at that poor seal," Martha said. She set bowls of chowder around the table and sat down beside her husband. "Isn't anybody going to do anything about it? It's going to start smelling up the whole cove."

"Chris and some game warden dragged her off," Lyle said. "They think that's the end of it."

"Oh, sure it is," said Frank. "It'll go straight to the bottom."

"They never bothered to weigh her down."

Frank showed surprise, the spoon halted for an instant before his opened mouth. He finished the motion and swallowed. "That's a dumb thing," he said. "They could have got an old anchor down at the landing."

"They didn't," Lyle said. "She'll come back with the tides."

"Who shot it, Gramps?" asked the oldest boy.

"I don't know."

Frank coughed contemptuously. "The hell you don't."

"Frank."

He glanced from his wife to his two sons and went on:

"I didn't tell you what happened this morning. Lou Keeley and me took his boat out past the Needle just before noon, and you know what I fished out of the water near that red channel buoy? A big cormorant with his silly head shot half off."

Martha put both hands to her face. "Oh, my," she said.

"You know how they perch on top of the marker," Frank said. "The kid must have picked it off for the fun of it."

"No sense to it," Lyle agreed.

"He's wild, and that's not the first dead thing I've seen floating in the channel. Gulls, lots of times. The seal's the biggest thing he's killed yet. One of these days he'll get himself a man, and then the cove'll wake up."

"He wouldn't ever shoot a man, would he?" said the youngest boy.

Frank shrugged. "It wouldn't surprise me."

"You've seen him?" Lyle asked.

"He hangs around the landing, nights. Always wears a black sweatshirt with a hood on it—name of some college on his chest. He never talks, and I never heard anybody talk to him."

"Queer," said Martha.

"He's got that power boat of his father's," said Frank. "That big mahogany-looking thirty-footer."

"I've never noticed it," Lyle said.

"He never goes near it, that's why. You'd think he'd spend his time fishing from it if he's so damned bored on the island. He could run out ten or fifteen miles past Monhegan and drift all day. There's fish out there, too."

Frank wiped his mouth with his palm and pushed his chair back from the table. As he stood up, he gave his wife a hard slap on the rump. "Good chowder," he said.

Lyle went on eating in silence; he found the chowder tasteless. "I think I'll go to bed early," he said, getting up from the table.

"Sleep late tomorrow," Martha said. The embarrassing concern was still in her voice. "You look peaked."

"Good night," he said.

Inside his room at the top of the back stairs, Lyle undressed slowly and got into bed without turning on the lamp. Some little of the diminishing daylight still discovered the objects around him. At the foot of his narrow bed was the antique cupboard where maps were stored; along one wall stood the high chifforobe, and on it a pewter pitcher and metal washbasin; under the window by the bed was the black captain's chair with its burden of clothing. There was little else to be seen. Hidden beneath the bed was the heavy porcelain vessel which Lyle used at night, and which Martha emptied—grumbling—in the morning. The bedroom was small and personal, secure and private.

Lyle did not immediately close his eyes, nor had he intended to when he left the kitchen. He could not remember how many months had gone by since he had last known a genuine desire for sleep. Even when he was most tired—and he realized as he lay looking about the darkening room that he had never before in his life been so exhausted—sleep no longer attracted him. Each night was a conflict not resolved; he feared that he might not again open his eyes to see day and then—after he had chided himself for an old man's fool cowardice—the assurance that he would indeed awaken to many more mornings yet unthought about struck with a special terror.

This evening, he found himself thinking about the nameless young man on the island, and he sought aimlessly after reasons for the actions of youth. He discovered none, not knowing if there were no reasons, or if they were only remote from his weak scrutiny. Lyle could no more comprehend the killing of poor sea creatures than he could understand his own struggles with sleep.

He lay still, hearing the sea below his window, the light breeze rustling through the curtains, the faraway clatter of supper dishes downstairs. All in a moment, he thought of tomorrow, of the seal coming back, and a feeling of elation seized him that put all panic and dullness from his mind. The final passing of twilight from his tiny room he did not notice. He was suddenly light-headed, and he slipped at once through giddiness into the drowsy beginnings of a dream.

He did not wake until shortly past noon. Then, he dressed himself in the clothes he had taken off the night before; downstairs, he poured and swallowed with a bitter face a cup of black coffee from the pot at the back of the kitchen stove, and went out to look at his half-world of water and horizon. The elation had not left him, but it was only in the clarity of day seen from the small porch that he sensed its vast influence.

What he saw, he had never seen. His eyes played incredible tricks with colors of the familiar: the calm channel was chalk-orange, the sea outside the cove a broad, swelling meadow of dull gold; the scrub fir and thin pines of the Needle had turned to hollow red as if they were the valleys and peaks of fire caught in one instant of burning, and the sky took up the strange hues of the earth in a pale wash of pink the color of turning petals. Far off, the tiny fin of a sail glided black over the copper waves, and the small cottage on the island appeared in an angular disguise of innocent blue.

Lyle faltered and stumbled to his chair. He was dizzy and disturbed. None of what he now saw stood still, but shimmered and warped as if he were perceiving this grotesque world from the near side of a wall of immense heat. Objects grew and wasted, in and out of focus, each in its turn as a disconnected image. When he closed his eyes, the brightness of his lids was dazzling; his ears rang with a shrill whine he could not identify. "I'm daft," he thought. He uttered the word "daft" louder than he had intended, and the echo of it came back from the barrier of the island as a high, unintelligible syllable. Then the hallucination passed as suddenly as it had seized him, and he sat overlooking his ordinary view, enervated, and cold with sweating.

All afternoon he waited for someone to come and tell him about the seal. He dared not purposely think of its returning; yet his mind accepted thoughts of nothing else. Anticipation haunted him, and hope hovered impatiently in the bright day that floated away on slow currents of light. When the sun had set, and the first gray mists blurred the horizon line, Lyle closed his eyes and clasped his hands into a figure of resignation. When he opened his eyes,

the youngest boy was standing at the foot of the porch steps, look-
ing up at him.

"It came back," the boy said.

Lyle parted his hands and smiled at the boy. "Where?" he asked.

"In just the same place as before—the way you said."

"You run along," said Lyle. He raised himself from the chair.
"Just run along."

"What are you going to do?"

"Take a little walk," said Lyle. "A little look-see."

The boy backed away. "It's all covered over with ropes," he said,
and ran up the path out of sight.

Walking as quickly as he was able, Lyle went to the ridge and
peered down toward the beach. The seal, still ropebound, was a
dark shadow in the twilit water close to shore; where the incoming
tide encircled it, a triangle of dry sand pointed away from it to the
higher land. As Lyle watched, Chris Simpson came up beside him.
The two men stood quietly, Simpson chewing on a cold pipe and
shuffling his feet.

"Won't Daniels raise Cain," Simpson said at last.

"I told him," said Lyle. "He ought to've listened."

"When he gets back from Damariscotta, he'll have to start all
over again." Simpson snickered. "I guess this time I'll rent him
my boat."

"No need. I'll take care of her."

"What for?"

"I should've done it in the first place."

Simpson hesitated. "You ought at least to get his permission."

"Then he'd best give me it right now," Lyle said. "I'm going
to take her off tonight."

"I told you: Daniels is in Damariscotta. He won't be back till
morning."

"I can't wait."

"Then I'm damned if I know what to say to you." Simpson
whacked the bowl of the pipe against his heel. He tucked the pipe-
stem into the corner of his mouth and scowled at Lyle. "You're a
stubborn so-and-so," he said; the words whistled between his
clenched teeth.

"I know how much stink I can stand," Lyle said, "and how much I can't."

Simpson gave the problem long consideration. "I won't stop you," he said finally. "I won't lift a finger to help you, neither, but I won't hinder you." He began walking away.

"I don't know if I can do it alone," Lyle said after him.

"That's your lookout," Simpson answered.

Lyle saw him go, then retraced his steps to the house. The kitchen was lighted, and the family seated around the table. Martha studied him as he entered, her gaze sharp and—he thought—more troubled than ever.

"Don't wash up," she said. "Your food's already cold."

"I'm not hungry," Lyle told her, "so I think I'll go upstairs."

"You didn't eat a thing all day," she said, her eyes still piercing him. "I left your lunch in the icebox, and you never even touched it."

"What's the matter?" asked Frank.

"I'll sit and talk," Lyle said, "but I'm not hungry." He took his place at the table and grinned foolishly at Frank. "The seal came back," he said.

Frank shook his head. "I'd like to know what's so interesting about that damned seal."

Lyle searched for a safe answer. "It gives a man something to think about."

"Waste of time," said Frank with his mouth full. He swallowed. "You know what that crazy kid did today?—early this morning, I guess. Went and shot up Lou's lobster buoys, those quart ale bottles he uses. How's that for a joke?"

"Poor Lou," Martha said.

"Poor Frank," Frank said. "I told him I'd help him drag for his traps tomorrow forenoon, and that's my time wasted. I'd like to tangle with that dumb sharpshooter, I'll tell you."

"That's not a good idea for you," Lyle said.

"It'd be a pleasure." Frank stopped, his knife suspended over his plate. "I'll have to put off driving you in to Doc Corbett's till day after tomorrow. I promised Lou."

"That's all right."

"You feel okay?"

"Pretty good," said Lyle, "today."

"But take it easy, will you?"

"I don't do a thing but sit," Lyle said.

"That's all you need to do," said Frank.

Lyle stood up. "You finish," he said. "I'll go upstairs and get some rest." He halted in the doorway and turned to Martha. "Wait breakfast tomorrow; I think I'll start getting up early again."

In his room, Lyle sat heavily on the edge of the bed and awaited the passage of time. He expected Martha to climb the stairs and insist that he drink some broth or a glass of milk, but she remained below. He considered getting out his maps and charts and spreading them across the bed to look up the familiar names of islands and reefs; he even thought about switching on the light and sewing a button he had lost from the cuff of his shirt. He did neither, but listened to the voices beneath his room as he waited in darkness. So much seemed now unimportant that he could not regret doing nothing. Changing his clothes, eating lunch, explaining to Chris Simpson and Frank his feeling for the seal—all were submerged in the same strange joy which the youngest boy had revived with the words: "It came back."

He sat in the dark for hours. It was not until he was sure that Martha and Frank were in bed asleep that he descended the back stairs, carefully, groping down the length of the slender railing with both his hands. He went across the kitchen, out the porch door, and into the cool night with its minor conflict of waves and crickets. The moon was rising, and barely lit his way to the narrow dock below the house.

His boat—an old, weathered dory that cast a bulky shadow on the water—was moored at the end of the dock. It swung sedately with the channel currents, its high bow bumping against the wharf edge, and Lyle made three trips to it from the land end of the dock. He put aboard the oars, then a dirty coil of rope. Finally, from under the dock, he dragged out two rust-covered pieces of ballast lead; he guessed their combined weight at something over a hundred pounds, and he lowered them with awkward slowness into the dory. This done, Lyle took a last look around him, as though he were cataloguing not only the contents of the boat, but all the objects and sounds of the cove; then he stepped aboard, cast off, and began rowing the few hundred feet to the beach where the seal lay.

It was midnight when Lyle reached the inlet. The moon was hidden by cloud, but a weak, phosphor glow rose from the muted sea and cast pale blue reflections all around him. The edge of the narrow beach was brilliant where the small waves burst and slid shell-shapes of light over the level shelf of sand. Above the shore, the hill and the shabby grove of pines were dim pretensions to reality. No sound reached him here but the slap of his oars and the restless noise of the ocean.

Close to land, when he felt the keel crunch across pebbles, Lyle shipped the oars and squirmed out of the boat into shallow water. Calf-deep in the sea, he pulled the dory as far up on the beach as he could manage. The action winded him, and he paused for several minutes, leaning against the boat to rest.

The outline of the rotting seal was vivid at the water's edge, a few yards to his left. No one had moved it; with the nudge of every wave it glimmered in the false light like an absurd gelatin. It appeared larger now than Lyle had remembered, but he began. He began by undoing what Daniels had done, throwing off the loose cords which crossed and recrossed the seal's bulk, until he had laid the creature bare and ready for his own rope. He knelt and pushed the first strand of his line under the seal, drawing out his arm wet with sand and decay.

Sweating, trembling, choking on the foul air of another world, Lyle worked for an hour to prepare the soft carcass for burial. The labor of it sickened him and insulted his senses; his muscles shuddered with wave upon wave of nausea; his lungs burned from the friction of each false breathing movement; his eyelids turned raw and stung with tears. Everywhere, his fingers operated stiffly over wet layers of flesh that ruptured and peeled at a touch; the feel of the cold skin was like the backwater slime, running and soft, of stagnant sea-grasses. When he was forced to stop and turn his back, desperate for a clean breath, Lyle heard behind him—or was it imagination?—the ghostly sigh of the seal endlessly dying; it was a sound like thousands of tiny mouths of foam opening out of the tide with a continuous hiss that had nothing to do with mortality. Once, he spun around with an angry curse to provoke the huge creature into a single last living movement, but no part of the beast responded: when Lyle fell off balance his hand plunged to the wrist in a swamp of dead matter, and when he tightened the last length of rope into a knot below the seal's small head, the cord cut down through flesh until it drew tight around invisible bone.

Lyle had not imagined the weight of the carcass, and the effort of half-carrying, half-dragging it to the dory and tumbling it into the stern was excessive for him. His hands and arms trembled from cold and fatigue; his clothes—the front of his shirt and over-alls and the tops of his shoes—were stained from contact with the seal. By now, his senses were caught at a pitch of sensitivity amounting to numbness.

Numbed, too, were his perceptions of time and space, with the result that from the time he pushed off from the beach and hauled himself into the dory, all the minutes of the early morning crowded close against one another in his mind, and all distance seemed none. He rowed for hours without knowing how long or how far, his back bowing and coming erect in the rhythm of his work, his feet buried and wet in the corpse before him. He only guessed when he was beyond the onshore currents, in water deep enough for his purpose. Then he put aside the oars to let his boat drift on the pale sea; he attached weights to ropes with careful knots, and plucked at the wound cords with testing fingers which reassured him.

Near daylight, Lyle wrestled the lead and the burden of the seal over the side of the dory. He saw the carcass sink, carried down by the stubborn weights, leaving a surface trail of yellow, hissing foam and fat bubbles of putrid air. For a few moments he knelt resting in the bottom of the boat, drawing in deep breaths. He did not watch the last traces of the animal disappear on the water; it could not even be said that he felt satisfaction with what he had done. When he was rested, he gripped the oars and rowed shoreward.

The dawn was a memorable red, that sort of vivid announce-ment of day which is like a burst of blood over the horizon, nothing about it faint or timid. It was a glorious warning of heat and a merciless sun. It turned the eastern sea scarlet, and Monhegan Is-land stood out of the water to the northeast, looking the color of rust. Lyle kept the sunrise before him as he rowed, his back to the land, thinking of nothing. The small crests of the ocean slapped against the boat; the trailing path of slick water spun itself into filaments of green and white froth; the tiny black whirlpools from the oar blades were swept by the hundreds out of sight in the tide. Lyle rowed mechanically, feeling the sharp pain of his unusual labor in the muscles of his shoulders and belly.

He had reached the southern tip of Needle Island, only two hundred yards from the mainland, when he heard one rifle shot, and then another. Startled, he shipped the oars and drifted closer. At the sound of the shots, a colony of gulls had cried up from the dark rocks, looking like streaks of spray in the sunlight. Their bright wings carried them upward in protesting spirals, in and out of shadow; their clamor as they circled above the dory was like children's voices.

When the side of the boat bumped on the rocky shore of the Needle, Lyle stepped over to dry land, leaving the dory to bob unmoored behind him, knowing that it would drift away into the slow currents of the channel. Before him was a barrier of scrub pine and yellow brush, and behind that wall—in one instant singled out from all the rest—he heard the four-syllabled sound of a rifle bolt opened and closed. Wearily, he started toward it, his face hot with the dawn and his eyes dazzled by the low, red sun. What now moved his aching legs was little more than the same durable elation which had sustained him through his first thirty-six hours of death.

WILLIAM CARPENTER

Man Climbing Katahdin

After a final quarrel with his wife, after
they'd agreed it was all over, a man drove up
to Maine, to climb Katahdin. On the way, Haydn
was playing on the radio, but it seemed violent,
like a Prussian army marching upon his home
and taking his wife prisoner. He thought of her
in leg irons with a plate of lobster salad
just out of reach. He thought of her walking
towards it, reaching the end of her chain,
then falling back. He envied his friend Morris,
who lived with a student majoring in Health.
They spent Sundays in bed reading the *New York
Times,* and Morris had told him that her breasts
hid under the newspaper like turtles, so that
the man thought about turtles as he started
up Katahdin. It felt as if his own body wore
a thick shell, making him climb slowly, making
him stop often to read the *Katahdin Guide.*
In 1843, it said, Henry Thoreau took the same
route up this mountain. As the man thought of
Thoreau, his shell seemed to burn off, and he
felt larger, he felt almost the same size
as Thoreau, and he imagined that Thoreau
gave him a hand at a place on the Knife Edge
where the snow was waist deep even in June, so
he could reach the summit and rest and look out
over the wilderness and the blue river snaking
to the sea. He wanted to say something to his
wife, he wanted to tell her that he'd climbed

the mountain with Thoreau, and from that height
the world looked different, it made sense, the way
music makes sense of feeling, or a book can make
sense of a human life. He wanted his wife to
be there on the summit, he wanted to show her
the alpine flowers, the log huts thousands
of feet below. He wanted to show her his hands,
how they were cut from the sharp granite, how
beneath the cuts there were the engraved lines
of the palms, like rivers, how some of these lines
were his—his wealth, his death—but one was hers,
and it would be easier to cut off his left hand
with his survival knife and leave it on
the Appalachian Trail than to erase that line.
He wanted to buy something at the campers' store,
even something stupid, like a shovel, and show up
in the middle of the night, holding the shovel
as a sign of peace, and say *this is a shovel,*
this is from Thoreau, so she would have to take it,
she'd have to let him in and give him coffee while
he told his story. She'd have to believe him, since
you have to believe what's there. It's all there is.

Where the Deer Were

It's always hard to form a true picture
of what is happening, isn't it?
difficult to know what's what.

                            For instance,
the moving tenderness of the desiring man,
the gentle vanity of the desired woman,
sliding their bare arms and legs together
in the grass across the stream.

                            It's late summer,
a misty day, but warm.
                        I can't see their faces.
So what is happening, really?
Perhaps they are fighting—very evenly.
Perhaps those sounds are groans of pain.
                              Now the mist
closes my eyes.

                When it lifts once more
I see nothing over there
but a hollow in the long grass
like the places where deer have been lying,
and the only thing I hear
is shallow water making excuses to stone.

PATRICIA O'DONNELL
_____

Unexplained Lights

In October of 1954 Wilhelm Reich, creator of "orgone energy" (the discoverer of orgone energy, Albert would say; the name of what already existed) drove his car three thousand miles, from Maine to Arizona, to cause rain to fall on the desert. Thirty-six years later Albert Moss, twenty-eight-year-old believer in orgones, packed his sleeping bag, one suitcase, and a camping stove into his Volkswagen, and set off on a quest of his own. He didn't know where he was going but he imagined dry dust springing into life, dead trees blooming, water flowing from rocks.

He left behind his job at a social services agency in Boston, and a wife who had already left him. Roberta had moved out in the spring, taking with her their eleven-month-old daughter, Stardust Blue. Albert had chosen the name as a tribute to orgone energy, which makes the sky blue and causes the stars to shimmer. Roberta had thought the name was pretty at the time the baby was born but later grew to dislike it. She had taken to calling the baby Alicia. "When she gets older then she can choose which name she likes herself," Roberta said. Roberta had also said, "You're impossible to live with. You're in some other world, it's like we don't even exist for you. It's not normal," she said, "for a twenty-eight-year-old man to think the way you think." She wanted him to care about the things other people cared about, wanted him to think about backyard barbeques and lawn chairs, savings bonds and college tuition. "Come down to earth," Roberta said. "Grow up," she said. "Wake up and smell the coffee," she said. "I'm leaving you."

The sky was heavy with gray clouds when he set out, but a crack of pale blue showed to the west, near the horizon. As he drove, the clouds moved slowly to the east. When he neared the

Massachusetts border sunshine spotlighted the hills, the sky still dark behind him. Albert rolled down the window and shouted into the wind, singing along with songs on the radio. The End of the Innocence.

In his billfold Albert carried several twenties and a five. In a cardboard box in the trunk were seven crisp hundred dollar bills. He had sold the few pieces of furniture Roberta had left him, and closed his checking account. Roberta had taken a course in how to be a real estate agent, and an agency had taken her on. She was so easily satisfied, he thought. Easily satisfied with everything but him and his impossible longings. He quoted parts of Reich's *The Function of the Orgasm* to Roberta, asked her to read it. "I don't need to," she replied. "I know what an orgasm is for. It's to make me feel good."

Albert drove all day. When the sun was low he stopped at a Howard Johnson's for dinner. He ordered a club sandwich, salad, and milk. The waitress didn't look at him as she took his order. Albert leaned back against the plastic-covered cushion of the booth. The other customers looked dazed, insulated from the people around them. The waitresses and the young man waiting behind the cash register all had the same expressionless faces. They walked without energy or stood motionless, like sticks. The cashier tossed a pencil in his hand. DOR was rampant, Albert thought, and wondered why more people weren't concerned. Deadly orgone radiation, the negative principle in the universe, was draining the vitality from human beings, animals, and plants. Reich had believed that spacemen were spreading DOR. The existence of DOR had become obvious to Albert as he rode the Green Line to work: the drained, ashen faces all around him, the cheeks and shoulders sagging as if pulled by sorrow. Roberta had been impatient: "That's life," she would say. "Besides, people just don't like the T. They never look happy there."

What worried Albert, then and as he sat in the Howard Johnson's, was the weariness that came over him. The sadness and futility of the lives around him seemed to seep into him, infecting him. It was a sort of dry despair he felt, as if he could die tomorrow, and it wouldn't really matter all that much. He leaned his arms on the Formica-covered table as he waited for his sandwich.

Albert drove a few more miles, then took an exit off the interstate. It was dark by now. His car jounced down unpaved roads until he crossed a small bridge. A stream ran below the bridge. He locked the car and slid down a slope, carrying his sleeping bag. He spread it out on a level spot, far enough from the stream to be dry, but close enough to hear the gurgle of water. Pulling a carefully rolled joint out of his wallet, he lit up. The sky was completely clear now. Leaning back on his elbows, he held the smoke within him, looking up. The stars were very bright, pinpoint holes punched through the black. He let the smoke out and breathed in the warm air, the smell of grass and crushed leaves. A light flashed above his head, making its way slowly across the sky.

When Albert reached Iowa he camped in a state park. The night before, cows had come down to drink at the creek near where he lay. He heard the thuds of their hooves on the ground; one had sniffed at his head.

He found an empty space by the river. Only one camper was in sight, a blue pick-up with a white topper. An elderly man and woman sat on lawnchairs, staring at the road. Albert sat on the grass and pulled out a book by Reich. "Contact with nature, with the universe, is achieved in the full genital orgasm and undoubtedly in babies during the oral orgasm." Albert thought of Roberta nursing Stardust. The dark nipple melting into the white skin, the baby's mouth stretching it to one side. Roberta had said he didn't love either her or Stardust, didn't really care.

He put the book down. Lights flickered through trees at the water's edge, on the other side of the river. He guessed he might go into town.

The business district was one short block. Albert's car was the only one driving on the street, although a few were parked diagonally. A kid on a bicycle, arms dangling by his sides as he rode no-hands, passed on the other side of the street. Albert parked in front of the "Sportsman's Lounge." The sign on the front of the building showed a bear raised up on its hind legs, pawing the air. Next to it was the Hatchery. "What's a hatchery?" Albert had asked the man in the lawn chair who gave him directions.

"It's where they keep the hot chicks," the old guy had said, his face unexpectedly creasing in a grin.

Albert took a seat at the bar, and ordered a beer. The bartender was a stocky woman, wearing a pink tee-shirt which read "Super Mom" on the front. When she turned Albert saw that the back read "Four Times Over." Above her head a waterfall churned, a light turning behind the picture giving the illusion of movement.

The music was country rock. At a pool table off to one side a young woman wearing white jeans put down her cue and moved in time to the music, snapping her fingers. A man at the bar laughed. "Go, Janine!"

The people who rode the T, or who sat in bars in Boston, seemed tireder than these people, more folded into themselves. Hopeless. Albert wondered if DOR spared those who worked the earth, who plowed and planted and harvested. He imagined the earth's positive forces getting into their systems along with the dirt under their fingernails.

The girl from the pool table leaned at the bar next to him. "Another beer, Gladys." Albert rested his cheek on his fist and looked at her. She wasn't anything terrific—short hair curled back from her face, wide hips—but her face interested him. She was all there, somehow, not held back or disguised. When she turned to look at him, he held his gaze steady.

"Creatures from outer space draining off our energy?" Janine looked at Albert doubtfully, a hint of a smile around the corners of her mouth.

"Why not?" Albert said. "I mean, it just could be true, couldn't it? No one has ever proved that there aren't creatures from outer space."

Janine turned a beer can slowly between her hands. They were sitting on the fire escape behind the Sportsman's Lounge. Below was an alley with trash containers next to a pickup.

"Well, suppose it were true," Janine said. "There's nothing we could do about it, right?"

"Well, the government could do something." Albert felt a familiar sense of agitation begin, the slight pounding in the chest, the feeling as if something were too large for his brain to hold. "I mean, they'd have to do something, if they only took it seriously. I think the government knows more about these things than they're letting us know."

He felt Janine's long gaze on him. A car went slowly down the street, under the streetlight. "Why worry so much?" she asked softly. "Why not enjoy your life? No one is stopping you from that." She set the empty beer can carefully beside her, and Albert felt his tension leave him in a long, shuddering sigh. Janine leaned against the brick wall of the building, staring up into the sky. "If anything drains off my energy," she said, "it's this town. Nothing ever happens. It's the same as it has always been. I feel like I've been here forever." From a neighboring yard came the rising curve of the locust's cry, reaching a peak then ending abruptly. Albert felt Janine's shoulder, warm against his. She was solid through the thin cotton blouse. He felt like leaning into her, immersing himself in her steady warmth.

In Janine's bedroom they lay naked on top of her bedspread. The bedspread was white, covered with little crocheted bumps. They had entered the apartment through a side door, whispering so the landlady upstairs wouldn't know Albert was there. The bedroom window was open and Albert heard a breeze shaking the leaves outside.

"What's Boston like?" Janine asked.

"Crowded. Dirty. Rude. Much nicer around here, actually." His whispered voice sounded boyish and hoarse.

"I bet it's wonderful." Janine stroked a hand across his chest. "Why did you leave?"

Albert remembered the desert, the dry dust springing to life. The thought embarrassed him. Here there were no deserts, no mountains or valleys; just the steady green farmland, giving and reliable. His own needs seemed impetuous and childish, somehow. "I don't know," he whispered. "I just wanted to get away," but a breeze outside the window swallowed the last of his sentence. In the darkness he was unsettled, as if the edges of himself were no longer clear. As if there were something he needed to do, some words he needed to say or action he needed to take, and he didn't know what it was. Then he felt Janine's hand between his legs, and the definition of his necessity became clearer.

He lowered himself onto Janine's soft weight. They made love slowly. Albert closed his eyes and it seemed, for a moment, as if he were back in the bedroom he shared with Roberta in Boston. It had been dark there, with the shades pulled. The sound of the wind in the trees was a little like the sound of traffic out the window. He knew it was Janine he was with, not Roberta, but he moved more forcefully as if to shake the weight of some giant mistake. He would make it right, he would, he would. Janine moaned softly beneath him.

In the moment of peak intensity he heard a high-pitched calling sound. He raised his head, and opened his eyes. "Stardust?" he asked. In the dark room he was pure hope, pure energy and excitement, about to see his baby's face. "Stardust?" he asked again, and heard his foolish voice in Janine's room.

Janine was giggling in his ear. "Stardust? That's kitty. She wants in."

"Oh." Albert relaxed, resting his weight on her. It was a cat, then. Not his child. He was a father, he would always be a father, "father" was part of who he was. The thought made him feel weak.

Janine moved her hands over his back, caressing him. She sighed. Through half-closed curtains he saw the shadows of trees moving outside. He imagined he could hear the fields breathing around where they lay. The fields stretched back to the east where he came from, and to which he would soon return, to the hills rising gently, their slopes rippling like the folds of a skirt. The sky was huge above them, shimmering with energy, with twinkling lights. Some of them were stars, and some of them unexplained lights which moved by at great speeds.

"That's okay," Janine whispered, and he didn't know to what she referred. "That's okay," her hands on his back as another breeze rustled the leaves, pushing aside the curtains to touch their bodies.

This Room

Each thing given
place in the pattern
rather find
place in mind

a diverse face
absent past
shelf of habits
bits pieces

eye lost then
love's mistakes
aunt's battered house
off foundation

children's recollection
tokens
look back
chipped broken

room goes on
dark winter's edge
now full with sun
pales the worn rug.

Waldoboro Eve

Trees haze in the fog coming in,
late afternoon sun still catches the stones.

Dog's waiting to be fed by the empty sink,
I hear the people shift in their rooms.

That's all finally there is to think.
Now comes night with the moon and the stars.

Some Clear Night

Some clear night like this,
when the stars are all out and shining,
our old dogs will come back to us,
out of the woods, and lead us
along the stone wall to the cove.
There will be foxes, and loons,
and a houseboat floating on the lake.
The trees will lean in, a lantern
swinging over the water, the creaking of oars.
Now we will learn the true names of the stars.
Now we will know what the trees are saying.
There is wood in the stove.
We left the front door open.
Does the farmhouse know
that we're never coming back?

Totally

I'm raking leaves and singing in my off key voice
a mangled version of Madonna's "Like a Virgin,"
a song I thought I hated;

that's how it goes when your head and heart
are in different time zones—
you often don't find out till tomorrow
what you felt today.

I know I do not understand the principles
of leaf removal; I pile them up
in glowing heaps of cadmium and orange,

but I identify so much more
with the entropic gusts of wind
which knock them all apart again.
Is it natural to be scattered?

When I look at the sky I am often dreaming
of a television program that I saw some months ago;
when I walk into a dinner party

I am thinking of the book I mean to read
when I get home—you might say
my here is dislocated from my now,
so never am I entirely anywhere,

or anyone. But I won't speak cruelly
of myself: this dividedness is just what
makes our species great: possible for Darwin

to figure out his theory of selection
while playing five-card stud;
for surgeon Keats to find a perfect rhyme
wristdeep in the disorder
of an open abdomen.

For example, it is autumn here.
The defoliated trees look frightened
at the edge of town,

as if the train they missed
had taken all their clothes.
The whole world in unison is turning
toward a zone of nakedness and cold.

But me, I have this strange conviction
that I am going to be born.

RICHARD PEEK
_____

Piles

I just had a day off, first one I've had in ages, so I decided to spend my time carrying on an old family tradition called moving the pile. I had to move my pile to get it further away from the road so the "city folk" that come up to ski in the winter wouldn't complain.

I'm not sure how far back our tradition of moving the pile goes. It's existed all my life and I'd be willing to bet, my ancestors brought something from the family pile when they came to this country.

My Dad moved the pile many times. Every time we moved we had to move the pile. We also moved it occasionally to clear out an area or try and make things more attractive around the house. I've kept a pile at every place I've ever lived. When I went on the road I left my pile with my parents and when I moved to Maine I drove down and got it.

Different people's piles contain different things. Mine has an interesting assortment of steel, some aluminum and some tin. I've got a welder in the barn and my boy has sheet metal tools and between the two of us we can do almost anything with our pile.

Guys are judged by what kind of stuff they keep in their piles. If my buddy, Roger, needs a widget and can't find one he'll call me.

_____

If I can find one I am heaped with praise and granted one favor, usually an opportunity to choose some item or treasure from his pile when I need it.

I used to think women didn't keep piles so I asked one. She assured me they do, "we just keep ours in closets while you men put yours outside," she said.

I believe pile keeping is a country thing. I don't believe people in cities keep piles. In fact, I think strict laws prohibit pile keeping in the city, that's why city people are so mean and nervous.

You see, in the city, if you need a widget you won't find one in a neighbor's pile. You have to go to the widget store and buy a new one. Widgets are more expensive now than they've ever been before. Last time I checked, they were getting somewhere between $250.00 and $1,000.00 for new widgets.

I've got a bunch of widgets in my pile, some of 'em have been around since my granddaddy took them off his tractor back in 1948. They still work good and those old widgets are a darned sight better than any of this new fangled stuff they make today. Good old made in America widgets I've got. They'll still be around when my kids have kids.

Recently our town officials got all up in arms over some guy's pile. Seems the neighbors didn't want to pay their taxes 'cause they thought Mr. Bumbles' pile de-valued their land. How disgusting, of course, city people don't appreciate pile keeping because they aren't allowed to have piles. If they do, pile police come around and issue fines; people's piles are loaded onto trucks and hauled away.

Since city people aren't allowed to have little piles, every city has a big pile, sometimes bigger than buildings. The piles fill up several blocks and big cranes load them on trains so they can be hauled away to factories where they melt them down and ship them to China, so they can make new widgets out of them.

I never cared much for living in the city. Never cared much for people coming around trying to tell me what to do with my pile, either. After all, it ain't hurting nothing. It ain't endangering the planet or anything like that. Not unless some genius scientist has discovered that rust is a hazardous material.

The Other Maine

I have a dream. Not like Martin Luther King had a dream. Not that kind of dream. What I've been having is more like a nightmare. It is always good to wake up and see that it hasn't happened yet.

At first, in this dream we are all pretty much as we really are. I park outside the post office and grocery store where the people of my small Maine town nod hello or stop to gossip. I love my people here. They are visible people. When you look at the face of one of them passing you in the produce aisle, you know the history of that face—the gossip, the rumors, the truth. You see a complete person. Here in my town you don't have to fix yourself up glamoury, wallow or wriggle about in the latest fashions, load on makeup, diet to the brink of starvation, like they have to in some other places. In those other places, you are a stranger. Nobody lives there long enough to make a history, gossip, rumors, truth. In those places your exterior is most important. You become to others just skin, just hair, just clothes—no deep waters. How expensive it must be to live there! How time-consuming.

My people here in this town have beautiful eyes, beautiful hands—especially the hands—some hands scarred by work, some not. Some have slender inexpensive rings, the kind that show if you are married, though everybody knows who is or isn't. Clothes are mainly for warmth or to keep the blackflies and deerflies from mutilating you. My people are mostly underweight or over-weight—however it is they turned out, like good bread.

What is also wonderful here is our homes. Most of us in my town still live far enough apart so we can't see our neighbors from our doorways or windows. Being able to see your neighbor's house is like seeing them in bed or on the toilet. It's indecent.

Home is supposed to be private, isn't it? Lots of us have assorted useful stuff around our yards—tractors, tractor parts, truck tires, wooden skids, plastic industrial pails, rolled up chicken wire, treehouses (the lopsided kind made by kids), old cars, old appliances. This comes from freedom, from not worrying what other people think. Visitors don't look at your stuff anyway (except maybe to make a trade). They mostly look at *you*. They come to visit *you,* the person they know quadriptillions of rumors and truths about. They know you to the bone. When you hear their car or truck pull up under the old maple trees by your door, you don't run to put on fifty layers of makeup and your best leather skirt. There's no hiding *you*. You don't need to. *That's* freedom.

Here we are in heaven. Life as it should be. That's how the office of tourism has been advertising Maine lately. That's how the realtors have been selling Maine. But what they show in the ads are models in tailored reindeer sweaters on thick carpets toasting with champagne in front of a fire. Stretched out at their feet is a six-hundred-dollar dog. I couldn't know those people, not even if I tried. They are untouchable, unknowable, artificial, dangerous. Dangerous because lately many Mainers are trying to be like the artificial people. Some actually believe that the artificial life is worth aspiring to.

Holy Toledo.

A lot of developers are putting homes between the homes—not homes really, some real showboats—what some would call investments. Also, there are beginner houses. Something like beginner bicycles. Or training pants. All of us can now see our new neighbors' skin, hair, and fashions as they come in and out of their "nice" homes—strangers that look like the ads, living life as they should be, nothing useful piled around their yards, nothing, just the two or three or four glossy cars. You can imagine these strangers relaxing on their rugs, looking into the fireplace. But you can only imagine it. You can't find out anything about them. They don't have cousins you can ask, or uncles or brothers or grammies. And they themselves won't talk. They only ask questions,. Mainly, "How are you today?" They never answer questions unless you ask them "How are you today?" and they always say "Fine." Most of our regular people here talk back and forth, like, "My mother is still sick . . . I'm taking her to the doctor's at two . . . she won't listen to anybody and take her medicine." And, "You want those flower drapes? Brad's cat wrecked the ones on the long window and now I've only got the ones to fit the short windows . . . Muriel's giving me that plum-colored fabric left over from Frannie's wedding and I'm going to see what I can do with it." It is hard to get anything going with these new Life-As-It-Should-Be neighbors because they don't talk. And when they look at you, you can tell by their eyes making the quick cool sweep over you that they are only registering your clothes, your teeth, what car you are driving, and making a quick guess at your weight . . . and now that they're living only a few yards from you, they can see your home, too. Somehow the word "privacy" has taken on new meaning. Now the home is highly visible but the soul is hidden.

This would be fine—a little disconcerting, but bearable—but what's happening is a lot of us Mainers are having a peculiar reaction. Life as these strangers say it should be has gotten into the blood and hearts of some of my people, like in that movie *The Thing*, and it's taking them over, sucking out their humanity, scaring them or something—it's unexplainable. Not only are the regular Maine people fixing up their homes (with loans they can't afford) to look like the Life-As-It-Should-Be people's, but our town lawmakers are changing the codes to say that we've *all* got to do it. Codes. Rules. Laws. (The opposites of freedom.) Laws that say you have to at least *look* like you're living life as it should be. Laws against inexpensive homes. Since most Mainers have bosses who pay inexpensive pay, inexpensive not-at-all-showy homes are sometimes all you can get (if you are lucky to get any). You build it or buy it, and you live in it whether it meets the new codes or not. A lot of Mainers are now outlaws because they are not living life as *they*, whoever *they* are, think it should be.

Now here's where the nightmare begins. Up till now has been the real part. Or is this all really happening?

The nightmare laws say that because tourists like to think we are all sitting up here in front of the fireplace with fashionable sweaters, pedigreed dogs, perfect teeth, softly waved honey-colored hair, and the faces and figures of models, inside our manicured white New England houses with short grass and two to four sleek little cars on the hot-top driveway, that we all must now pave our driveways, paint our houses white (black or green trim only). Keep them at all times in perfect flawless repair, cut the grass to three quarters of an inch (absolutely no weeds), no clotheslines, no butterflies, no bugs of any kind, no hoods up on the cars, glossy cars only, no mixed-breed dogs, no loose cats. Anybody who can't afford to or chooses not to obey these laws is fined a thousand dollars a day.

Next the code makers decide that tourists and strangers coming to purchase their pieces of Maine might be put off by those Mainers who have managed to keep up with the white paint, etc., but who themselves look shabby. Like fat, boney, or bald, or with a pimple or red hair or long noses or a crooked tooth or a receding chin or smallish eyes or—heaven forbid—a birth defect, little short arm or something. The codes stipulate that these people must not spend any time lingering in their front yards, but must get in or out of their vehicles and make a mad dash. *Backyards only* for these unsightly individuals who aren't looking as they should look. And those men with *stained hands* who work under cars or with plumbing. They are ordered to wear gloves on the way home from work or to carry wipettes in their cars and trucks. And no trucks that look like trucks allowed. Only the newer trucks that look like cars. Trucks, real trucks, as everybody knows look . . . nasty.

Now, as the nightmare continues, the tourists and buyers drive up and down the roads of Maine, and they see a storybook New England. "Lovely, isn't it?" they whisper. But one day the Maine office of tourism notes with alarm that tourism has slackened. They set up a committee that costs thousands to study what happened. They do a survey asking tourists of the past why they don't come up any more. "Too dull," the ex-Maine tourists sneer. "Too . . ." Too something, they aren't sure what. They are taking their vacations now in other countries to look at the real people, to view humanity.

The Maine Office of Tourism and the town and state code people race to their desks and phones. "Bring the tractors back! The real trucks! The rusty hay rake! The redheads. The old grammies with no teeth. The pink and lavender and yellow ochre houses. The trailers. The mixed-breed dogs. Washing machines. Broken snowmobiles. Car parts. Unsightly treehouses. Plastic toys strewn around. Loose cats. Bring back the hunched-over people, the black hands, the weeds, the butterflies and grasshoppers, the pin curlers, stained aprons, the blue industrial pails, the clotheslines, the re-tarded people, the one-legged people, the fat ones, the boney ones, the ones with thick glasses. Bring back humanity. What did we do with them? Where did we put them all? All those lawbreakers who broke the codes! Find them! They were beautiful."

Ghosts, Balloons, Some Martians

Ghosts seem to prefer their usual occupations.
They are humdrum, opening and shutting doors
or creaking their old rocking chairs in our dreams,
or perhaps one of them steps forward
to sell you gas as you drive into
a boarded-up station by mistake—and then
disappears, fated to repeat the habitual
moments of his life, never
the extraordinary;
                  and just so
we encourage a taste for the quotidian
in the arts. We call for a plain poetry
that is "true," austere, and thoroughly
uninflated.
                "No more balloons!"
we swear, and turn our backs on the gaudy ride
going up with a roar. If we look after it
wistfully, if we strain to watch
the people waving from the dangling wickerwork
as they sail off into the blue sky drinking champagne,
isn't it natural, wouldn't anyone want
to catch sight of a wonder?
                     My old neighbor
woke her husband up one night to see Martians
passing by right outside with their lamps
and strange cries in the air. Next day, of course,
the truth came out; it had been nothing
but a late balloon, a bit lost, trailing its basket
between house and barn at the level

of the upstairs window, its lights
searching the way.
                        Are you smiling
at that? Why shouldn't we smile
as if night weren't a mystery?
                              "Come here,"
says our visiting Irish friend, her voice
tight and small. I hurry
to the screen door where she is standing and peer out
over her shoulder. Why is she scared? All I see
is the steep fall of the field in the summer dusk,
the darker shapes of the apple trees by the house,
and the hundreds of flickering sparks from fireflies
skimming over the tops of the long grass and turning
their little greenish lights on and off, on and off, on and off.

GEORGE GARRETT

How It Is, How It Was,
How It Will Be

How it is
on the next day after
the blizzard
how the sky clears   blues   brightens
cloudless and clean with the old moon
floating here and there quiet and grinning
and the quiet fallen snow
glinting   winking   glittering
(is there one and only word for it?)
with abundance   opulence   extravagance
of (one and only) sunlight
how my breath and the river's
do steam and ghost and shimmyshake
in this purely cold air
how now we know
that we shall surely live forever
how now we want to

ROBERT KIMBER

Afloat on Snow

All our most pleasurable means of travel make use of water, and when I say water, I include ice and snow—water in its solid as well as its liquid form. They also make use of what I suppose would nowadays be considered technologically rather primitive devices: canoes, sailboats, snowshoes, cross-country skis.

Travel in just about any kind of conveyance has its moments—floating above a carpet of clouds in a jetliner, for example. Or, on shipboard, watching the coast of Maine rise out of the sea. Even the lowly automobile can show you some wonderful sights as it winds down a mountain pass in Austria or, closer to home, tops Indian Hill overlooking Moosehead Lake. But for all that, I still find the *process* of petroleum-powered travel singularly dreary. One does, after all, very little but sit on one's duff and watch the landscape go by. It's a sedentary business for which passive words like "I was flown" or "I was shipped" seem more appropriate than active ones like "I flew" or "I sailed."

Travel utilizing "primitive" technologies, on the other hand, is endlessly engaging and enchanting. Part of the fascination comes, I think, from the interplay of our own minds and bodies with natural elements and natural forces. That is a rather abstract way of saying there's a thrill quite unlike any other in feeling the tug of accelerating water as it seizes your canoe at the head of a rapid, the tug of a fresh breeze as it fills your sails, the tug of gravity as you head down a hill on skis. In skiing, sailing, and paddling, there is a thrill not of conquest but of harmony, an almost musical thrill. You use skis and your own weight, sails and tiller, canoe and paddle, to play the forces of gravity, wind, or current like an instrument. The thrill is not a cheap one. It takes years of practice to play well, and if you play badly, the results can be uncomfortable, if not worse. Depending on terrain, wind, weather, and I don't know how many other variables, the demands on your own muscle power and alertness can vary hugely. Are you floating along on an easy current without a rock in sight, or are you bucking a heavy chop on a windswept lake? Are you swooping down a long, gentle slope from ridge to valley floor, or are you pushing your way up a steep trail? There are moments of ease, exhilaration, and illumination. There are moments of excruciating exertion, near-terror, and bone-weariness. There is never alienation, ennui, or isolation from land and weather.

In the winter, when snow transforms the surface of the earth into an almost liquid one, travel in the forest becomes much closer akin to canoeing or sailing than it is to walking on bare ground in the spring, summer, and fall. Ski and snowshoe language reflects this liquefaction of the land: "flotation" is what keeps you on top of the snow, and if your snowshoes don't provide enough of it for your body weight, you'll sink. And if you go out on cross-country skis in powder snow, you'll need wide touring skis, not skinny little racers, to keep you afloat. Then, too, the motions of cross-country skiing seem almost a blend of running and swimming. The adjectives that come to mind to describe them are "liquid" and "flowing." The snowshoer, of course, does not glide. He still walks. He still has to pick 'em up and put 'em down. But even for him snow eases the way. It fills in the holes, covers up the snags, smooths out the bumps. Isaiah would have loved snow. It exalts the valleys and makes every mountain and hill low (well, not quite). It makes the crooked straight and the rough places plain.

For bears, winter may be a time of closing up and tucking in; but for human beings who avail themselves of this primitive technology, land travel is never so easy and elegant. Winter is a time of release and opening up. The landscape becomes transparent, spreading out like a map in front of you. The hillsides that are hidden from view when you walk the summer woods are right before your eyes now. You can almost reach out and caress them and feel the shape of this little valley, the backbone of that ridge. I put on my skis and go places I can't go at any other time of year. Bogs I wouldn't dream of wallowing through in the summer become oases. Places where you would slog your way through bugs and alders and knee-deep mud become highways of white silk under your feet. The water-killed spruce and fir rise more delicately and lovely than any minarets in the moonlight. The tapestry of tracks of fox and coyote and squirrel and snowshoe hare reassure you that the web of life is unbroken.

Just south of Attean Lake near Jackman is Number 5 Bog. On the map it looks to be about four miles long and four miles wide and just about one of the last places on earth you'd want to be on foot. If you beach your canoe and climb up the bank of the Moose River, which flows along the bog's edge, you'll see nothing but alders, hummocks, and mud. Not very inviting in June, but downright possible in January. Maybe this January I'll finally get up in there.

The swiftness of skis and the clarity of winter let me fit and piece my world together in a way I can't at any other time. Weld, which is so far away from my home in Temple by car, is a half-day's jaunt over Wilder Hill on the snow. If I want a couple of hours off closer to home, I can hop from Drury Pond to Pickerel Pond to Ballard Pond, skimming through the puckerbrush and beaver bogs between them where, in the summer, no way would open. In winter, my skis let me get to know my world—from my back fields to the Canadian line—with an intimacy impossible at any other time. And so I've come to feel that winter may be about the warmest season of the year after all, and my skis (along with my canoe) among the most advanced means of transportation I know.

RICHARD FOERSTER

Spring Tide

York, Maine

Ten eel-necked cormorants, journeying
somewhere north, rest on the rocks' last knuckle

that points from this cove out toward the indefinable
line. There a beacon, bleared by thin fog,

searches the evening's depths beyond Boon Island.
The sea lies flat as rippled slate.

One could think of walking out on it,
except that the imperceptible heaving

cracks into whiteness at the cormorants' feet.
Suddenly I'm caught up in the hush

of ritual. The birds splay their ancient wings
to the tentative air, hold them, poised

and priestly, as if inviting a necessary prayer.
There's such trembling in this waiting

for a sign. But the moment passes, and the birds
bend their awkward bills to preening.

The light grows dim. The wheel-eyed beacon stares
and turns. What could I recite if now, on the verge

of losing sight of them and wanting
home, they'd assume their singular grace and fly?

Presence

after George Oppen

That we are here: that we can question who
we are, where; that we relate to how deer

once small have grown bold in our back garden;
that we can ask, ask even ourselves, how

to the other we may appear, here in the always near place
we seem to ourselves to inhabit, who sleep toward

and wake from steeped hills, the sea opening into our eyes
the infinite possibility of infinity

we believe we're neither beyond nor shy of,
here as we are, without doubt, amid then, there,

and now, falling through dark into light, and back,
against which we cannot defend, wish as we might, as we do.

Still, as the physicist said, *the mystery is*
that we are here, here at all, still bearing with,

and borne by, all we try to make sense of:
this evening two does and a fawn who browse

the head lettuce we once thought was ours.
But no. As we chase them off mildly, and make

an odd salad of what they left us, the old stars
come casually out, and we see near and far we own nothing:

it's us who belong to all else; who, given this day,
are touched by, and touch, our tenderest knowing,

our lives incalculably dear as we feel for each other,
our skin no more or less thin than that of redwing,

rainbow, star-nose, or whitethroat, enfolded like us
in the valleys and waves of this irrefutable planet.

About the Contributors

Richard Aldridge has written five volumes of poetry, most recently *Driving North*. He has also edited three anthologies of poetry, including *Speaking of New England,* which appeared last year. A retired secondary school teacher, he lives and writes on the Maine coast.

Paula Anderson is an elementary education student with a writing concentration at the University of Maine at Farmington. She lives with her two sons on Millay Hill in New Portland, Maine, a location that appears often in her work. This is her first published poem.

Kate Barnes is the daughter of Maine writers Henry Beston and Elizabeth Coatsworth. Her latest book of poetry is *Where the Deer Were,* and she has published her poems widely, appearing in such magazines as *Harper's* and *The New Yorker.* She lives on a blueberry farm in Appleton.

Alice Bloom lives in Mount Vernon, Maine, and teaches in the English department at the University of Maine at Farmington. Her essays and reviews have appeared in *The Yale Review, Harper's,* and *The New England Review,* among other magazines, and in several anthologies.

Philip Booth, the author of nine volumes of poetry, lives in Castine, Maine. He has received Guggenheim and Rockefeller fellowships and has won numerous awards for his poetry, including the Lamont Prize, the Maurice English Poetry Award, and an award in poetry from the National Institute of Arts and Letters.

Franklin Burroughs has taught English at Bowdoin College since 1968. He is the author of *Billy Watson's Croker Sack* and *Horry and the Waccamaw.* His work has been included in *Best American Essays* and *The Pushcart Prize Anthology,* and has appeared in *The Kenyon Review* and *The Georgia Review.*

William Carpenter's three volumes of poetry are *The Hours of the Morning, Rain,* and *Speaking Fire at Stones,* with the artist Robert Shetterly. His novel *A Keeper of Sheep (Ein Huter den Herden)* was just published in Europe. He teaches at the College of the Atlantic in Bar Harbor.

Thomas Carper, a professor at the University of Southern Maine, has published poems in *Poetry* and other journals, as well as in a recent collection, *Fiddle Lane.* He has also performed Renaissance a capella trios in live and broadcast concerts in New England and France.

Carolyn Chute is the author of three novels, the most recent of which is *Merry Men.* The recipient of a Guggenheim Fellowship in 1992, she lives in Parsonsfield, Maine, with her husband Michael, where, in her words, "three grandkids visit and often complain about no TV."

Robert M. Chute, retired from his position as a biology professor at Bates College, lives in Poland Spring, Maine. He has written several volumes of verse, the latest being *Woodshed on the Moon: Thoreau Poems.* He is a winner of the Maine Arts Commission's chapbook competition.

Amy Clampitt has published *Westward* and three other volumes of verse, each of which contains poems about coastal Maine, where she summers. She has won a MacArthur Fellowship, a Guggenheim Fellowship, and many other honors for her work.

Elizabeth Cooke is the author of the novel *Complicity* and several short stories, which have appeared in *McCall's, Redbook,* and other magazines. She teaches writing at the University of Maine at Farmington and recently made western Maine, her summer retreat in childhood, her year-round home.

Robert Creeley went to college in Maine and now returns each summer to Waldoboro, where his sister Helen lives. For Creeley, E. A. Robinson remains "a primary measure" in his poetry. A member of the American Academy of Arts and Letters, he has published numerous collections of poetry and prose.

Theodore Enslin lives and works in Milbridge, Maine, making periodic trips around the United States and Canada for readings of and lectures on his work. His main interest is a poetry grounded in musical procedure. His latest book is *The House of the Golden Windows.*

Richard Foerster, a resident of York Beach, received the "Discovery/*The Nation*" Award in 1985 and the Bess Hokin Prize from *Poetry* magazine in 1992. The author of two collections of poetry, *Sudden Harbor* and *Patterns of Descent,* he has published his poems widely.

Elaine Ford has written four novels, the most recent of which is *Monkey*

Bay. She was awarded NEA Fellowships in 1982 and 1986, and a Guggenheim Fellowship in 1990. She is Associate Professor of English at the University of Maine at Orono and lives in Milbridge.

Jacquie Giasson Fuller lives in Gorham, Maine, and grew up in Lewiston. A writing instructor at the University of Southern Maine, she has published poems, articles, and stories that often include Franco-Americans in *Yankee, Canado-Americaine,* and several other periodicals.

George Garret, who has summered for years on the coast of Maine, has written 25 books and has edited or co-edited 18 others. He is Henry Hoyns Professor of Creative Writing at the University of Virginia and was elected last year as Chancellor of the Fellowship of Southern Writers.

Richard Gillman, author of two poetry volumes and of essays for the *New York Times Book Review,* co-edited *Poets, Poetics, and Politics,* a collection of Rolfe Humphries' letters. A resident of Waterville, Maine, he has recently published poems in *The Sewanee Review* and *The New England Review.*

Tony Hoagland, who lives in Waterville, won the 1992 Brittingham Prize for his collection of poems, *Sweet Ruin.* He has received an NEA Fellowship and two Pushcart Prizes. His poems and essays about poetry have been published in *Poetry, The Georgia Review, Harper's,* and other magazines.

Edward (Ted) Holmes, professor emeritus in the honors program at the University of Maine at Orono, has been a Maine resident since 1939. His latest books are *Two If By Sea* and *Harriet Beecher Stowe: Woman and Artist*; other publications include collections of short stories.

Susan Kenney has authored three Roz Howard mysteries, as well as two novels. She has won first place in the O. Henry Awards and received the Quality Paperback Book Club New Voices Award for her novel *In Another Country.* She is Dana Professor of Creative Writing at Colby College.

Robert Kimber lives on an old farm in Temple. His three books, featuring outdoor life in Maine, are *Upcountry, Made for the Country,* and *A Canoeist's Sketchbook.* He writes regularly for *Country Journal, Down East* and other prominent upcountry journals.

Gary Lawless was born in Belfast, Maine, in 1951. He is co-owner of the Gulf of Maine Bookstore in Brunswick and editor/publisher of Black-

Contributors

berry Books. The author of seven volumes of poetry, he lives as caretaker at Chimney Farm in Nobleboro, home of writers Henry Beston and Elizabeth Coatsworth.

Carl Little's books are *Three Thousand Dreams Explained,* a collection of poems, and two volumes of art history, *Paintings of Maine* and *Edward Hopper's New England.* He is Director of Public Affairs at the College of the Atlantic on Mount Desert Island, where he lives with his wife and two children.

Patricia O'Donnell teaches fiction writing in the BFA program at the University of Maine at Farmington. Her stories have been published in several magazines, including *The New Yorker, The North American Review,* and *Agni Review.* They have also appeared in *The Eloquent Edge* and other anthologies.

Richard Peek, who, as he puts it, "lives to write" in Razorville, Maine, is regularly featured in *The Kennebec Journal* and on Maine Public Radio's *Maine Things Considered* radio program. His work has also been selected for broadcast on National Public Radio.

Cathie Pelletier was born and raised on the banks of the St. John River. Her four novels, all about northern Maine, include the recently published volumes *The Weight of Winter* and *The Bubble Reputation.* She is the 1992 winner of the New England Book Award for Fiction.

Mary Peterson has received an O. Henry Award, a Pushcart Prize, and an NEA Fellowship for her fiction. In addition to her volume of short fiction, *Mercy Flights,* she has published stories in *Ms., Ploughshares, North American Review, Fiction International,* and other magazines. She lives in Kittery.

Sanford Phippen of Hancock, Maine, has written three collections of anecdotes and stories, the latest being *Cheap Gossip.* A regular columnist for *The Maine Times,* he has published articles in many forums, and is the editor of *High Clouds Soaring, Storms Driving Low: The Letters of Ruth Moore.*

A. Poulin, Jr., was born in Lisbon, Maine, the son of immigrant Quebecois parents. His work includes two volumes of poems, *A Momentary Order* and *Cave Dwellers,* and a book of translations, *Anne Hebert: Selected Poems.* He is founding Editor/Publisher of BOA Editions, Ltd., a house devoted solely to poetry.

Bill Roorbach is the author of *Summers with Juliet,* a memoir. Other work has appeared in *Harper's, New York, Granta,* and *The Iowa Review,* and has won special mentions in *Pushcart Prize XVI* and *Best American Essays, 1992.* He teaches in the BFA program at the University of Maine at Farmington.

Kenneth Rosen lives in Portland and teaches at the University of Southern Maine. He founded and directed the Stonecoast Writers' Conference. His recent poems have appeared in *The Massachusetts Review* and *Paris Review.* His collections of poems include *Whole Horse,* nominated for the Pulitzer Prize, *Longfellow Square,* and *Reptile Mind.*

Ira Sadoff is the author of four collections of poetry, most recently *Emotional Traffic.* He has published a novel, *Uncoupling,* and award-winning short stories, which appear in his *Ira Sadoff Reader,* together with selected poems and essays. He teaches at Colby College.

Susan Hand Shetterly has written four children's books and a collection of essays. She has been a nature essayist for *The Maine Times* and last year won an NEA Fellowship, which has sponsored work on short fiction and an extended essay about the salt marsh and bay in Surry, where she lives.

Betsy Sholl won the 1991 Maine Arts Commission chapbook competition for her collection, *Pick a Card,* and the Associated Writing Programs contest in poetry for *The Red Line.* The author of five volumes of poetry, she lives in Portland and teaches at the University of Southern Maine.

John Thorne is the author of *Simple Cooking* and, with his wife Matt, *Outlaw Cook,* winner of the 1992 IAPC/Julia Child Cookbook Award for literary food writing. He currently lives in Steuben, Maine, where he is completing a new book, *Serious Pig,* which is partly about surviving Maine food.

Robley Wilson, who grew up in Sanford and has frequently returned to Maine, is the editor of *The North American Review* and teaches at the University of Northern Iowa. A Guggenheim Fellow in fiction, he is the author of four story collections and a collection of poems.

Monica Wood, a Portland resident, recently published fiction in *Redbook, The North American Review,* and the anthology *Sudden Fiction International.* Her stories, including "Wish," have been featured on National Public Radio. *Secret Language,* her first novel, was published in 1993.

Baron Wormser lives in Mercer and works as a librarian. His third and latest volume of poems is *Atoms, Soul Music and Other Poems.* The recipient of an NEA Fellowship and a prize from *Poetry* magazine, he teaches part-time in the BFA program at the University of Maine at Farmington.

About the Editor

A 1993 resident of the Rockefeller Foundation's Bellagio Center in Italy, Wesley McNair has held a Guggenheim Fellowship, two NEA Fellowships, and a Fulbright Lectureship in Chile. He has also received the Devins Award for Poetry, the Eunice Tietjens Prize from *Poetry* magazine, and the Theodore Roethke Prize from *Poetry Northwest.* A series aired by PBS television on Robert Frost for which he wrote the scripts was awarded a New England Emmy. His volumes of verse are *The Faces of Americans in 1853, The Town of No, My Brother Running,* and a chapbook, *Twelve Journeys in Maine.* He teaches in the BFA program in creative writing at the University of Maine at Farmington, and he lives with his wife, Diane, in Mercer, Maine.

Acknowledgments

ARRIVALS

Richard Gillman. "Together Among Monarchs." First published by *Sewanee Review* CI (Summer 1993), copyright © 1993 by Richard Gillman. Reprinted by permission of *The Sewanee Review.*

Paula Anderson. "Apparition." Copyright © 1994 by Paula Anderson. Reprinted by permission of the author.

Susan Hand Shetterly. "Mallards." Copyright © 1994 by Susan Hand Shetterly. Reprinted by permission of the author.

William Carpenter. "The Ecuadorian Sailors." From *Rain,* copyright © 1985 by William Carpenter. Reprinted by permission of Northeastern University Press.

Ira Sadoff. "Brief Afternoons." From *Emotional Traffic,* copyright © 1989 by Ira Sadoff. Reprinted by permission of David R. Godine, Publisher, Inc.

Franklin Burroughs. "Of Moose and a Moose Hunter." From *Billy Watson's Croker Sack,* copyright © 1991 by Franklin Burroughs. Reprinted by permission of W. W. Norton.

Jacquie Giasson Fuller. "Cecile's Dog Bo." First published in *Yankee* magazine, copyright © 1993 by Jacquie Giasson Fuller. Reprinted by permission of the author.

Bill Roorbach. "Into Woods." First published in *Harper's Magazine,* copyright © 1993 by Bill Roorbach. Reprinted by permission of the author.

Edward Holmes. "Blitzkrieg and the Nautical Plow." Copyright © 1994 by Edward Holmes. Reprinted by permission of the author.

Richard Aldridge. "Moth at My Window." From *Red Pine, Black Ash,* copyright © 1980 by Richard Aldridge, originally published by Thorndike

Press, Thorndike, Maine, with rights now held by North Country Press, Belfast and Unity, Maine. Reprinted by permission of North Country Press.

TRAVELERS' ADVISORIES

Baron Wormser. "Somerset County." Copyright © 1994 by Baron Wormser. Reprinted by permission of the author.

Elizabeth Cooke. "Northern Lights." Copyright © 1994 by Elizabeth Cooke. Reprinted by permission of the author.

Robert M. Chute. "The Bird Feeder." First published in *Potato Eyes,* copyright © 1990 by Robert M. Chute. Reprinted by permission of *Potato Eyes.*

Robert Kimber. "No Night Life." From *Upcountry,* copyright © 1991 by Robert Kimber. Reprinted by permission of Lyons & Burford, Publishers, New York.

Theodore Enslin. "Vespers." From *From Near the Great Pine,* copyright © 1988 by Theodore Enslin. Reprinted by permission of the author.

John Thorne. "Maine Eats." First published in *Simple Cooking,* copyright © 1992 by John Thorne. Reprinted by permission of the author.

Richard Aldridge. "The Cornfield." Originally published as "Which Frightened Both the Heroes So," in *Red Pine, Black Ash,* copyright © 1980 by Richard Aldridge, by Thorndike Press, Thorndike, Maine, with rights now held by North Country Press, Belfast and Unity, Maine. Reprinted by permission of North Country Press.

Susan Kenney. "For Those in Peril on the Sea: A Meditation." Copyright © 1994 by Susan Kenney. Reprinted by permission of the author.

Amy Clampitt. "Handed Down." Copyright © 1994 by Amy Clampitt. Reprinted by permission of Alfred A. Knopf.

Carl Little. "3,000 Dreams Explained." From *3,000 Dreams Explained,* copyright © 1992 by Carl Little. Reprinted by permission of Nightshade Press.

Acknowledgments

Robley Wilson. "On the Island." First published in *The Pleasures of Manhood,* copyright © 1977 by Robley Wilson. Reprinted by permission of the author.

William Carpenter. "Man Climbing Katahdin." From *Rain,* copyright © 1985 by William Carpenter. Reprinted by permission of Northeastern University Press.

Kate Barnes. "Where the Deer Were." From *Crossing the Field,* copyright © 1992 by Kate Barnes. Reprinted by permission of Blackberry Books.

Patricia O'Donnell. "Unexplained Lights." First published in *Short Story,* copyright © 1991 by Patricia O'Donnell. Reprinted by permission of *Short Story.*

Robert Creeley. "This Room" and "Waldoboro Eve." Copyright © 1994 by Robert Creeley. Reprinted by permission of the author.

Gary Lawless. "Some Clear Night." Copyright © 1994 by Gary Lawless. Reprinted by permission of the author.

Tony Hoagland. "Totally." Copyright © 1994 by Tony Hoagland. Reprinted by permission of the author.

Richard Peek. "Piles." Copyright © 1994 by Richard Peek. Reprinted by permission of the author.

Carolyn Chute. "The Other Maine." Copyright © 1989 by Carolyn Chute. First published in *Mirabella Magazine.* Reprinted by permission of the author.

Kate Barnes. "Ghosts, Balloons, Some Martians." From *Crossing the Field,* copyright © 1992 by Kate Barnes. Reprinted by permission of Blackberry Books.

George Garrett. "How It Is, How It Was, How It Will Be." Copyright © 1994 by George Garrett. Reprinted by permission of the author.

Robert Kimber. "Afloat on Snow." From *Upcountry,* copyright © 1991 by Robert Kimber. Reprinted by permission of Lyons and Burford, Publishers, New York.

Richard Foerster. "Spring Tide." From *Patterns of Descent,* published by

Acknowledgments

University Press of New England publishes books under its own imprint and is the publisher for Brandeis University Press, Brown University Press, University of Connecticut, Dartmouth College, Middlebury College Press, University of New Hampshire, University of Rhode Island, Tufts University, University of Vermont, and Wesleyan University Press.

Library of Congress Cataloging-in-Publication Data
The Quotable moose : a contemporary Maine reader / edited by Wesley McNair.
p.   cm.
ISBN 0–87451–673–0
1. Maine—Literary collections.   2. American literature—Maine.
3. American literature—20th century.   I. McNair, Wesley.
PS548.M2Q68   1994
810.8′032741′09045—dc20   93–38324